TEMPLE
AT THE
CENTER OF TIME

TEMPLE
AT THE
CENTER OF TIME

NEWTON'S BIBLE CODEX DECIPHERED AND THE YEAR 2012

DAVID FLYNN

OFFICIAL DISCLOSURE

A DIVISION OF ANOMALOS PUBLISHING HOUSE

CRANE

Official Disclosure
A division of Anomalos Publishing House, Crane 65633
© 2008 by David Flynn
All rights reserved. Published 2008
Printed in the United States of America
08 2
ISBN-10: 0981495745 (paper)

EAN-13: 9780981495743 (paper)

Cover illustration and design by Steve Warner

All scripture quotes are from the King James Version unless
otherwise noted.

A CIP catalog record for this book is available from the Library of
Congress.

CONTENTS

AUTHOR'S NOTE

All geographic distance calculations in this book are based on the 1909 Federal Aviation International Sphere Model, the standard for international aeronautic and avionic navigation for nearly a century. The (FAI sphere) is most closely based on the *sacred* methods of measuring distances on the earth from antiquity (measure along a great circle on a sphere with a mean radius of 3,958.75 statute miles) and agrees with the numeric systems found in the ancient texts of the Bible.

INTRODUCTION

*I suspect that my theories may all depend upon a force for which
philosophers have searched all of nature in vain.*

—ISAAC NEWTON

During the formation of modern science and philosophy of the
17th century, the highest achievement lay not in the realm of discovery, but in rediscovery. The Renaissance began at the end of
the Byzantine Empire in 1453, when Constantinople fell to the Turkish Ottoman Empire. Volumes of Classical Greek manuscripts were
made available to Western Europe for the first time, brought by waves
of Greek refugees.[1] One of the greatest philosophical influences transferred to Western Europe from Constantinople was the work of the
Neo-Platonists. This philosophy continued the ideas of Plato, who
believed that all the workings of knowledge and civilization had been
conveyed to humanity from a divine source, and was not conceived
by the mind of man.[2] Through a series of disasters on a world scale,
civilization and the knowledge that had produced it was lost.

Whereas just when you and other nations are beginning to
be provided with letters and the other requisites of civilized

1

life, after the usual interval, the stream from heaven, like a
pestilence, come pouring down, and leaves only those of you
who are destitute of letters and education; and so you have to
begin all over again like children…Plato, *The Timaeus.*[3]

Further in this work is the story of Atlantis, the greatest and oldest
civilization the world has ever seen, that had disappeared "in a single
day and night of misfortune." There exist no earlier sources of the
legend of Atlantis besides the work of Plato. *Timaeus* was one of the
most copied and widespread of Plato's works in the Renaissance. In
the Neo-Platonic philosophy, the story of Atlantis was considered allegory with underlying truth, or in some cases, a true historical account.
It provided the intellectual framework from which the Neo-Platonists
searched for lost knowledge. The Neo-Platonist manuscripts of Hippolytus, Proclus, Arisophanes, Plutarch, Apuleius, and many others
from antiquity developed the theme that knowledge had been given to
man from a divine source. Through its misuse resulting in the corruption of mankind, it was lost by a subsequent judgment from heaven.

Neo-Platonic views of the time also sought to link the celestial
and natural world with the divine, an idea borne out of a reawakening
to the scientific value of the ancient texts of the Greeks. Ancient religious, scientific, and esoteric works were reassessed within the context
of Judaic-Christian thought.

Historically, the Scientific Revolution was united with an Occult
Renaissance, the vestiges of which can be seen even today within the
names of established branches of modern science. For example, *chem*-
istry originated from al*chemy*, (the dark art) from the Arabic word
meaning "from Egypt" or from the land of Kemet, meaning "darkness."[4] Men like Heinrich Agrippa, John Dee, Kercher, Descarte, and
later Leibnez and Newton created amalgamations of the religious and
natural world, a world divinely ordained and regulated.

Theologians of the Renaissance proposed that because all natural
mechanisms of creation originated from God, the resolution of these

aspects through natural magic would validate Christianity. Ideas stemming from pure occult writing contained in various ancient sources were deemed compatible with the hidden knowledge in the ancient texts of scripture. This transition of thinking from the realm of occult and religious, to one of pure science was one of the hallmarks of the age. Geometers, mathematicians, chronologists, philosophers, and theologians of the age searched the texts of the ancients for the "lost pure knowledge" or *prisca sapienta* that would merge all sciences.[5]

Late medieval thinkers such as Descartes, Francis Bacon, and John Dee were obsessed with re-obtaining the *prisca sapientia*. They poured over the records of antiquity to recover it, believing that the ancients had distilled the essence of it in mathematical truths or some in a symbolic language.

In 1657, the English scholar Robert Turner published *Ars Notoria*, which purported to contain the pure knowledge of the ancients. The key to understanding the nature of lost knowledge, according to Turner, who had borrowed from earlier works, was the prayers of King Solomon, builder of the first temple of Jerusalem. In the forward of the text, Turner's editor explains that, "It is called the Notory Art because in certain brief notes it teacheth and comprehendeth the knowledge of all arts."[6] In practical application, *Ars Notoria* did little to produce a pure science, but it did reveal the direction in which the intellects of the Scientific Revolution were searching in order to recover it. They viewed the Biblical account of King Solomon as a tantalizing glimpse of knowledge that had once been *and* might be recovered by any man that was deemed worthy by God. Solomon was regarded as having obtained the pure science through divine providence. Many of the Late Medieval and Renaissance intellects patterned themselves after Solomon, learning as much as possible about the ancient Hebrew language and rituals. The languages of other ancient civilizations were considered important to the quest as well. The more ancient the language, the closer it may have been to the original and purest expression of knowledge. Suspecting that the ancient Greek geometers had once

possessed part of this whole, Rene Descartes, one of the key figures in
the Scientific Revolution, wrote:

> We have sufficient evidence that the ancient geometers made
> use of a certain "analysis" which they applied in the resolution
> of their problems....These writers, I am inclined to believe,
> by a certain baneful craftiness, kept the secrets of this math-
> ematics to themselves. Acting as many inventors are known to
> have done in the case of their discoveries, they have perhaps
> feared that their method being so very easy and simple, would
> if made public, diminish, not increase public esteem. Instead
> they have chosen to propound, as being the fruits of their
> skill, a number of sterile truths, deductively demonstrated
> with great show of logical subtlety, with a view to winning
> an amazing admiration, thus dwelling indeed on the results
> obtained by way of their method, but without disclosing the
> method itself—a disclosure which would have completely
> undermined that amazement.[7]

Groups of Jewish mystics living in France and Spain during the
12th and 13th centuries believed that all the mysteries in the universe
could be derived from names, phrases, and especially numbers contained in the writing of Moses.[8]

Through this reasoning, they developed a tradition of Kabbalah,
meaning "received" or "revelation." Its adherents believed that the
highest knowledge of ancient Scripture was dispensed by God and *received* by men of sufficient scholarship and character. This knowledge
was passed down to generations through tradition. The fundamental
books of Kabbalah were the *Bahir* (brightness) and *Heichalot* (Palaces)
from the 1st century AD, and the *Zohar* (radiance) from the 13th century. These included the ideas of the Jewish sages Isaac the Blind and
Nahmanides and were also based on earlier works such as the traditions of Enoch.[9]

Following the expulsion of the Jews from Spain in 1492, the mystic writings of Judaism were distributed and translated throughout Europe. Works previously not available to European intellects were suddenly attainable, albeit for extensive sums of money. Of these, one of the most significant was the Hebrew Talmud, a collection of scholarly works on the Old Testament that were compiled in the 6th century AD; it also had many texts from much earlier periods, some that dated from the 2nd century AD.[10] The Talmud explained that generations of humanity were molded, one out of another, in successive catastrophes. In the rabbinical concept of the "Seven Earths," the generation inhabiting the Fourth Earth built the tower of Babel but went on to the Fifth Earth when men became oblivious of their former origin and language. Their generation was called "the people who lost their memory." The Fifth Earth was called "the generation of oblivion." In the Hebrew *Tractate Sanhedrin* 109a it is said that, "The place where the tower once stood retains the peculiar quality of inducing a total loss of memory in anyone who passes it."[11]

The Neo-Platonic philosophers of the 4th century AD wrote commentaries on the works of Plato and myth from Egypt that addressed the same ideas. The belief in a lost world language that retained the essence of all knowledge played a fundamental part in this school of thought.[12] They tied the loss of the pure knowledge and its recovery with the "messenger to the gods." In his Commentary on the *Timaeus of Plato*, Proclus wrote, "The deity Hermes was responsible for distinguishing and interpreting things, recalling to memory the sources of intellect."[13] Macrobius wrote similarly concerning the Roman version of the same deity, stating that "We know Mercury to have power over the voice and over speech, he recalls all what had been forgotten."[14]

John Dee for example, wrote a treatise on what he called the "one symbol," or *Monas Hieroglyphica*, that was published in 1564. Dee believed that he wrote the secret of all knowledge in this work through the divine providence of God: "[I am] the pen merely of [God] Whose

Spirit, quickly writing these things through me, I wish and I hope to be."[15] Dee's "monad" was, in essence, the sign of Mercury.

MONAS
HIERO
GLYPHI-
CA.

Fig. 1. Image by author based on John Dee's *Monas Hieroglyphica* (Cambridge: C. H. Josten Ambix Journal XII,1964), 2.

In the late medieval period of Europe, Hebrew mystics began to address the *mercurial* theme of lost knowledge.[16] They focused primarily on the etymological source of the earliest name for the Roman god Mercury in Egyptian myth, Thoth or Tahuti. The sages explained that the name "Thoth" is a combination of the last letter of the Hebrew alphabet, tawv, and the word for promise, *oath*.[17] The letter tawv has the literal meaning, "a mark or sign."[18] A "tau-oth" or "tah-ut" was therefore a symbol connected with divine promise.

The Semitic (Hebrew and Phoenician) and Egyptian cultures were in contact with each other from greatest antiquity. When the Israelites entered the Promised Land, which was also called Canaan/Phoenicia, at the end of the Exodus, ca. the 14th century BC, the area extended from the border of Egypt to the south to the edge of the mountains of Ararat in the north. The core theology of Egypt (the Osiris, Isis, and Horus myth) incorporated the city Byblos on the coast of Phoenicia as central to its narrative. "Byblos" is the origin of the Latin word for book, Bible, and the phonetic alphabet is so called because of its establishment in Phoenicia. Renaissance theologians believed that Moses was the inventor of the first "sound-based" script in the ancient world. They derived this understanding from the writings of Eupolemus ca. 158 BC that states: "Moses was the first wise man to

teach the alphabet to the Jews who transferred them to the Phoenicians and the Phoenicians passed to the Greeks."[19] In Genesis, the first
man marked with the sign of God's promise to protect him was Cain,
and the Lord said to him,

> What have you done? The voice of the blood of your brother
> cries to me from the ground....You shall be a vagabond and a
> fugitive on the earth. And Cain said to the Lord, My punish-
> ment is greater than I can bear....And it will be that anyone
> who finds me shall kill me. And the Lord said to him, If any-
> one kills Cain, he shall be avenged sevenfold. And the Lord
> set a mark on Cain, so that anyone that found Cain should
> not kill him. (Genesis 4:10–15)

According to this etymology, the *first* wisdom spread throughout
the earth by the exile Cain, the one closest to the origin of humanity in
his purest and divine sense. The Omniscient God had spoken to him
directly as He had spoken to Adam and Eve. Similarly, in Egyptian cos-
mology, Thoth was not only the inventor of writing but also the "lord
of time" and "he whom reckons years and measures the earth."[20]

The Egyptian *ankh*, meaning life, was closely associated with
Thoth. The ancient circle-cross glyph of mercury and the combination of the Greek letters (the consonant tau and vowel omega) forming the word *t-auw* loosely resemble it and have similar meaning.
Both are related to the *tauv* mark of Cain as a symbol that "preserved
his life."

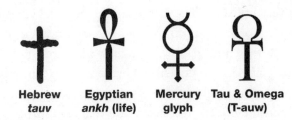

| Hebrew | Egyptian | Mercury | Tau & Omega |
| *tauv* | *ankh* (life) | glyph | (T-auw) |

Fig. 2. Image by author

The Jewish sages explained that Cain built the first city and therefore was the founder of civilization. Cain named this city Enoch after his first son (Genesis 4:16–17). Also according to the sages, the names of Enoch's grandson and great grandson, *Mehujael* and *Methusael* (man smitten by Elohim and man who is of Elohim) show that for a time the knowledge of Elohim, the name of God recorded in Genesis, was preserved, *but soon disappeared.* Their reasoning was that the lineage of Cain had died in the flood. However, the human race survived through Noah and his family descended from Seth, Adam's third son. The Mystics focused on the two Enochs that lived before the great deluge of Noah. The first, the son of Cain, had transferred the sacred knowledge from Eden into the first civilization that was later destroyed due to its corruption and evil. The second Enoch, from the line of Seth, preserved the pure knowledge apart from this corruption. This body of knowledge had been incorporated in ancient structures geometrically. Its decipherment needed a key thought to exist in a universal language that was lost. Ironically, the event that caused its loss corresponded with the development of writing and the birth of civilization. Although biblical chronology renders it impossible for Noah to have met Enoch from the line of Seth, he would have known Methuselah, Enoch's son. Methuselah lived for 967 years. There was a belief among biblical scholars that Noah would have possessed the learning of Enoch, particularly because it had been recorded in writing. In 1614, Walter Raleigh's *The Historie of the World in Five Bookes* gave this explanation:

> …It is very probable that Noah had seen and might preserve this book. For it is not likely, that so exquisite knowledge therein (as these men had) was suddenly invented and found out, but left by Seth to Enoch, and by Enoch to Noah, as hath been said before. And therefore if letters and arts were known from the time of Seth to Enoch, and that Noah lived with Methusalem, who lived with Adam, and Abraham lived with

Noah, it is not strange (I say) to conceive how Moses came to the knowledge of the first Age, be it by letters, or by Cabala and Tradition, had the undoubted word of God need of any other proof than self-authority.[21]

Regardless of whether Noah preserved the written knowledge of Enoch, or the knowledge was recorded in some other fashion, the name Enoch in the Old Testament was of prime importance to the medieval and Renaissance thinkers in the search for a universal language. There was a special geometry expressed in the letters, chronology, and meaning of Enoch's life on earth. Occult mystics referred to themselves as "initiates" of the ancient sciences. The Hebrew name Enoch was itself a word meaning "initiated" or "experienced."[22] He lived for exactly 365 years, a number equaling the days in a solar year.

The books *Polychronicon* of the Medieval Alchemist Ranult Higdon (AD 1350), the *Cooke Manuscript* (AD 1410), as well as the *Antiquities of the Jews* by Flavius Josephus recorded the knowledge from Enoch of Seth's line that was preserved geometrically in the architecture of ancient temples. This was especially the case for the Great Pyramid of Giza in Egypt and the Temple of Solomon in Jerusalem.

Within this Judaic-Christian framework, the intellects of 17th century Europe searched for the *prisca sapientia*. The Cambridge Neo-Platonists in England maintained the tradition of philosophy interrelated with theology as well. Through their establishment in Britain at the highest academic institution of the time, the progress of several centuries towards the attainment of knowledge was preserved. The Cambridge Neo-Platonists included many notable intellects of the occult and scientific renaissance, men like Henry More, John Smith, Ralph Cudworth, and Benjamin Whichcote. The University of Cambridge's motto, "From this place, we gain enlightenment and precious knowledge," produced scientific geniuses whose theories are still used in modern academics. These were notably Isaac Newton, Lord Kelvin, James Clerk Maxwell, and Lord Rayleigh.[23]

Isaac Newton, the greatest of the natural philosophers was in close association with the Cambridge Neo-Platonists. They influenced his views concerning the physical laws manifested in the universe. In fact, it was by embracing their tenet of the existence of an original pure knowledge that he produced his greatest works.

Many books have investigated whether Newton believed that an original pure knowledge existed. Some conclude that he did in fact search for it, but that is the whole of their investigation. A few have written that Newton actually discovered "something" and try to fit his existing research into a *prisca sapientia* of their own design, claiming his beliefs fit modern realms of philosophy or Eastern religions, but these speculations are not upheld by the body of his work. Although Newton had solved riddles of space, time, gravity, light, and invented mathematics to predict the motion of objects, this was not the *priscia sapienta*. Since the time of Newton, no one has revealed the true form and nature of the original knowledge, or from whence it came; that is the greatest question of all.

Some of Newton biographers have speculated that the evidence for Newton's search for the "key" to all things was demonstrated by the sheer vastness of his works. The biographer Gale Christianson described Newton's motivation for studying alchemy as having been a means to an end, and that Newton was searching alchemy for a symbolic key that could unlock the *prisca sapientia* from the writing of the ancients. He concluded also that, "The theological manuscripts [in Newton's collection] reveal that he no less ardently pursued a parallel religious wisdom or *prisca theologia*…"[24]

Dr. Christianson makes a good point; the volume of Newton's work does show his dedication to both the "pure thought" and the "pure words of God"; however, the *majority* of Newton's works were theological. Newton produced three times as many theological papers than scientific. These manuscripts consistently recorded Newton's belief in the author of creation as one and the same as the author of the

Law and prophecy contained in the Bible. This one tenet is also the most pervasive in all of Newton's scholarly manuscripts.

A strange condition remains; despite the resolve in which Newton searched for the *prisca theologia* and the *prisca sapientia*, he did not leave any *direct* assertions concerning the matter. If he had discovered a unifying theme to "all thought," or realized the direction towards which such a value might be found, he seems to have left no explanation.

However, it can be demonstrated that Newton did *rediscover* the *prisca sapienta* and imbedded this information within his writings that addressed the laws of creation. In this way, Newton intended that his discoveries would be revealed in a future age; an age in which we *presently* exist.

NOTES

1. Sir Steven, Runciman, *The Fall of Constantinople* (Cambridge UK Cambridge University Press, 1965).
2. Columbia Encyclopedia, H. L. Strack, translator. Columbia Universty Press. London, UK. 1963 entry for Plotinus.
3. Plato. *The Timaeus,* translated by Benjamin Jowett. (New York: Liberal Arts Press, 1949).
4. Webster's New International Dictionary, 3rd Ed., Unabridged; G. & C. Merriam Company, Springfield, Massachusetts, U.S.A.; 1961.
5. Edward Zupko, *Revolution in Measurement: Western European Weights and Measures Since the Age of Science* Published by Amer Philosophical Society, Philadelphia USA (May 1990).
6. Robert Turner. *Ars Notoria* London, Printed by F. Cottrel, Lamb at the East-end of Pauls. 1657. Transcribed and converted to Acrobat by Benjamin Rowe, July 1999. www.Sacred-magic.com
7. Rene, Descartes, (Regulate, 1958b Rule IV) *Key Philosophical Writings* translated by.Elizabeth Haldane. Wordsworth Classics of World Literature, 1997 Hertfordshire: Wordsworth UK.
8. Frances, Yates. *Giordano Bruno and the Hermetic Tradition* (Chicago: University of Chicago Press, 1991).
9. Author's note: Enoch the patriarch before the great flood of Noah was reputed to have spoken with the angels and visited heaven. His record of these events is recorded in the pseudopigraphic book of Enoch.
10. Columbia Encyclopedia. H. L. Strack, translator. Columbia University Press London. 1963. The Babylonian Talmud was available to the natural philosophers of the 17th century and contains works dating from the 1st and 2nd centuries AD.
11. Louis Ginzberg, *Legends of the Jews.* Published by the Jewish Publication Society of America. Philadelphia 1920.

12. Rossi, Paolo, *Logic and the Art of Memory: The Quest for a Universal Language,* trans. Stephen Clucas. (Published by University of Chicago, Illinois. Athlone Press, 2000).

13. Felix. Buffiere, *The Myths of Homere et la pensee grecque.,* Vol. V, p. 237. (Publisher, Society of Editions, Paris, France 1956).

14. Proclus' Commentary on Plato's dialogue *Timaeus.* Translated by Dirk Baltzly. (Printed in the United Kingdom at the University Press, Cambridge. 2006)

15. James Orchard Halliwell *The Private Diary of Dr John Dee, and the Catalogue of his Library of Manuscripts.* Facsim.of 1842 edition (March 1997) by pg. 43. Kessinger Publishing Kila MT 59920 U.S.A.

16. Frances Yates, *Giordano Bruno and the Hermetic tradition.* (Chicago: University of Chicago Press, 1991 pg. 13).

17. James Strong's Hebrew dictionary entry # 226. Strong's Exhaustive Concordance of the Bible. AMG Publishers edition, World Bible Publishers, Inc. 1986 Iowa Falls, IA.

18. Ibid. Strong's Hebrew dictionary entry # 8420.

19. James H. Charlesworth *Pseudepigraphia,* Volume 2, ed., (New York: Doubleday, 1985), Pg. 43, 122. 124.

20. E. Wallis Budge, *The Gods of the Egyptians.* Vol. 1 p. 400 the Pyramid texts. Dover Publications, London; New Ed edition (June 1, 1969)

21. Walter Raleigh, *The Historie of the World in Five Bookes* (University Press, Oxford 1829) Book 1. Pg. 156, 157.

22. Ibid Strong's Hebrew dictionary entry # 2596

23. Elizabeth Leedham-Green, *A Concise History of the University of Cambridge.* (Cambridge University Press, Cambridge UK: 1996). Pgs. 1–4.

24. Gale E. Christianson, *In The Presence Of The Creator. Isaac Newton and His Times* (Connecticut, USA, The Easton Press. 1989).

1

PRINCIPIA APOCALYPTICA

saac Newton came further in understanding the physics of time and space than any man in his age, which is why his mathematical and natural philosophical works are considered the foundation of scientific exploration to this day. Yet, Newton's investigation of the primary causes of nature was consistently fashioned in relationship to the theological framework of the ancient Hebrews. His vast research on chronology and interpretation of biblical prophecy was as brilliant as his work in physics. According to John Locke, "Mr. Newton is really a very valuable man, not only for his wonderful skill in mathematics, but in divinity also, and his great knowledge is the Scriptures, wherein I know few his equals."[1]

Within the empirical scientific work for which he is most famous, *Principia Mathematica,* Newton wrote of the inseparability of the order of time and space from the existence of God:

> The true God is a living, intelligent, and powerful being. His duration reaches from eternity to eternity; His presence from infinity to infinity....He governs all things and knows all

8

DAVID FLYNN

things that are or can be done. He is not eternity and infinity, but eternal and infinite; he is not duration or space, but he endures and is present. He endures forever, and is everywhere present; and, by existing always and everywhere, he constitutes duration and space. This most beautiful system of the sun, planets, and comets could only proceed from the counsel and dominion of an intelligent and powerful Being....He is omnipresent not virtually only, but also substantially; for virtue cannot subsist without substance. In him are all things contained and moved. [2]

It had not been realized until fairly recently that Newton wrote far more concerning theology, philosophy, and even alchemy than he did in natural philosophy. The family of the Earl of Portsmouth inherited Newton's vast collection of writing and stored it in the library of Cambridge University. These papers were held in Cambridge until 1936 when they were purchased in auction from John Maynard Keynes.[3] Many biographers up until that time avoided mention of Newton's esoteric interests. This was borne not only out of the lack of information concerning their existence, but also to the negative impact they might have on his reputation as a scientist or the veracity of his most famous works.

Within these papers, it was apparent that Newton believed the ancient mathematicians possessed methods for calculating the exact dimensions of the Earth. Newton also reasoned that they purposely obscured these methods in their works. In researching the ancient Greek attempts to solve the prediction of location for objects in motion, Newton wrote, "But they accomplished it by certain simple proportions, judging that nothing written in a different style was worthy to read, and in consequence concealing the analysis by which they found their constructions."[4] The revolution of science that Newton single-handedly achieved in *Principia* was primarily that the laws of motion and gravity, and the nature of space and time, had not manifested apart from his belief in the immutable truths of the Bible. From its pages, Newton found the path towards discovery in the natural universe. By his own words, the Bible was his source of inspiration for every theory that he conceived.

Newton believed that the code of civil and religious truth that God gave to Moses on Mount Sinai also contained the physical laws of creation. Because the central focus of the Torah was the "Ark of the Law" and later the temple that housed it, Newton reasoned that the unifying theory of dimension should also be contained within both. He understood that this creational blueprint was not only embedded within the structure of the law presented in Exodus, but also echoed in the works of the ancients having lived closer to the time of the Exodus. This was also the consenting view of the Renaissance Neo-Platonists with whom Newton had been associated.

In 1593, the Spanish biblical scholar Arias Montano proposed that the proportion of creation was concealed in weights and measures given to the Hebrews by God through Moses.[5]

In 1690, the independent minister Thomas Beverley wrote concerning the dimensions of a future temple of Jerusalem, described in the book of the prophet Ezekiel:

> And as Number, Weight, and Measure are so Essentially necessary to All the Great Things, that are perform'd in the World, as to Astronomy, Observation of the Heavens, and their Course, Geometry, Architecture, Statics, Navigation, Survey, Experimental Philosophy, and to all Commerce, and Traffick, and even mutual Cohabitation of Mankind; So under these Measures in this Vision are shaded the Sublimity of the Divine Communion with his Saints, and Servants; and of Angels, and Saints one with Another; and those Lines of Communication signified by Jacobs Ladder, Gen. 28.12. between the New Heaven, and the New Earth.[6]

It was in awareness of this principle that the British architect Sir Christopher Wren (1632–1723) wrote, "Architecture aims at Eternity; and therefore, is the only thing incapable of modes and fashions in its principles."[7]

An overview of Newton's scientific works reveals a consistent incorporation of thought from ancient Jewish sages, prophetic studies, Bible chronology, and history. He studied the writings of the Jewish sages before producing his theories of natural philosophy. While a student at Cambridge, Newton learned Hebrew from Isaac Abendana, the first person to translate the *Mishnah*, a treatise on the five books of the Old Testament, into Latin.[8] He was also able to read the early mystic works of Jewish scholars through his access to the Latin commentaries on the Hebrew Scriptures at the Cambridge library. The works of Moses Mamonides were considered the greatest in Judaism. His writings, the *Mishneh Torah* (1180) and the *Guide of the Perplexed* (1190), are still the foremost Jewish studies of the Old Testament in existence. Maimonides was the greatest theologian of Rabbinic Judaism, and his influence ranged beyond Jewish thought to influence Christians like Saint Thomas Aquinas and Newton himself. The biographer John Maynard Keynes described Newton as "rather a Judaic monotheist of the school of Maimonides."[9]

The importance of the ancient Hebrew religion as the original form of God's communication to humanity was central to Newton's search for clarity of universal laws:

> So then the first religion was the most rational of all others till the nations corrupted it. For there is no way (with out revelation) to come to the knowledge of a Deity but by the frame of nature.[10]

This belief had been reinforced not only through Newton's familiarity with the works of ancient Jewish sages, but also by the writings of Francis Van Helmont (1614–1698), whose books were housed at the library of Cambridge where Newton taught as a professor. Helmont believed that great and undiscovered knowledge existed in the original Hebrew versions of the Old Testament, as he explicates in *The Language of the Prophets*:

> Is there no key to be found with which the Mysteries of Scripture might be opened? And forasmuch as the Old Testament was written in Hebrew and that it cannot be translated into another language so as to retain its own proper force and energy, may not we therefore suppose that in the Hebrew language (as we consider the same to be a living language) this key is to be found?[11]

Newton understood the words of God in prophecy as a reflection of the design in God's creation. He expressed these views within his theological studies and works of chronology, history, and natural philosophy, each of which was incredibly vast. However, due to his strong rejection of the Trinity—a belief considered heretical in the "Trinitarian" Church of England, and one that Newton occasionally wrote of within his theological research—these biblical works from several decades of his life remained a secret. Newton may have intended that this research would surface after his death, leaving the providence of God to decide its fate. However, his interest in cryptograms in nature paralleled his pursuit of the riddle of prophecy. The code that unlocked all prophetic writing was a topic that Newton explored extensively. He wrote:

> He that would understand a book written in a strange language must first learn the language....Such a language was that wherein the Prophets wrote, and the want of sufficient skill in that language is the main reason why they are so little understood. John did not write in one language, Daniel in another, Isaiah in a third and the rest in others peculiar to

themselves, but they all write in one and the same mystical language....For the language of the Prophets, being Hiero-glyphical, had affinity with that of the Egyptian priest and Eastern wise men, and therefore was anciently much better understood in the East than it is now in the West. I received also much light in this search by the analogy between the world natural and the world politic. For the mystical language was founded in this analogy, and will be best understood by considering its original.[12]

This opinion was not exclusively Newton's, however. For example, in 1657 Robert Turner wrote of knowledge of a "key" in his work *Ars Notoria*, a book of orations and prayers that Solomon had allegedly used upon the altar in the temple in Jerusalem. Apart from being an unusually esoteric and occult work, it reveals an overriding view of philosophers of the time that the language of the Hebrews contained a supernatural power that could unlock the secrets of nature. A brief explanation was inserted in a footnote by the publisher in 1657:

It is called the Notory Art because in certain brief notes it teacheth and comprehendeth the knowledge of all arts....It being a Science of so Transcendent a purity, that it hath its Original out of the depth and profundity of the Chaldee, He-brew, and Grecian Languages; and therefore cannot possible by any means be explicated fully in the poor Thread-bare Scheme of our Language.[13]

Newton devoted his entire life in the quest of a pure science and theology. If he had discovered the *prisca sapientia*, and further evidence will show that he did, he would not have resorted to leaving such a discovery in the hands of the unworthy. It is likely a unifying theory of the laws of creation with the laws of God would be best suited to a code. This form of writing and encryption, in Newton's reasoning, was the modality in which the Bible itself had been written. As God revealed the Law of Moses to men with supernatural power, with its words revered and protected, a unifying law of creation should be presented in like manner. Similarly, the dispensation to men of such a powerful truth would only take place with the full intent and providence of God; Newton, however, would not write of its discovery openly. He would seal it within his papers exploring the laws and the creation of God. These vast works, ranging from chronology, natural philosophy, and theology suggested its presence, visible only to those given the eyes to see.

It is not without precedent then, that Keynes made this statement concerning Newton's view of reality:

> He regarded the universe as a cryptogram set by the Almighty—just *as he himself wrapped the discovery of the calculus in a cryptogram when he communicated with Leibniz* [emphasis added]. By pure thought, by concentration of mind, the riddle, he believed, would be revealed to the initiate. He did read the riddle of the heavens. And he believed that by the same powers of his introspective imagination he would read the riddle of the Godhead, the riddle of past and future events divinely foreordained.[14]

Here, Keynes highlights one of the most significant and overlooked aspects of Newton's work: an obsession with the cryptography of God's design of the natural world.

The methods of encryption that Newton employed display the same genius that was manifested into his theories of gravity, light, and motion.

Newton encrypted his discovery of calculus to Leibnez due to fear that others less skilled in mathematics might plagiarize it. His first open statement of calculus was inserted in the appendix of *Optics*, published in 1704. Later, Newton added a copy of a letter that he sent to Leibniz in 1676, in *Principia* (the Scholium to Book II, Section II, Proposition VII) in order to establish the date of his discovery. He wrote:

> I cannot proceed with the explanation of the fluxions [the calculus] now, I have preferred to conceal it thus: 6accdae13eff7i3l9n4o4qrr4s8t12vx.

This encryption defined the meaning of calculus by giving the number of different letters in a Latin sentence: *Data aequatione quot-cunque fluentes quantitates involvente, fluxiones invenire: et vice versa.*

Newton waited twenty years before giving this translation of this anagram, which in English reads: "Given an equation involving any number of fluent quantities, to find the fluxions: and vice versa."[15]

The code lists the number of times each letter appears in the Latin sentence in alphabetical order. Newton's technique for encrypting the discovery of calculus manifests in a distinctive framework. Only a reader sufficiently familiar with the mathematical topic and Latin could understand it. However, it awaited interpretation by the one who made it. This was akin to the methods in which Newton ascribed man's discernment of prophecy, about which he explained:

> God gave the Prophecies of the Old Testaments, not to gratify men's curiosities by enabling them to foreknow things, but that after they were fulfilled they might be interpreted by the event; and his own Providence, not the Interpreters, be then manifested thereby to the world. For the event of things pre-dicted many ages before, will then be a convincing argument that the world is governed by providence.[16]

Newton held an exception to this belief, however. He believed that certain prophecies were opened through divine providence at ap-pointed times for the benefit of the true Church on earth. He searched for the timing of prophetic events from the past in order to establish the scene of prophetic fulfillment in his time:

> That the benefit which may by understanding the sacred Prophecies and the danger by neglecting them is very great and the obligation to study them is as great may appear by considering the like case of the Jews at the coming of Christ. For the rules whereby they were to know the Messiah were the prophecies of the Old Testament. And these our Saviour recommended to their consideration in the very beginning of His preaching and afterward commanded the study of them for that end saying…. Hypocrites can ye discern the face of the sky but can ye not discern the signs of the times.[17]

This statement seems to contradict Newton's statement that prophecy was not given to predict future events. However, he was convinced that the end of days was upon the earth in his lifetime, and therefore, the formula for the correct interpretation of prophecy was satisfied. This drove him to establish a chronology for events that was soon to be fulfilled. In keeping with the pattern of prophetic encryption in the Bible, Newton wrote his interpretations within the same framework.

The greatest Hebrew cryptographer in antiquity was a subject of several books that Newton wrote during his lifetime: the prophet Daniel. In 1733, six years after Newton's death, only one of his studies of the Bible was published, *Observations upon the Prophecies of Daniel and the Apocalypse of St. John.* It was in this book that Newton revealed the motivation for his research of prophecy:

> He who denies Daniel's prophecies, undermines Christianity, which is founded on Daniel's prophecies concerning Christ…. For Daniel's Prophecies reach to the end of the world; and there is scarce a prophecy in the Old Testament concerning Christ, which doth not in something or other relate to his

second coming. If divers of the ancients, as Irenaeus, Julius
Africanus, Hippolytus the martyr, and Apollinaris Bishop of
Laodicea, applied the half week to the times of Antichrist;
why may not we...[18]

In casual reading, this statement displays Newton's faith in the
veracity of the Bible, especially the writing of the prophet Daniel.
There are many biographical works of Newton explaining his pursuit
of natural philosophy in the direction that was shaped by his theological beliefs. However, Newton had a much loftier goal in his pairing of
the theological world with the scientific. Every intellectual work that
he achieved was an effort to understand the prophecies of God for the
time and manner of the return of Christ.

Newton believed, as did the great body of early church scholars
up until his age, that the book of Daniel contained the most time-
centered prophecies in the Bible. In the *Prophecies of Daniel*, Newton
wrote, "Daniel is most distinct in order of time, and easiest to be understood, and therefore in those things which relate to the last times,
he must be made the key to the rest." Flavius Josephus, in his 1st century AD work *The Antiquities of the Jews*, wrote that Daniel "was not
only wont to prophecy future things, as did other prophets, but he
also fixed the time at which these would come to pass."[20]

Newton wrote *Observations upon the Prophecies of Daniel and the
Apocalypse of St. John* several years after his discoveries of light, gravity,
and time. The reinforcement of his previous scientific works with the
theological were not so much a change in his thinking but a statement
of his frame of mind during the most productive and inspired time in
his life—and the most tragic.

EXPECTATIONS OF THE END OF DAYS

After Newton graduated from Trinity College at Cambridge in the
spring of 1665, the university was closed because of an outbreak of

the bubonic plague, known historically as the Great Plague. Over the course of two years, the plague killed nearly 100,000 people in Europe. The death toll in London alone was 70,000, nearly 15 percent of the city's population. Although the Great Fire of London destroyed much of the city in 1666, it also killed most of the rats and fleas that carried the plague bacteria. In Britain, many religious minds of the time viewed the plague and the destruction of London as fulfillment of the prophecies in the Book of Revelation. The number of the year 1666 also stood as an ominous sign of the end for many prominent theologians of the time.

Between 1642 and 1661, England experienced three civil wars over the governing of the British Isles. During this time, King Charles I was replaced by the first Republican government of Britain until the coronation of Charles II in 1661. A major influence of the Republican government between these Kings was the religious-political movement of the Fifth Monarchists from 1649 to 1661. The Fifth Monarchists took their name from the belief that the four world powers outlined in the prophecies of Daniel 2:4: Assyria, Persia, Greece, and Rome had ended and the Fifth Monarchy, and that of the saints under Jesus Christ, would soon be at hand.[21] The proponents of this view produced many books of this prophetic interpretation that circulated throughout England even after the re-establishment of Charles II. Their apocalyptic expectations for the year 1666 were well established during Newton's education at Cambridge.

During the seventeenth century, the view of the apocalypse changed from an allegory to the life of man and the reward of heaven, to a literal expectation of the return of Christ to establish his kingdom. This view was popularized by John Foxe's *Book of Martyrs,* which was published in 1563. Foxe believed that the millennium had begun at the conversion of Constantine in AD 312 and that the Second Coming and Last Judgment of Christ were imminent.[22] The writings of Martin Luther contributed to the 17th century view of English theologians that the

Pope was the Antichrist and that England would be the divine tool in the overthrow of Rome.[23]

In 1642, Henry Archer's book *The Personal Reign of Christ Upon Earth* predicted the second coming of Christ in 1666. This exegesis of the prophecies of Daniel and the Revelation of St. John was followed by other books from English authors like John Tillinghast, Peter Sterry, and John Rogers in the 1650s also claiming that the year 1666 was a likely date for the return of Christ.[24] The Arabic numerals of 1666 represented a statement of the mark of the beast in Revelation, according to Mr. Francis Potter's book, published in England in 1642, *An Interpretation of the Number 666.*[25]

Joseph Mede (1586–1638), a prominent Anglican professor of Greek at Cambridge, endorsed Potter's book and wrote considering Potter's theory of 1666, "If it be not a truth…it is the most considerable probability that I have ever read in that kind."[26]

Joseph Mede was the greatest theological influence of Isaac Newton. He possessed a compilation of Mede's works published in 1665, which included *Clavis Apocalyptica* (Key to the Revelation) and *Heaven Upon Earth.*[27] It would be hard for Newton to disregard the prophetic interpretations of the events of 1665 and 1666, especially when considering the contemporary prophecies that came before them. The fire of London was actually predicted by an obscure British author named Walter Gostelo in 1658 who wrote,

The coming of God in Mercy, in Vengence; beginning with fire, to convert of to consume, at this so sinful city London: Oh! London, London. If fire make not ashes of the city, and thy bones also, conclude me a liar forever!…[T]he decree is gone out, repent, or burn, as Sodom and Gomorrah![28]

In addition, astronomical portents heralded the plague and London fire, as recorded in this historical account from Hamburg, Germany in December 1664:

The great Comet lately seen here, appears no longer with us; but here is now another, much less then the former, rising Southeast, and setting North-West. They write from Vienna by the last [mail], of a great Comet seen there also, shewing itself first from the East, and pointing toward Hungary. There has been likewise seen in the air the appearance of a Coffin, which causes great anxiety of thought among the people. We have had our part here of the Comet, as well as other Places, besides which, here have been other terrible Apparitions and Noises in the air, as Fires, and sounds of Canon, and Musket-shot.[29]

And from London:

A blazing star or comet appeared for several months before the plague, as there did the year after another, a little before the fire....The comet before the pestilence was of a faint, dull, languid colour, and its motion very heavy, Solemn, and slow; but the comet before the fire was bright and sparkling, or, as others said, flaming, and its motion swift and furious; and accordingly, one foretold a heavy judgment, slow but severe, terrible and frightful, as was the plague; but the other foretold a stroke, sudden, swift, and fiery as the conflagration....The apprehensions of the people were likewise strangely increased by the error of the times; in which, I think, the people, from what principle I cannot imagine, were more addicted to prophecies and astrological conjurations, dreams, and old wives' tales than ever they were before or since. Whether this unhappy temper was originally raised by the follies of some people who got money by it—that is to say, by printing predictions and prognostications—I know not; but certain it is, books frighted them terribly, such as Lilly's Almanack, Gadbury's Astrological Predictions, Poor

Robin's Almanack, and the like; also several pretended religious books, one entitled, Come out of her, my People, lest
you be Partaker of her Plagues; another called, Fair Warning; another, Britain's Remembrancer; and many such, all,
or most part of which, foretold, directly or covertly, the ruin
of the city.[30]

During Newton's last few months as an undergraduate at Trinity
College, he studied amidst the apocalyptic fervor that pervaded the
country. He recorded his observation of the comet of 1664–65 in a
notebook, and on December 23,1664, he wrote, "I observed a comet
whose rays were round her, yet her tail extended itself a little towards
the east and parallel to the ecliptic."[31]

For two years during the fearsome plague and the fire of London,
he lived with his mother at his home in Woolsthorpe, England. It
was during this time, termed by biographers as "the two miraculous
years," that Newton developed every revolutionary scientific work for
which he is famous. It is a distinct possibility that the productivity of
Newton's miraculous years stemmed from his conviction that the end
of the age was upon the earth. From his viewpoint of prophetic interpretation, a framework that he inherited from Joseph Mede, Henry
Archer, and many other theologians, the time for research would have
soon come to an end. Any scientific advances that could be made
necessarily had to be done in earnest. For Newton, every theoretical
revelation that he achieved stood as verification of Daniel's prophecy
as reads in Dan12:4: "Even to the time of the end…knowledge shall
be increased." Newton viewed the book of Daniel as a missive extending through time to him, addressed to his intellect, a mind divinely
inspired to value and solve its riddles. The body of these scientific
accomplishments as being concentrated within the plague years was
explained much later in a letter Newton wrote to the scholar Pierre
Des Maizeaux in 1718:

In the beginning of the year 1665, I found the Method of approximating series & the Rule for reducing any dignity of any Binomial into such a series. The same year in May I found the method of Tangents of Gregory & Slusius, & in November had the direct method of fluxions & the next year in January had the Theory of Colors & in May following I had entrance into the inverse method of fluxions. And the same year I began to think of gravity extending to the orb of the Moon & (having found out how to estimate the force with which a globe revolving within a sphere presses the surface of the sphere) from Kepler's rule of the periodical times of the Planets being in sesquialterate proportion of their distances from the centers of their Orbs, I deduced that the forces which keep the Planets in their Orbs must be reciprocally as the squares of their distances from the centers about which they revolve: and thereby compared the force requisite to keep the Moon in her Orb with the force of gravity at the surface of the earth, and found them answer pretty nearly. All this was in the two plague years of 1665 and 1666. For in those days I was in the prime of my age of invention & minded Mathematics & Philosophy more than at any time since.[32]

In the decades that followed, Newton's research turned away from the scientific, and towards questions of biblical interpretation, prophecy, and chronology. The study of the events preceding the return of Christ would take precedence in Newton's intellectual focus. He did not abandon the topic even until his death. He wrote of the duty presented to him having been molded by the times:

Why should we not think that the Prophesies which concern the latter times into which we are fallen were in like manner

intended for our use that in the midst of Apostacies we might
be able to discern the truth…and consequently that it is also
our duty to search with all diligence into these Prophesies.[33]

Newton returned to Cambridge in 1667 and remained as a lec-
turing Professor of Mathematics for twenty-nine years. During this
period, Newton published his scientific works developed during the
upheaval of 1665 and 1666 and began intensive study of biblical
prophecy.

In 1696, Newton moved to London to begin a new job as the
Warden of the Royal Mint. It had become apparent to Newton over
the passing years that the return of Christ he had anticipated early in
his career was less imminent. However, Newton retained his belief of
the time-dependant nature of Daniel's prophecies and their eventual
manifestation in the world. Toward the end of his life, knowing that
he was not of the generation that would see the fulfillment of end
time prophecy, Newton concentrated on the clear interpretation of
its chronology. This work was dedicated to theologians of the future.
All that was left for Newton, as a summation of his great theological
work, was to supply the *direction* in which others were to proceed
after his death, the manner of which followed the design of Daniel's
prophecies. "As for you, Daniel, obscure the matters and seal the book
until the time of the End: let many muse and let knowledge increase"
(Daniel 12:4).

In this version of Daniel 12:4, from a literal translation of Hebrew
based on the *Targum* that Newton used in his studies of Daniel, the
mode of communication to a future audience was described. Compre-
hension of the prophecy was dependent on time and the providential
influence of God.[34]

Believing that his theological and chronological works would serve
the investigations of scholars in the future, and that they addressed the
same theme as the prophecies of Daniel, Newton recorded them in
like manner. The information in these works extended far beneath

the surface. Only those wise enough to discern the clues would be awarded the secret of understanding in the time of the end.

> [A]bout the time of the end, in all probability, a body of men will be raised up, who will turn their attention to the prophecies, and insist upon their literal interpretation in the midst of much clamor and opposition.[35]

NOTES

1. Franz Kobler, *The Jewish Frontier,* March 1943 "Newton on the Restoration of the Jews," p. 21.
2. Isaac Newton, *Mathematical Principles of Natural Philosophy and System of the World,* trans. Andrew Motte, rev. with an Appendix by Florian Cajori. (Los Angeles: University of California Press, 1966)
3. Milo Keynes, *Essays on John Maynard Keynes.* (Cambridge University Press, Cambridge UK 1975).
4. Isaac Newton, *Veterum loca solida restitute: Principles of Mathematics,* University of California Press Berkeley CA. 1999. pgs. 4, 277.
5. Benito Arias Montano *Antiquates Judaicae* (León: University of León Press, Spain, 1999) pgs. 108–112.
6. Thomas Beverley, *The Pattern of the Divine Temple* (London, 1690) Library of Congress, Washington Gov. Printing office. Washington D.C. U.S.A. 1868 pg.9
7. Christopher Wren, *Tracts on Architecture* Tract I. ed. Lydia M. Soo. Cambridge University Press, Cambridge UK. (November 13, 1998)
8. Jose Faur "Newton, Maimonides, and esoteric knowledge," *Cross Currents: The Journal of the Association for Religious and Intellectual Life* no. 40, (1990): Pg. 528.
9. *One Hundred Twentieth-Century Philosophers,* ed. Stuart Brown, Diané Collinson, and Robert Wilkinson (London: Routledge publishers, 1998).
10. Isaac Newton, MS. Yahuda 41, p. 7r. Professor Rob Iliffe., Newton Papers Project University of Sussex, East Sussex. UK.2007 www.newtonproject.sussex.ac.uk
11. Francis Mercury Van Helmont, *The Natural Alphabet* (1614–1698) Allison P. Coudert (Translator) Brill Academic Publishers, Boston, MA. U.S.A. (June 30, 2007)

12. Isaac Newton, *The Language of the Prophets*, in Theological MSS, ed. Herbert McLachlan.Manchester University press. Liverpool UK 1950 pg. 14.

13. Robert Turner *Ars Notoria: The Notory Art of Solomon*, Transcribed and converted to Acrobat by Benjamin Rowe, July 1999. www. Sacred-magic.com.

14. John Maynard Keynes 1947, *Newton, the Man* (New York: Meridian Books, 1956). Pg. 36.

15. Ibid.

16. Isaac Newton, *The Prophecies of Daniel and the Apocalypse* (Hyderabad, India Printland Publishers, 1998) Pg. 14.

17. Isaac Newton *Observations upon the Prophecies of Daniel and the Apocalypse of St. John*. Jewish National and University Library, Jerusalem, Transcribed by Shelley Innes 1998.Pg. 14. The Newton Project—University of Sussex, East Sussex London: 2007 www.newtonproject.sussex.ac.uk

18. Ibid. Newton. *Observations* Pg. 13.

19. Ibid. Newton. *Observations*, p. 14.

20. Flavius Josephus *Antiquities of the Jews* 10.11.7. 267; John J. Collins *Cosmos and Salvation: Jewish Wisdom and Apocalyptic in the. Hellenistic Age*. History of Religions 17.2 Minneapolis, Minnesota USA University of Minnesota Press 1977: pg. 153.

21. Bernard Capp *Fifth Monarchy Men: Study in Seventeenth Century English Millenarianism*, (Faber and Faber, London UK 1972)

22. Richard Bauckham, *Tudor Apocalypse: Sixteenth Century Apocalypticism, Millenarianism and the English Reformation* (Oxford: Sutton Courtenay Press, 1978).

23. Patrick Collinson, *Biblical Rhetoric: the English Nation and National Sentiment in the Prophetic Mode*, Pg. 12 Cambridge UK: Cambridge University Press. 1997.

24. Henry Archer, *The Personal Reign of Christ Upon Earth* (1642), cited by Philip Rogers, *The Fifth Monarchy Men* (London: Oxford University Press, 1966), p. 11–13.

25. The full title is: An Interpretation of the Number 666, was written by wherein not only the manner how this number ought to be interpreted is clearly proved and demonstrated; but it is also showed that this number is an exquisite and perfect character, truly, exactly, and essentially describing that state of Government to which all other notes of Antichrist doe agree. With all known objections solidly and fully answered, that can be materially made against it." Sidney Lee. *A Dictionary of National Biography* Vol. 16. Published by Smith, Elder & Co. London, UK 1909

26. "Mede's Works". vol. ii. lib. iv. p. 1058.: Translated by R. Bransby Cooper London. 1664. Christian Classics Ethereal library 2007 Pg. 851. http://www.ccel.org/ccel/mede/key.html

27. J.E. Force and R.H. Popkins, eds. *Newton and religion: Context nature and influence.*, (Boston: Dordrecth publishers, 1999).

28. Sir Egerton Brydges *Titles, Extracts, and characters in English Literature*, Revived. Published 1815 by T. Bensley for Longman, Hurst, Rees, Orme, and Brown Digitized Nov 15, 2006 Original from the New York Public Library. Volume 8. pg. 73.

29. An excerpt from the Hamburgh, newsletter, December 24, 1664 (published in Newes, January 5, 1665) The Historical Sources of Defoe's Journal of the Plague Year. Copyright 1920, The Stratford Co., Boston, Mass U. S. A. pg., 67.

30. Daniel Defoe. A Journal of the Plague Year 1722 University of Adelaide Australia. Library Electronic Texts Collection. 2006. http://ebooks.adelaide.edu.au/d/defoe/daniel/

31. J.E. McGuire and Martin Tamny (eds), *Certain Philosophical Questions:* Newton's Trinity Notebook (New York: Cambridge University Press, 1983), pp. 377–9.

32. Ibid. *Certain Philosophical Questions:* Newton's Trinity Notebook. Pg. 85.

33. Isaac Newton, *Treatise on Revelation* Jewish National and University Library, Jerusalem, Yahuda Ms. 1.1. The Newton Project—University of Sussex, East Sussex London: 2007 www.newtonproject.sussex.ac.uk

34. Stone Edition Tanach. Artscroll series. Published by Mesorah Publications, ltd. Brooklyn, New York 11232, 2007.

35. Rev. J. W. Brooks *The Literalism Elements of Prophetical Interpretation.* E. G. Dorsey, Printer.Philadelphia USA 1840. V. Preface. page VI

2

CLAVIS TEMPORALIS

For as the few and obscure Prophecies concerning Christ's first coming were for setting up the Christian religion, many and clear Prophecies concerning the things to be done at Christ's second coming are not only for predicting, but also for effecting a recovery and re-establishment of the long-lost truth.

—ISSAC NEWTON,

Observations upon the Prophecies of Daniel and the Apocalypse of St. John[1]

In the book *Chronology of Ancient Kingdoms Amended*, Newton laid the timeline of events and reigns of kings for Greece, Egypt, Assyria, Babylon, and Persia in six chapters. In chapter four, he dealt with the fall of Babylon, and explained the timing of the destruction of the temple of Jerusalem and the line of kings of the Medes and Persians. In the midst of this order of events, Newton inserted, "The Kingdom of Babylon was numbered and finished and broken and given to the Medes and Persians."[2] This was a statement given by the

prophet Daniel in answer to the riddle that had stricken King Belshazzar on the eve of the fall of Babylon. It was distinctly time-oriented.

On the surface, it seems that Newton inserted it in *Chronology* to
establish Babylon's fall within the chronicles of the Jews. He did not
mention the prophetic implications of the event, a subject he me-
ticulously examined in *Observations* and other works where he also
defined the parallels of the Revelation with the Book of Daniel. However, both these prophetic books, according to Newton, hinged on
the fall of Babylon.[3] The fall of Babylon, the rebuilding of the temple
of Jerusalem, and even the name of Babylon's conqueror, Cyrus, was
predicted more than 160 years before these events by the prophet Isaiah: 44:28:

> Thus saith of Cyrus, he is my shepherd, and shall perform
> all my pleasure: even saying to Jerusalem, Thou shalt be
> built: and to the temple, Thy foundation shall be laid. (Isaiah
> 44:28)

The designation by God of Cyrus as "my shepherd" was a messianic title that distinguished him as a gentile type of Christ. "For
Jacob my servant's sake, and Israel mine elect, I have even called thee
by thy name: I have surnamed thee, though thou hast not known me"
(Isaiah 45:4).

The implications were that both Cyrus and Christ would be irre-
sistible conquerors of Israel's enemies (Isaiah. 45:1; Revelation 19:19–
21) and both would restore Jerusalem and especially *the temple*. This
was Newton's thematic bridge between the Revelation of John and the
prophecies of Daniel.[4]

BABYLON

Plinii the Elder wrote that Babylon was, for a long time, the most
famous city in the world, and according to Herodotus, Babylon dis-

played many of the mightiest works of mortals concentrated in one spot on earth.[5] Its walls were reckoned one of the seven wonders of the world, and it was from there that the treasure of Solomon's temple was removed before being burned and razed to the ground by the Babylonians ca. 587 BC.[6] The Jews that survived the war and were deemed useful were exiled to Babylon. In ca. 539–540 BC, the King of Babylon, Belshazzar, made a great feast for thousands of his nobles. This feast toasted his gods with the golden vessels that his predecessor, Nebuchadnezzar, had removed from the Temple of Solomon.[7] During their festivities, he and his guests witnessed a frightening omen:

> In the same hour came forth the fingers of a man's hand, and wrote over the candlestick upon the plaster of the wall of the king's palace: and the king saw part of the hand that wrote.[8]

Fig. 3. Image by author based on Daniel 5. The words in the inscription on the wall have been interpreted by Rabbinic scholars to have been written in "top down" vertical columns starting from the right and moving to the left, confusing the magi who normally only read letters from right to left. However, the words were known at the time as common monetary values, so that the descriptive aspects of the words, though intact, may not have been realized.

The terrified King consulted his wise men, an elite group of mystics and scholars gathered from the farthest reaches of his kingdom:

> Any man who can read the writing and reveal its meaning shall be clothed with purple, and have a chain of gold around

his neck. And he shall rule third in the kingdom. Then all the king's wise men came in, but they could not read the writing, or make the meaning known to the king. [9]

Newton understood the Magi of Babylon and their prowess for solving riddles. Once again, Keynes provides insight with respect to the "Babylonian" focus of Newton's cryptology, stating that Newton

> ...looked on the whole universe and all that is in it as a riddle, as a secret which could be read by applying pure thought to certain evidence, certain mystic clues which God had laid about the world to allow a sort of philosopher's treasure hunt to the esoteric brotherhood. He believed that these clues were to be found partly in the evidence of the heavens and in the constitution of elements (and that is what gives the false suggestion of his being an experimental natural philosopher), but also partly in certain papers and traditions handed down by the brethren in an unbroken chain back to the original cryptic revelation in Babylonia. [10]

Newton was an expert in the history of the Babylonian Magi, knowing they had been in direct contact with the Prophet Daniel. Those Magi brought to Babylon from Egypt had also encountered traditions of the Prophet Joseph. In fact, the rulers of their respective countries of exile appointed both Hebrew prophets chief of the Magi. In the chapter preceding the description of the Temple of Solomon, Newton included the wise men's resume:

> At that time [of the founding of Babylon by the Assyrians] *Sabacon* the *Ethiopian* invaded *Egypt*, and made great multitudes of *Egyptians* fly from him into *Chaldæa*, and carry thither their Astronomy, and Astrology, and Architecture, and the form of their year, which they preserved there in the

Æra of *Nabonassar:* for the practice of observing the Stars began in *Egypt* in the days of *Ammon*…But Astrology was invented in *Egypt* by *Nichepsos,* or *Necepsos,* one of the Kings of the lower *Egypt,* and *Petosiris* his Priest, a little before the days of *Sabacon,* and propagated thence into *Chaldæa,* where *Zoroaster* the Legislator of the *Magi* met with it: so *Paulinus, Quique magos docuit mysteria vana Necepsos:* And *Diodorus, they say that the* Chaldæans *in* Babylonia *are colonies of the* Egyptians, *and being taught by the Priests of* Egypt *became famous for Astrology.* And *Diodorus, they say that the* Chaldæans *in* Babylonia *are colonies of the* Egyptians, *and being taught by the Priests of* Egypt *became famous for Astrology.*[11]

Despite the world renown of the Magi, the Bible records that Daniel was master over them all. He had been appointed over the horoscopists, conjurers, Chaldeans, and fortunetellers by Belshazzar's father, Nebuchadnezzar.[12] Daniel had interpreted a dream that not only troubled Nebuchadnezzar greatly, but that the king had also forgotten.

The dream was of an image of a man with a head of gold, the arms and shoulders of silver, torso of brass, legs of iron, and feet of iron mixed with clay. Daniel explained it as a symbol of all the great empires of the world from Babylon until the "End of days." The Queen remembered Daniel's interpretation of this dream, and the esteem that Nebuchadnezzar had for him and his god, as "a revealer of secrets" (Dan. 2:47), saying, "An excellent spirit, and knowledge, and understanding, explaining of dreams, and *revealing of hard sentences, and the unraveling of knots* [emphasis added] were found in Daniel."[13]

Here again was the theme of cryptography and God's design of time as Daniel explained the meaning of the writing:

And this was the writing that was written: MINA, MINA, TEKEL, UPARSIN. This is the meaning of the thing: A

MINA, God has numbered your kingdom, and finished it. A TEKEL, You are weighed in the balances and found lacking. UPARSIN, you kingdom is divided, and given to the Medes and Persians.[14]

While Daniel explained the writing to the King, the Medes had already diverted the river Euphrates that ran through Babylon into a canal up river. That same evening, the armies of Cyrus had entered through the river conduit under its great walls. Belshazzar was killed and the great city passed into the rule of Darius the Mede. The next year, in 538 BC, the Persian King Cyrus the Great released the Jews from their captivity of seventy years to Jerusalem and arranged for the rebuilding of the temple.[15]

Newton had been employed as an authority of the standards of weight and measure for currency in Britain during his work on the *Observations upon Daniel.* He was appointed Warden of the Royal Mint in 1696, and in 1699 he was given the position of Master of the Royal Mint of Britain based on his knowledge of ancient standards of weight and measure. For him, it would have been abundantly clear, with respect to his dual understanding of both the ancient languages of the Bible and his profession, that the words MENE MENE TEKEL UPARSIN, were actually monetary values. These are described as the standards of weight for use in Ezekiel's future temple in Jerusalem: "And the shekel (TEKEL) [shall be] twenty gerahs: twenty shekels, five and twenty shekels, fifteen shekels, shall be your maneh (MINA)."[16] The numeric quantity represented were units of ancient Chaldean weights and measures.

The *gerah* was the smallest proportion of weight used in Babylonian commerce at the time. Mene (1,000 gerahs), Mene (1,000 gerahs), Tekel (20 gerahs), and the Peres, to divide the Mene (500 gerahs) equals 2,520.[17]

Despite the fact that Newton would have clearly recognized this feature in Daniel's interpretation of the writing, he made no mention of it in his *Chronology*, though this number surfaces again in both the prophecies of *Revelation* and *Daniel*, leaving the reader to wonder *why* it was disregarded.

With respect to Newton's intention of providing direction for the future revealing of prophecy, leaving out such an integral point stands in bold relief. He may have intended it as a clue to deciphering the underlying meaning of his *Chronology*. In fact, the number 2,520 is the key to Newton's hidden prophetical direction, and the metaphysical design of prophecy and time itself. It is a theory of the *prisca sapientia* that Newton intuitively believed existed, but did not have the resources or data to investigate. He did, however, anticipate that the means for its proof lay in the future.

Throughout *Chronology*, Newton assigned the dates of civilizations not based on the Christian calendar, which started at the birth of Christ, but the Nabonassar era (AN—Anno Nabonassari) was considered the inception of the Neo-Babylonian Dynasty. This was the point that King Nabonassar founded his kingdom in Babylon in 747 BC. The Greek astronomer Claudius Ptolemaeus and later astronomers used this point in chronological calculations, but the era was not used by the Babylonians or, for that matter, the average British subject.[18]

The omission of Julian dates was consistent throughout Newton's *Chronology*. He stated that the fall of Babylon occurred in the year of Nabonassar 209 or 210. (The Julian date corresponding to the start of Nabonassar's reign is 747 BC–209 or 210 would be 539 or 540 BC.) The reader would need to be familiar with this timetable to find the correspondence with the birth of Christ. The full interpretation of the text of *Chronology*, especially chapter four, with its focus on Babylon, was left to one skilled in the application of various eras as well as the history of the Bible. Any further interpretation was dependent on the reader having comprehensive understanding of the subject in advance. Chapter five was dedicated solely to the measure of *lengths* of the Temple of Solomon, in a book dedicated to the measure of *time*.

What was Newton's intention?

According to the Jewish sages, the specific location of God's temple on the Earth was as important as its internal geometry. This was because no man had established the site for its construction, but it had been given by the law of God. Ezekiel 43:12 states,

> This *is* the law of the temple: The whole area surrounding the mountaintop *is* most holy. Behold, this *is* the law of the temple.[19]

Because God had set the location for the temple, the divine proportion evident within its architecture would have also manifested in its placement relative to everything around it. The temple of Jerusalem was the only building ever known to be directly designed by the Almighty; the same was also the designer of creation itself.

> [Its dimensions]…were made clear by the writing from the hand of the Lord concerning it, all the work to be done according to the plan. (1 Chronicles 28:11–19)

The Ark had found a permanent resting place there as the focal point of the temple and of Jerusalem and Israel, and not from man's point of view, but God's. Through this reasoning, its location on earth intersected time and dimension. Newton's study of its measurements within his *Chronology* underscored his belief that God had somehow inserted this metaphysical property within the geometry of the temple of Jerusalem.

Returning to the book Chronology

After describing the kings and events of Babylon, Newton abandoned *sequences* altogether, and instead focused upon the *linear* dimensions of Solomon's temple. He produced a meticulous drawing of the temple's courts, rooms, and gates calibrated to the "sacred cubit."[20]

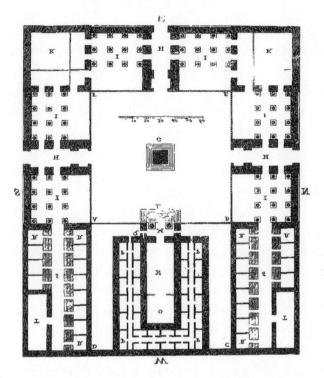

Fig. 4. Reprinted from Isaac Newton's *The Chronology of Ancient Kingdoms Amended* (London: 1728),11. The Newton Project—University of Sussex, East Sussex London: 2007, www. newtonproject.sussex.ac.uk.

Newton opens chapter five with, "The Temple of Solomon, being destroyed by the Babylonians, it may not be amiss here to give a description of that edifice."[21]

By inserting a geometrical study of the Temple of Solomon in a masterful work otherwise not wavering from a precise historical order of ancient nations, the variation stands out in bold relief. Newton seems to be directing the reader to look more closely at the temple's relationship to time and chronology. From the perspective of one not well-versed in 17th century thought pertaining to the *prisca sapatientia*, this deviation from the tone of his book seems unrelated and even unnecessary, but this is clearly not the case.

In an earlier book, *A Dissertation upon the Sacred Cubit of the Jews and cubits of the several nations,* Newton opened with this statement:

> To the description of the Temple belongs the knowledge of the sacred cubit: to the understanding of which the knowledge of the cubits of the several nations will be conductive.[22]

Newton held the divine dimensions within the Temple of Solomon equal with the physical order of God's creation, an order that was preserved in the length of the sacred cubit. Newton included statements of the temple's design in context with the form and fulfillment of prophecy in his work *Lexicon Propheticum,* (Dictionary of Prophecy), in which he says, "This structure commends itself by the utmost simplicity and harmony of all its proportions."[23]

When Newton wrote this study, his acquaintance with the Jewish books on the dimension and supernatural properties of the first and second temples had already been well established. The Library at Cambridge held a copy of the book, *Sha'ar Ha-Heshek*[24] of Yohanan Alemanno, which was a study of the wisdom of King Solomon and its deposit in the temple of Jerusalem. Alemanno described the temple as a microcosm of heaven in its design and rituals. The book of Rabbi Abraham Portaleone of Mantua, *Shilte Ha-Gibborim,* also at Cambridge, described the temple's building and ritual in relation to all known architectural and scientific skills.[25]

In the late 1500s, the Spanish Jesuits Hieronymo Prado and his student Juan Bautista Villalpando wrote *Explanationes in Ezechielem,* in which he described the dimensions of Ezekiel's temple in relation to the platonic structure of music, the order of the heavens and the design of creation. This work brought into focus the Renaissance idea of the temple as a microcosm of God's creation, embodying the order of the universe. This study was inserted into the London Polyglot Bible that Newton owned.[26]

Newton also studied *Synopsis Mathematica* (1626), the work of

Father Marin Mersenne, which explored the math and number contained in the temple as well as the *Ex Talmudis Babylonici Codice Middoth* that detailed the architecture of the temple from the Babylonian Talmud.[27] Along the same lines of reasoning portrayed in these early works, Newton described the visions of John in Revelation as a microcosm of earth and heaven:

> In the Apocalypse the world natural is represented by the Temple of Jerusalem & the parts of this world by analogous parts of the temple: as heaven by the house of the temple; the highest heaven by the most holy; the throne of God in heaven by the Ark; the Sun by the bright flame of the fire of the Altar, or by the face of the Son of Man shining through this flame like the Sun in his strength; the Moon by the burning coals upon the Altar convex above & flat below like an half Moon; the stars by the Lamps; thunder by the song of the Temple & lightning by the flashing of the fire of the Altar; the Earth by the Area of the courts & the sea by the great brazen Laver. And hence the parts of the Temple have the same signification with the analogous parts of the world.[28]

Later in the same work, Newton furthered the idea of the temple's universal symbolism to address the structure and timing of prophecy, underscoring the significance of each vision of John as dependent upon its temple orientation.

Within its context, Newton connected the secret for interpreting the book of Revelation to the temple itself. However, Newton did not give a clear explanation of why the temple of Jerusalem was the key to prophetic interpretation. Although he did *encrypt* the key:

> For it was revealed to Daniel that the prophesies concerning the last times should be closed up & sealed until the time of the end: but then the wise should understand, & knowledge

should be increased. Dan 12.4, 9, 10. And therefore the longer they have continued in obscurity, the more hopes there is
that the time is at hand in which they are to be made manifest. If they are never to be understood, to what end did God
reveal them?…I suspect there are still more mysteries to be
discovered. And as Mr. Mede laid the foundation & I have
built upon it: so I hope others will proceed higher until the
work be finished.[29]

Newton had specifically addressed the statement "the wise will
understand" to those with the knowledge of biblical history; even
modern Sunday Bible students know that the wisest man of the Old
Testament was King Solomon, for God told him:

Behold, I have done according to thy words: And God said
unto [Solomon]…lo, I have given thee a wise and an understanding heart; so that there was none like thee before thee,
neither after thee shall any arise like unto thee.[30]

Newton's comment ends with, "Mr. Mede laid the foundation &
I have built upon it." Solomon also built the first temple of God in
Jerusalem.

Many scholars—even before Newton—believed that the geometry of the future temple of Jerusalem and the "heavenly city
of Jerusalem" of Revelation possessed some key to the unfolding of
prophecy itself. God as a "divine geometer" pervaded early Christian thought. This was the belief that both the natural creation and
architecture of the temple were from the same designer. The temple
was, then, a microcosm of the universe in which God's structure
of time was represented both symbolically and geometrically. The
Bible records that the Israelites constructed two temples, the first
built by Solomon and the second by Zerubbabel. Daniel, and John
in Revelation, mention a third future temple existing at the second

coming of Christ. Some theologians believe that Ezekiel described this third temple in chapter 40 through the end of his book. Still others contend that Ezekiel's temple is in fact a fourth temple that will be built after the great cataclysms described in Revelation. However, theologians are in agreement that Ezekiel's temple is designated for the 1,000 years of peace after the return of Christ, termed the "millennium" in Christianity.

By virtue of the temple being set in that future time, it was suspected of also containing a geometric framework of the prophecies of Christ's return. Many theological researchers of Newton's time focused primarily on the temple of Ezekiel for this reason. However, Newton deemed the sacred proportion of each to be equally instructive and valuable in the search for *priscia sapientia*. He compared Ezekiel's future temple with Solomon's from 1 Kings 6 and the second temple from descriptions of Flavius Josephus and the Talmud in order to reconcile their proportions into a complete *prophetic* symmetry. In *Lexici Prophetici Partem Secundum*, Newton wrote,

> So now we must consider the world of the Israelites, & the meaning of its parts and ceremonies must be explained. And before anything else we must take a look at the Sanctuary in which these deeds of the law were enacted, and which had a three-fold form: The Tabernacle until the time of Solomon, the first Temple until the Babylonian captivity, and the second Temple until the captivity under the Romans. We must look at the shape of these three if we wish to follow the meaning correctly.[31]

Origen, considered the first to formulate the concept of biblical interpretation in the form of analogy, wrote,

> If one wished to obtain means for a profounder contemplation of the entrance of souls into divine things...let him

peruse at the end of Ezekiel's prophecies the visions...and let him peruse also from the Apocalypse of John what is related of the city of God, the heavenly Jerusalem, and of its foundations and gates.[32]

As a Neo-Platonist himself, Origen assumed that his readers would investigate the prophecies in Ezekiel within the context of God as the "divine geometer." He combined the Neo-Platonic tenet "all is number" from Pythagoras with the numeric texts of the Old Testament. Consistent with this view, the temple of Ezekiel and John's city of Jerusalem were primarily "architectural" treatises.

Theological visionaries before Newton took Origen's suggestion a step further. The temple was a consistent subject in works of astrology/astronomy up through the ages, and various models of Ezekiel's temple were mapped out according to the text that revealed its geometric proportion as a representation of the distance of planets in their orbit from the sun.[33]

These ideas were founded on an inclusive biblical theme. Though every ancient civilization claimed establishment by a god, Israel claimed its God created not only the universe itself, but every other god. The God of Israel personally gave the design of His temple to King David and transferred the pattern for the furnishings of the temple to Moses at Mount Sinai. It took a labor force of 150,000 men, the most skilled masons and artisans from Phoenicia, seven years to build the temple. Some of the largest building stones of all time were laid in its foundations. The cost of the construction was an immense 3,000 tons of gold and 30,000 tons of silver set aside by King David. Knowing that the temple was to be God's dwelling place on earth and the repository of the Ark of the Covenant, King Solomon did not take the preparations of the temple's dedication lightly.

The ancients regarded the area where the temple stood as an intersection between dimensions set by God. It was a place on Earth that constituted a divine and central "pivot" from where God interacted with mankind. Jerusalem was known as Ur Salem, "City of Peace," before Abraham. As stated in the Old Testament in Hebrews 11:8–11, "For he [Abraham] looked forward to the city, which has foundations, whose builder and maker is God."[34]

The early Neo-Platonic and Jewish literature was very clear concerning Jerusalem's supernatural location. The description of Jerusalem as a terrestrial center point, "situated in the center of the world," is found in Philo's *Legatio ad Gaium*.[35] The Babylonian Talmud states,

> The world is like a human eyeball. The white of the eye is the ocean surrounding the world, The iris is this continent, The pupil is Jerusalem, And the image in the pupil is the Holy Temple.[36]

Flavius Josephus described Jerusalem as the "navel" of Judea and said that "Jerusalem, as the seat of royalty, is supreme, exalted over all the adjacent region, as the head over the body."[37]

These statements from history aided Newton in his studies of the temple's prophetic centrality, an idea further reinforced in his mind through his investigations of ancient languages. Newton's fluency in ancient Greek, Hebrew and Latin helped him a great deal, granting him understanding that the word "temple" was related to "time."

> For example, "temple" in Latin has the meaning:
> [tempus, tempor, time.] [templum,a space marked out, a building dedicated to a god, temple.] [tempora pl., the fitting or appointed time,].[38]

In the same way the word *temple* is related to words associated with time itself, the dimensions of the temple are related to the divine "template" of God for the fulfillment of prophecy. In addition, the metaphorical quality of the phrases, the *Ark* of the *Temple,* and *Arc* of the *Temporal* are not coincidental. The etymology of these words stemmed from the occult/theological views leading up to the age of the Renaissance. It was common for scientific constructs to be paired with the words that best suited them from the ancient religious Greek and Hebrew texts. In the same manner of the linguistic transfer from the religious to the scientific, it is probable that the Ark of God and His temple were inspirational in Newton's ideas of *movement through time.*

In modern understanding, time is explained as a point between two eternities that is dependent upon motion to be perceived. This concept was represented in a common Hebrew saying hundreds of years before Newton, "HaMakom V'HaZman Echad Hu,"[39] which translates to "Time and Space are One." The great scholar Maimonides embellished this ancient Jewish view of God's creation and its connection with time in his work *The Guide to the Perplexed,* with which Newton was well acquainted:

> Time is an accident consequent upon motion and is necessarily attached to it. Neither of them exists without the other. Motion does not exist except in time, and time cannot be conceived by the intellect except together with motion. And all that with regard to which no motion can be found, does not fall under time.[40]

Maimonides produced this work using basic information from the Torah. The Hebrew name of God provided the basis of Maimonides' theory for time and God's relationship to it. The Jews even before the Renaissance avoided pronouncing the "Tetragrammaton" or four-letter name of God, יהוה, because the name was considered too holy to be spoken incorrectly. The four letters of this name spell the words, היה הוה ויהיה, "He was," "He is," and "He will be," establishing the eternal nature of God from man's perspective of God in the dimension of time.[41]

The arc is the measure of movement through time and can represent the measure of all time between eternities. In the same way, the Ark represented the influence of the eternal God within temporal existence.

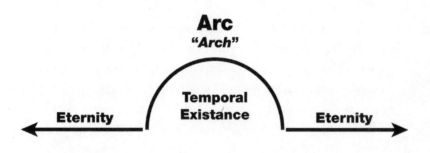

Fig. 5. Image by author

In this model, time is linear, and moves from a beginning to an end. Travel through space is similar. Movement begins from a point of origin and ends at a terminus.

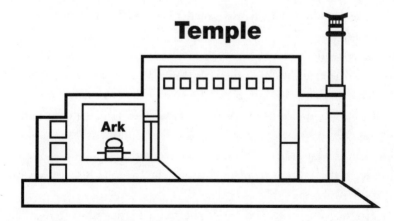

Fig. 6. Image by author

Here, the Ark of God resides inside the Temple, or metaphorically the temporal plane. The Ark of God represented the "arc" of his interaction between eternities. God, omniscient, omnipresent, and omnipotent, set the Temple at the focus of his influence in the world. It is a mirror image of the model of time. In 1909, Reverend C. I. Scofield made an observation that

> All begins with the Ark, which was placed in the holy of holies, because, in revelation, God begins with Himself, working outward toward man: as, in approach, the worshiper begins from himself, moving toward God in the holy of holies.[42]

The Ark of the Covenant had been removed from its place in the Holy of Holies in the temple of Jerusalem before the invasion of Babylon in 587 BC. However, according to the ancient Jewish sages, the site where it had rested was considered almost equally important. Its location was God's eternal residence on Earth, the significance of which was described in the Talmud, a compilation of studies of Jewish law.

After the Ark was taken away (near the end of Bayit Rishon, i.e. the first temple period), a stone remained there from the time of the first Prophets, and it was called Eben ha-Shetiya, "Foundation Stone."[43]

The name Eben ha-Shetiyah is a combination of two Hebrew words: "the eben (rock) of shetiyah (foundation, array or weaving)"[44] literally translates to "the rock from which the world was arrayed" and "the foundation stone of the world." This remarkable meaning of shetiyah, of weaving or warping, fits the metaphysical sense of the location as wrapping the fabric of time around itself. This idea is reinforced in the Talmud that explains that the Eben ha-Shetiya was the first physical object that God created.[45]

In the Mishnah Kelim 1:6–9, the Temple is described in relationship to degrees of holiness radiating outward from the Holy of Holies where the Ark of the Covenant stood. These areas are listed in order from least holy to most holy as: the land of Israel; the walled cities of Israel; the city of Jerusalem; the temple mount; Rampart Court of women; Court of the Israelites; Court of the Priests; between the porch and the altar; the Sanctuary; and finally the Holy of Holies. In the pseudopigraphic book of Jubilees, the temple mount in Jerusalem is described as the center point of the world: "And he [Noah] knew... that Mount Sinai [is] the center of the desert, and Mount Zion the center of the navel of the earth...."[46]

This idea is mentioned in several places in the Old Testament. For example, Judges 9:37 and Ezekiel 38:12 describe the location of the temple, or the mount upon which it stood, as the "highest place or center of the earth itself" or *tabur ha eretz*.[47] The Septuagint Greek translation of these texts rendered the word "tabur" (highest place), as "omphalos," or navel.

The forms of "shetiyah" encompass a full sense of the foundation stone upon which the Ark of the Covenant was placed. The ancient Hebrew sages consider the combined meaning of "shetiya" as consistent with a point existing metaphysically outside of time.[48]

In addition to the meaning "to warp," the root *shayth* also forms the Hebrew words: (1) *Shathaw*, meaning a foundation or basis; (2) *Shawtham*, meaning to unveil; (3) *Shawthaq*, meaning to subside or be calm; (4) *Shawthah*, meaning to drink; and (5) *Shawthan*, meaning to produce water.[49] These ideas combined produce the sense of a metaphysical intersection between eternity and time, the terrestrial and the heavenly. The sages extended the implication of the foundation stone as a fountain of the water of life to the point from which all the world's water emanates. As heaven is the origin of the stone, so also is the source of all water on the Earth, falling as rain from heaven.[50]

The process of water on the Earth fits the conception of time as well the Ark's relationship to it. Like time, the water of a river flows in a linear path towards its destination at a uniform rate. The ark that navigates upon it can move with the water's course, or independently from it. Like rain from heaven, time falls upon the earth based on the movement of the heavens. Ultimately, the rivers empty at their destinations. Moses floated his Ark upon the Nile, Noah rode the flood of the Great Deluge, and the Ark of the Covenant traversed the ocean of the Sinai desert. All three were guided by the Spirit of God (ruach), a word in Hebrew that is used both identically for breath and for wind.

In this light, it seems reasonable that a relationship should also exist between time and location of prophetic events directly affecting Jerusalem and the temple's location. The *prisca sapentia* framework of Newton suggests that the distance between the temple of Jerusalem and the capital city of any nation historically affecting Jerusalem would be supernaturally connected. This relationship would be significant with respect to units of time, expressing meaning in line with God's divine plan as recorded in the word of his prophets. The dualistic word "ruler," as both the arbitrator and enforcer of law as *a device of linear measurement,* is implied. God is the author of perfect law, both of morality and of nature. Ezekiel recorded the dimensions of this future temple in chapter 40 of his book, starting with the lengths of the temple gates, chambers, courts, walls, and its exterior. After this, calibrations of weights and measures for the temple functions were given in detail. Finally, the distance of land outward from the temple was measured.[51]

> And he brought me thither, and, behold, [there was] a man, whose appearance [was] like the appearance of brass, with a line of flax in his hand, and a measuring reed; and he stood in the gate. (Ezekiel 40:3)

The measure of distance away from Jerusalem in this text implies a spiritual significance. A relationship between Jerusalem and the nations has existed from the foundation of the temple, but has not been completely perceived—and could not be until the conventions of modern science.

If a measurement is arced from the point of the temple of Jerusalem's foundation stone to the palace of Balthazar, the political center of Babylon, and the exact location the writing on the wall occurred, the distance should relate to the pivotal period that the city most influenced Jerusalem. According to current knowledge, such a relationship exists, and is the distance of 539.86 statute miles.

According to the Babylonian chronicles, Babylon fell to the Medes and Persians on the sixteenth day of Tishri of the Jewish calendar, which is also October 12, 539 BC.[52]

Modern satellite measurements between the temple mount in Jerusalem and the center of ancient Babylon correspond perfectly to the year and month of Babylon's fall.

At this defining point in history, the Jews were released from captivity in Babylon and returned to Jerusalem to rebuild the destroyed Temple of Solomon. Newton described the exact location of Nebuchadnezzar's palace in the West half of the city of Babylon in *Chronology of Ancient Kingdoms Amended*:

Babylon was a square city of 120 furlongs, or 15 miles on every side, compassed first with a broad and deep ditch, and then with a wall fifty cubits thick, and two hundred high. Euphrates flowed through the middle of it southward.... [I]n the middle of one half westward stood the King's new Palace, built by Nebuchadnezzar, and in the middle of the other half stood the Temple of Belus, with the old Palace between that Temple and the river: (Herodotus. l. 1. ca. 178 BC. This old Palace was built by the Assyrians, according to Isaiah 23:13.)[53]

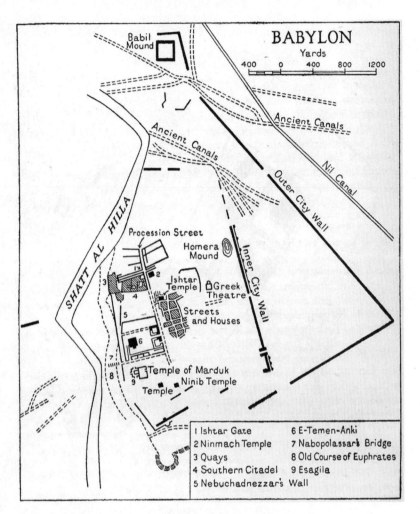

Fig. 7. Reprinted from George Stephen Goodspeed, Ph.D., *A History of the Babylonians and Assyrians* (New York: Charles Scribner's Sons, 1902), X-X.

Newton explains the location that Belshazzar would have witnessed the writing on the wall in the new palace as being on the west side of the Euphrates. This area, located exactly 32 degrees, 32 minutes north and 44 degrees, 25 minutes east, is the most precise fit with distance in relationship to the year of the fall of Babylon in the Gregorian calendar.

Fig. 8. Courtesy of NASA World Wind

The *prisca sapientia* relationship in the year of Babylon's fall and the distance between Babylon and Jerusalem is recorded in statute miles. However, this is not the only linear value that expresses this phenomenon. The nautical mile can also be used to establish significant prophetic and time based results.

NOTES

1. Newton, Isaac. *Observations upon the Prophecies of Daniel and the Apocalypse of St. John*. Part 2, Chapter 1 - Jewish National and University Library, Jerusalem, Yahuda Ms. 1.1 Transcribed by Shelley Innes summer 1998. The Newton Project—University of Sussex, East Sussex London: 2007 www.newtonproject.sussex.ac.uk

2. Isaac Newton, *Chronology of Ancient Kingdoms* CHAP. IV. Of the two Contemporary Empires of the Babylonians and Medes. The Newton Project—University of Sussex, East Sussex London: 2007 www.newtonproject.sussex.ac.uk

3. Isaac Newton *The Prophecies of Daniel and a Treatise on Revelation* in Chapter 10 "Of the relation which the Prophecy of John hath to those of Daniel; and of the Subject of the Prophecy". Source: Yahuda Ms. 9, Jewish National and University Library. The Newton Project—University of Sussex, East Sussex London: 2007 www.newtonproject.sussex.ac.uk

4. Isaac Newton. *Observations upon the Prophecies of Daniel, and the Apocalypse of St. John* (London: 1733). Part II, Chapter III: Of the relation which the Prophecy of John hath to those of Daniel; and of the Subject of the Prophecy. The Newton Project—University of Sussex, East Sussex London: 2007 www.newtonproject.sussex.ac.uk

5. Plinii, *Natural history*. Book 5. Cap. 26. H. Rackham, Translator. Loeb Classical Library, Harvard University Press. Cambridge, Massachusetts: 1989.

6. C. F. Pfeiffer, *Old Testament History*, p. 455. Grand Rapids. MI. U.S.A.: Baker Book House Co, 1973,

7. Ibid.

8. Daniel 5:5 Quoted from the Scofield Bible. Editor Rev. C. I. Scofield,. D.D. Oxford University Press, New York. 1945.

9. Daniel 5: 7 KJV

10. Gale E Christianson, *Newton the Man*, (New York: Free Press, 1984).

11. Isaac Newton, *Chronology of ancient Kingdoms* CHAP. IV Pg. 327. The Newton Project—University of Sussex, East Sussex London: 2007 www.newtonproject.sussex.ac.uk

12. Daniel 2:48 KJV

13. Daniel 5:12 The Scofield Reference Bible. Editor Rev. C. I. Scofield,. D.D. Oxford University Press, New York. 1945.

14. Dan 5:25–28 The Scofield Reference Bible. Editor Rev. C. I. Sscofield,. D.D. Oxford University Press, New York. 1945.

15. Herodotus, *The Histories* 1.191 John M. Marincola (Editor), Aubrey De Selincourt (Translator) Penguin Classics U.S.A. 1996. Author note: Cyrus's armies, under the command of Ugbaru had already defeated the Babylonians at Opis situated on the Tigris River. From there, the Persians had control of the canal systems of Babylon. The ancient historian Herodotus recorded that the Persians diverted the River Euphrates into a canal up river from Babylon until the Euphrates dropped "to the height of the middle of a man's thigh." On October 12, 539 BC, the Persian army marched through the river conduit under Babylon and took the city without a fight. Belshazzar was slain. His father, Nabonidus had fled at the fall of Babylon but eventually surrendered to Cyrus.

16. Eze 45:12 The Scofield Reference Bible. Editor Rev. C. I. Scofield,. D.D. Oxford University Press, New York. 1945.

17. *Oxford Cyclopedic Concordance.* (New York: Oxford University Press, INC, 1947).

18. Author's note: This era begins in the first year of the reign of Nabonassar on New Year's Day in the Egyptian calendar or Wednesday 26 February 747 B.C. in the Julian calendar.

19. Ezekiel 43:12. New King James Version © 1982 Thomas Nelson Publishers. Nashville, TN. U.S.A.

20. Isaac Newton, *The Chronology of Ancient Kingdoms Amended*
    Chapter V. (London: 1728). The Newton Project—University
    of Sussex, East Sussex London: 2007 www.newtonproject.sussex.
    ac.uk

21. Ibid.

22. Shalev, Zur – "Measurer of All Things: John Greaves (1602–
    1652), the Great Pyramid, and Early Modern Metrology",
    Journal of the History of Ideas - Volume 63, Number 4, October
    2002, pp. 555–575, The Johns Hopkins University Press.

23. Newton, *Lexicon Propheticum*, Yahuda MS 14, ff 1–8. The
    Newton Project—University of Sussex, East Sussex London:
    2007 www.newtonproject.sussex.ac.uk

24. Fabrizzio Lelli, "Alemanno, Yohanan ben Isaac," Encyclopedia of
    the Renaissance (New York,1999), Online version of the 1901–
    1906 *Jewish Encyclopedia*: www.jewishencyclopedia.com

25. Ibid. Jewish Encyclopedia, "Shilte Ha- Gibborim," Mantua
    1612.

26. The Catholic Encyclopedia, Volume XII. Published 1911. New
    York: Robert Appleton Company.

27. Gillispie, Charles. C. ed., Dictionary of Scientific biography. v
    13 p29–30. 16 vols. New York: Charles Scribner and Sons, 1970

28. Isaac Newton. *Theological notes.*Keynes MS. 5, Vr. 9. (Yahuda
    Library Jerusalem 9.2). The Newton Project—University of
    Sussex, East Sussex London: 2007 www.newtonproject.sussex.
    ac.uk

29. Isaac Newton, *Observations upon the Prophecies of Daniel and the
    Apocalypse of St. John.* Jewish National and University Library,
    Jerusalem, Yahuda Ms. 1.1 Transcribed by Shelley Innes summer
    1998. The Newton Project—University of Sussex, East Sussex
    London: 2007 www.newtonproject.sussex.ac.uk

30. 1 Kings 3:5–14 KJV

31. Isaac Newton, "A Treatise or Remarks on Solomons Temple,"
    Prolegomena ad Lexici Prophetici partem secundum, in quibus

agitur De forma Sanctuarij Iudaici. (Babson Ms. 434), Huntington Library, San Marino, California. Quoted in translation by David Castillejo, "Expanding Force in Newton's cosmos". Ediciones de Arte y Bibliofilia, Madrid Spain (May 1981) p 38.

32. "The Ante-Nicene Fathers" Origen ("Against Celsus," bk. Vi., Ch. 23.(Alexander Roberts and James Donaldson, editors); American Edition. 1885. Reprint, Schribners and Sons, New York. 1903

33. Villalpanda shows the camp of Israel around the tabernacle in the wilderness in a square form, with the zodiac situated around it. In addition the four evangelists are also arranged, corresponding to their symbols in the zodiac, found in William Stirling, *The Canon—An Exposition of the Pagan Mystery Perpetuated in the Cabala as the Rule of all the Arts*, London, 1897,-modern ed., p.39The Garnstone Press, London, 1974.

34. Hebrews 11:8–11 KJV

35. Vilnay, *Legends of Jerusalem*, pp. 128–132. Philadelphia: Jewish Publication Society of America, 1987.

36. Talmud-Derech Eretz Zuta 9. Translated by Michael L. Rodkinson. New York: New Talmud Pub. Co. c1896–c1903.

37. Flavius Josephus, *War of the Jews* (3:51–52), new trans. Rev. Robert Traill, P.D. M.R.T.A. Isaac Taylor , ed. Vol. 2. London: Houlston and Stoneman, Paternoster Row 1851).

38. Webster's Revised Unabridged Dictionary. Noah Porter, editor. (G & C. Merriam Co., 1913, Springfield, Massachusetts. U.S.A.)

39. Rabbi Yehudah Loew ben Bezalel Gur Aryeh al HaTorah. (the Maharal) 1525–1609. Online version of the 1901–1906 *Jewish Encyclopedia*: www.jewishencyclopedia.com

40. Maimonides, *The Guide of the Perplexed*, trans. Shlomo Pines, (Chicago: University of Chicago Press, 1963)

41. Chumash Rashi, *The Tanach* (New York: Mesorah Heritage Foundation Pub, 1996).

42. Rev. C. I. Scofield *The Scofield Reference Bible.* footnotes, pg. 101. New York, Oxford University Press. Copyright 1909.

43. Talmud Shemot 25:10–16 (Yoma 3:2). Translated by Michael L. Rodkinson. New York: New. Talmud Pub. Co. c1896–c1903.

44. Strong's Hebrew Lexicon # 8371 in Strongs Exhaustive Concordance of the Bible. AMG Publishers edition, World Bible Publishers, Inc. 1986 Iowa Falls, Ia.

45. Ibid. Talmud, Yoma 54a.

46. Book of Jubilees Trans. R. H. Charles, revised Ch. Rabin in H. D. F. Sparks (ed.), The Apocryphal Old Testament (Oxford: Clarendon Press, 1984), p. 38.

47. Ibid. James Strong's Hebrew Lexicon # 2872.

48. Ibid.

49. Ibid. # 8354–8371.

50. Psalms 1:3. KJV

51. And he brought me thither, and, behold, [there was] a man, whose appearance [was] like the appearance of brass, with a line of flax in his hand, and a measuring reed; and he stood in the gate. Ezekiel 40:3 KJV

52. James B. Pritchard, *Ancient Near Eastern Texts Relating to the Old Testament.* published by Princeton University Press. Princeton NJ. U.S.A. 1969.

53. Isaac Newton, *The Chronology of Ancient Kingdoms Amended* (London: 1728) Chapter 4: Of the two Contemporary Empires of the Babylonians and Medes page. 326. The Newton Project—University of Sussex, East Sussex London: 2007 www.newtonproject.sussex.ac.uk.

3

THE "TEMPORAL" NAUTICAL MILE

From greatest antiquity, the art of navigation has demonstrated a link between the heavens and earth. On the sea and in deserts without changing horizons, the sun, moon, and stars are the only reliable guides. The angle of North Star above the horizon reveals the latitude of the observer. However, the calculation of longitude (location east or west of a fixed point) is based on the precise timing of the sun or stars at their zenith (highest point in their travel across the sky). The timing of the transit of the sun or stars is compared to tables of their transit at a fixed location over a year, such as at the zero meridian at Greenwich. Both latitude and longitude are based on 360 degrees in a circle and the number of minutes and seconds in an hour (60).

To determine longitude, a navigator needs an accurate clock to compare the difference between noon at the Prime Meridian and noon at his location. Since the earth rotates 360 degrees in 24 hours, one hour difference correlates to 15 degrees difference in longitude from the Prime Meridian (15 x 24 = 360).

The average distance around the Earth in nautical miles is 21,600 miles (360 x 60). One degree of latitude is 60 nautical miles and about

69 *statute miles* on average. A nautical mile is 1.15 times greater than a statute mile, but about 796 feet longer.[1]

In the New Testament, the Greek word *naus* means both a "center of the temple," where the Ark stood in the Holy of Holies (Matthew 23:17), and "ship" (Acts 27:41).

The Greek *naus* was derived from the Hebrew word for "home" or "temple," pronounced either naw-veh or no-ah. As the former, it is the ancient etymological origin for the word "navy" and "navigation." As the latter, it is the phonetic translation of the name of the antediluvian patriarch Noah. *Naus* is also the origin for the word nautical (Greek, *nau-tes*[2] which is related to the Hebrew root *navta* meaning "to stretch out," "to move or travel," and even "a *measuring line*," found in Job 38:5, Isaiah 44:13, and Lamentations 2:8.[3]

Isaac Newton understood the significance of Noah with respect to sacred knowledge and the recovery of its pure form. Concerning his treatise on the origin of religion, Newton's colleague David Gregory wrote that Newton

> has composed a tract on the origin of nations. Religion is the same at all times, but religion, which they received pure from Noah and the first men, the nations debased by their own inventions.[4]

In the same work, Newton tied the pure religion of Noah to the temple itself:

> Twas one design of the first institution of the true religion to propose to mankind by the frame of the ancient temples, (of Solomon and Nehemiah) the study of the frame of the world as the true Temple of the great God they worshipped.[5]

The Hebrew name Noah is pronounced "noe" or "noach" and its spelling, נח, is subtly different from naw-veh, נוה. Both words are a variation of the same Hebrew root *noe* meaning, "to rest," to "settle down," and "a home or dwelling place."

In nautical terms, time and distance are related. The speed that a ship travels across the water is the "knot," which is defined as one nautical mile per hour. The number of degrees of travel determines nautical miles over the Earth multiplied by 60 minutes in an hour. Distance in these degrees is calibrated using the terms "arc minutes" and "arc seconds." This is, of course, due to the curvature of the Earth. However, the play of meaning between the *Ark of Noah* and the *arc of navigation*, or minutes per degree of an arc is obvious. These words had their genesis in events from the book of Genesis.

There is a more extraordinary connection of distance between prophetic events and the temple. Although the Holy of Holies is termed a "Naus" in Greek, it was called the "debir" in Hebrew (1 Kings 6:5). The latter has the precise meaning "to arrange," but it is used figuratively to speak, answer, appoint, bid, command, commune, declare, destroy, give, name, promise, pronounce, rehearse, say, speak, be spokesman, subdue, talk, teach, tell, think, use (entreaties), or utter, among other things.[7]

"Debir" identifies the presence of God in the Holy of Holies as the *source* for the words of the prophets. The oracle function of the prophets resonated with the oracle of the temple, which connected in time and space.

The *prisca sapienta* correlation between time and distance in the prophecy of the book of Daniel should also relate to the Revelation of John. Newton viewed the book of Revelation in the New Testament as a mirror of Daniel's prophecies in the Old Testament. Revelation recapitulated the theme of Babylon's fall and focused on the temple as a unifying point of prophetic dimension, a fact that Newton closely detailed in *Observations*. Both Daniel and John addressed the theme of time of the end and the return of Christ:

The Apocalypse of John is written in the same style and language with the Prophecies of Daniel, and hath the same relation to them which they have to one another, so that all of them together make but one complete Prophecy; and in like manner it consists of two parts, an introductory Prophecy, and an interpretation thereof.[8]

John wrote Revelation while exiled on the island Patmos near Greece, which lies exactly 539.86 nautical miles from Jerusalem.

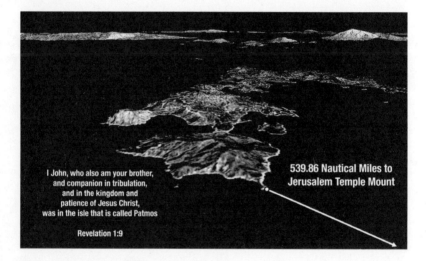

Fig. 9. Courtesy of NASA World Wind

In many instances the statute mile seems to reflect distance with respect to time before the birth of Christ and nautical mile, forwards or after the birth of Christ. In the case of Patmos, where St. John wrote Revelation, the distance in nautical miles seems to reflect the prophetic content of Daniel's writing of the last days.

Because the writing on the wall had the value 2,520 and occurred in 539 BC, both numbers should relate in some way with the pattern of time and prophecy. The last year of Babylon's power was 540 BC. It is the further working of knowledge that Newton suggested in the

Chronology cryptogram. The unifying constant 2,520 links the creation of God to His influence *within* creation. It is found in Genesis 2:1–3:

> And on the seventh day God ended his work which he had made….And God blessed the seventh day, and sanctified it: because that in it he had rested from all his work which God created and made.

As the solar day is measured by one 360-degree revolution of the Earth, seven days equals 2,520 degrees. The fall of Babylon in 539 BC reinforces the supernatural mathematics of the event, which is based on sevens:

$$7 \times 77 = 539$$

When the number of the last year before Babylon's fall, 540, is multiplied by 7, the result is 3,780, which is also 2,520 + 1,260 (half 2,520). When 540 is divided by 7, the result is 77.142857142857…, with a repeating decimal series.

Of the cardinal numbers between one and ten, seven is the only number that does not divide evenly into 360.

CIRCLE	DIVISOR	DIVIDEND
360	1	360
360	2	180
360	3	120
360	4	90
360	5	72
360	6	60
360	7	51.428571
360	8	45
360	9	40

Fig. 10. Image by author

Dividing 360 by 7 produces the same number as:

$$27{,}720 / 539 = 51.428571428571.$$

The persistence of 7 is seen redundantly in the prophetic unfolding of events written by Daniel. The number of the writing on the wall, 2,520, multiplied by seven is 17,640. There were 17,640 days (also 360 x 7 x 7) between the destruction of the temple in Jerusalem by the Babylonians and the fall of Babylon. If 17,640 days is divided by 365.25 days, it would equal 48.29 solar years. Thus, if the fall of Jerusalem in 587 BC is added to 48.29 solar years, it would equal the fall of Babylon in 539 BC.

The ancient "sacred year" consisted of 360 days, the numbering of which was a common practice among the ancients, according to the historian Immanuel Velikovsky:

> The old Babylonian year was composed of 360 days, a fact which was understood by scholars even before the cuneiform script was deciphered. The old Babylonian year consisted of twelve months of thirty days each. The Assyrian year consisted of 360 days; a decade consisted of 3,600 days. Assyrian documents refer to months of thirty days, counted from crescent to crescent. The ancient Persian year was made up of 360 days of twelve months of thirty days each. The Egyptian year was made up of 360 days before it was changed to 365 by the addition of five days. The calendar of the Eber Papyrus, a document of the New Kingdom, has a year of twelve months with thirty days each. The new moon festivals were very important in the days of the Eighteenth Dynasty, observed at thirty-day intervals. There is a statement found as a gloss on a manuscript of *Timaeus* that the calendar of a solar year of 360 days was introduced by the Hyksos after the fall of the

Middle Kingdom. The Book of Sothis, erroneously credited to the Egyptian priest Manetho, as well as Georgius Syncellus, the Byzantine chronologist, both maintain that originally the additional five days did not follow the 360 days of the calendar, but were introduced at a later time. The Mayan year consisted of 360 days; later five days were added, and every fourth year another day was added. In ancient South America the year consisted of 360 days, divided into twelve months. In China the year consisted of 360 days divided into twelve months of thirty days each. When the year changed from 360 to 365, the Chinese added five and one-quarter days to their year. Plutarch wrote that in the time of Romulus, the Roman year was made up of 360 days only, and various Latin authors say the ancient month was thirty days in length.[8]

There is additional evidence for the supernatural correlation of distance and year between Jerusalem and the nations. It involves the fall of Jerusalem and the city of the exiled prophet Ezekiel. This is significant with respect to Newton's studies of the temple dimensions. Although the temple of Ezekiel's vision has never been built, it provided the only concise measurement of the temple of God that could be used to establish the divine proportion, or as Newton supposed, the prophetic time scheme geometrically established in its layout.

The exile of the Israelites by the Babylonians occurred in two parts: the first in 596 BC, and the second in 587 BC. Before Daniel, the prophet Ezekiel was carried to exile in Babylonia by Nebuchadnezzar. Ezekiel began predicting the fall of Jerusalem and the destruction of its temple while living in a Jewish settlement near the city Nippur in Babylonia.

The word of the LORD came expressly unto Ezekiel the priest, the son of Buzi, in the land of the Chaldeans by the river Chebar; and the hand of the LORD was there upon him....Thus saith the Lord GOD; This is Jerusalem: I have set it in the midst of the nations and countries that are round about her. And she hath changed my judgments into wickedness more than the nations, and my statutes more than the countries that are round about her: for they have refused my judgments and my statutes, they have not walked in them.... Wherefore, as I live, saith the Lord GOD; Surely, because thou hast defiled my sanctuary with all thy detestable things, and with all thine abominations, therefore will I also diminish thee; neither shall mine eye spare, neither will I have any pity. Moreover I will make thee waste, and a reproach among the nations that are round about thee, in the sight of all that pass by.[10]

Here, the world centrality of Jerusalem is mentioned. In contrast, for thousands of years Nippur was the religious center of Mesopotamia. Sumerian myth deemed the city as the birthplace of humanity, created by the deity Enlil. In the same way that Rome legitimized political power in the Holy Roman Empire in Europe, Babylonian rulers looked to Nippur for spiritual favor and power. Nippur remained the religious heart of Mesopotamia throughout the reigns of Assyrian and Babylonian kings. Ezekiel's prophecy defined the polarization of spiritual centers on the Earth, Nippur of Babylon against God's center of power in Jerusalem. The Jews living with Ezekiel considered the destruction of Jerusalem impossible, believing that God would protect the city forever. Ezekiel's message of doom, delivered through Nippur, a city diametrically opposing the God of Israel, demonstrated the extent to which Israel had rebelled against God's covenant with them.

In 596 BC, Nebuchadrezzar set Zedekiah, the third son of Josiah, on the throne of Judah. Soon after, Zedekiah conspired with Egypt and revolted against Babylon. In 587 BC, Nebuchadrezzar sent a massive army against Jerusalem, which forced King Zedekiah to flee through a water tunnel under the city—known as Zedekiah's tunnel—but was captured, had his eyes put out, and was taken to Babylon. A month later, Jerusalem was destroyed, and the majority of the people of Judah were carried into exile. This began the second captivity.[11]

The settlement of Jews hearing Ezekiel's prophecy of the destruction of Jerusalem lived along the Chebar canal in the city Nippur, which was located 587 miles from the temple of Jerusalem.[12]

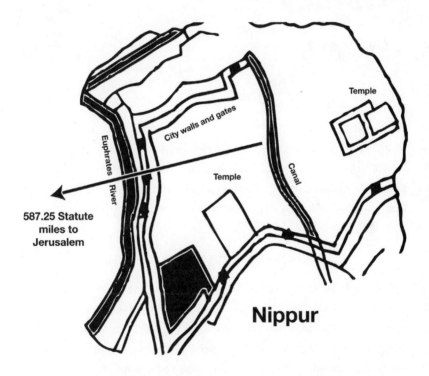

Fig. 11. Author's image based on H. W. F. Saggs, *Civilization Before Greece and Rome* (New Haven: Yale University Press, 1989), 119.

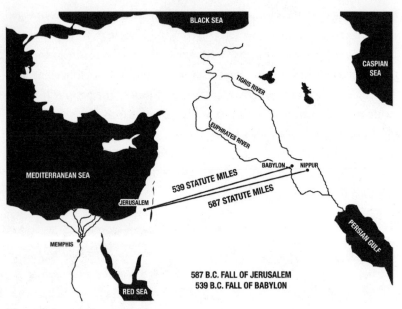

Fig. 12. Image by author

The year of the temple's demise agrees to its distance in miles from Ezekiel, the oracle of God that predicted its destruction. The year of return for the Jews to rebuild the temple agrees with its distance from Daniel, the prophet that predicted its restoration.

SUCH IS THE PROVIDENCE OF GOD

It is also a remarkable feature of the prophecy concerning the destruction of the temple that the nation of its destruction came to Jerusalem from the east. Both cities, Babylon and Nippur, can be sited from a straight line leading out of the eastern gate from the temple mount, which is extraordinarily significant in Ezekiel's prophecy.

As a show of acceptance of the sacrifices and dedication of the temple, the glory of the Lord entered the temple in the time of Solomon through the Eastern Gate. It was through this same gate that the Levite priests turned their backs to the temple of Jerusalem and worshiped the sun[13] (Ezekiel 8:16). In response to Israel's rebellion, Ezekiel saw a vision of the glory of the Lord removing itself from the temple through the Eastern Gate. With poetic justice, God judged the city in accordance to its idolatry. Instead of filling the temple with His glory, from the east came judgment. The object of worship in Israel's rebellion, the sun, determined the character of its destruction by the Babylonians.

Nebuchadnezzar, the king who destroyed Jerusalem and the temple, means "prince of the god Nebo (Mercury)," a deity closest to the sun. Nebo was the Babylonian version of Thoth, god of writing and illumination. Additionally, the Babylonian word *nebo* was associated with the Hebrew word *nebo-aw* meaning "to write prophecy." In the ominous scene of Ezekiel's *Neboaw* (prophecy) against Jerusalem in Ezekiel 9:4, an angel was told to "set a mark" (taveh tauv) upon the foreheads of men who lamented over its idolatry. This was in protection from God's judgment by the agency of the "prince of the god Nebo." This same mark is associated with Cain, and subsequently through pagan distortion of its meaning in antiquity; that is, it is the symbol of Thoth, Hermes, Mercury, and Nebo. Because the ancients associated the measuring of time with Thoth, the distance between Jerusalem and Babylon as an element of time seems a manifestation of this pagan god. However, it is a phenomenon that exists not by the workings of an idolatrous deity, but rather through the omniscient power of the God of Israel.

These manifestations of prophecy recorded in the earth are, in part, the *priscia theologia* for which Newton and the Renaissance intellects sought. It demonstrates God's control over time, space, the rise and fall of nations, and the fulfillment of prophecy. Because time has a beginning, a present, and an end, it is reasonable to believe that the time/distance phenomena should manifest with respect to prophetic events in the modern age, as well as those set in the future.

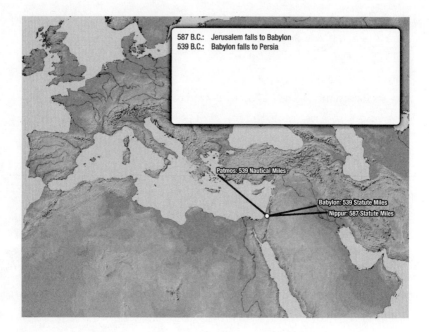

587 B.C.: Jerusalem falls to Babylon
539 B.C.: Babylon falls to Persia

Patmos: 539 Nautical Miles

Babylon: 539 Statute Miles
Nippur: 587 Statute Miles

NOTES

1. Columbia Encyclopedia. Third Edition. Edited by William Bridgewater and Seymore Kurtz. Columbia University Press. New York.1963

2. James Strong's Exhaustive Concordance of the bible. Greek Lexicon entry # 3485. World Bible Publishers, Inc., Iowa Dalls, IA. U.S.A. 1986.

3. *Gesenius's Lexicon* S. P. Tregelles trans. and ed in 1847, 1857. Baker Book House, Grand Rapids, Michigan, 1990.

4. H. W. Turnbull (ed.), *The correspondence of Isaac Newton*, Chapter 3. Pg.338 Cambridge University Press, New York 1961.

5. Isaac Newton Yahuda MS 41. ff. 8r and 9r-v. The Newton Project—University of Sussex, East Sussex London: 2007 www.newtonproject.sussex.ac.uk.

6. 1 Kings 6:5 KJV

7. Ibid., Strong's Hebrew Lexicon # 1696. James Strong's Exhaustive Concordance of the bible.

8. Isaac Newton. *Observations upon the Prophecies of Daniel Part II Chap II*, (London: 1733). The Newton Project—University of Sussex, East Sussex London: 2007 www.newtonproject.sussex.ac.uk

9. Immanuel Velikovsky, *Worlds in Collision*. New York: Simon & Shuster, 1977.

10. Ezekiel chapter 1 & 5. KJV.

11. John Roberts Dummelow, *A Commentary on the Holy Bible*, New York: Macmillan company, 1909.

12. Nippur's coordinates: 32°12.693857568549'N 45°23.078533531251 E.

13. Ezekiel 8:16 KJV

14. Ibid. James Strong's Exhaustive Concordance of the Bible. Hebrew Lexicon # 1509

4

THE LINE AND THE PLUMMET

Amongst the Interpreters of the last age, there is scarce one of note who hath not made some discovery worth knowing; and thence seem to gather that God is about opening these mysteries. The success of others put me upon considering it; and if I have done anything which may be useful to following writers, I have my design.

—ISAAC NEWTON,
Observations upon the Prophecies of Daniel and the Apocalypse of St. John [1]

It is notable that Newton did not render the dates in his book of ancient chronology from the Christian era. An *era* is defined as a period that begins from a fixed point in time. All dates are then rendered either forward to or backwards from that fixed point. The most commonly known eras for Western history are anchored to the points of the founding of cities: (1) the creation of the world by God (Jewish, equivalent to 3761 BC: Byzantine, 5508 BC); (2) the founding of the city of Rome (753 BC: year marked AUC for ad urbe condita, "from the founding of the city"); (3) the hegira, of the Moslem world, the

flight of Mohammed from Mecca (AD 622, abbreviation AH); and
(4) the founding of the Olympic games in ancient Greece (776 BC,
time in Olympiads).

The first to use the Christian era to mark years was Dionysius
Exiguus, a Roman monk, chronologist, and scholar in AD 525. Dionysius began reckoning years in history from the time of the incarnation of Jesus Christ. The birth of Christ is accepted in Christianity as
the manifestation of God's Word in the flesh, as stated in John 1:14,
and is closely related in meaning with the Ark of the Covenant. The
event was important to Newton, who believed that the Ark and the
temple served as a type or shadow that was fulfilled in the person of
Christ. Newton studied the works of St. Augustine (354–430) that
stated that the writing of Moses could not be fully understood but in
the reality of Christ:

> Thy Word, through Whom Thou madest all things…Thy
> Only Begotton, through Whom Thou calledst to adoption
> the believing people…I beseech Thee by Him Who sitteth at
> Thy right hand, and "intercedeth with Thee for us, in Whom
> are hidden all the treasures of wisdom and knowledge." These
> I do seek in Thy books. Of Him did Moses write; this saith
> Himself; this saith the Truth.[2]

The theme of Newton's studies of the "temporal properties" of
the Ark and temple in the Exodus was consistently Messianic in application. It was a means to solve the timing of His return. Newton
revealed his Christ-centric belief concerning prophecy in his *Treatise
of Revelation*:

> For the rules whereby they [the Jews] were to know the Mes-
> siah where the prophecies of the Old Testament. And these
> our Savior recommended to their consideration in the very
> beginning of His preaching and afterward commanded the

study of them for that end saying Luke 4:21: "Search the Scriptures for in them ye think ye have eternal life, and these are they which testify of Me."[3]

That numeric symbols in the Bible have correspondence with the work of Christ on Earth was a subject of a great many theologians in history. Joseph Mede, Newton, and their predecessors had focused on this issue in their studies of Bible prophecy. The regard that biblical numbers provided a valid means of interpretation was eventually abandoned in later theological circles through the course of history. This was due to the aversion of mixing esoteric and occult practices with pure exegesis and rational thought. However, the significance of numbers with respect to prophecy remains. The study of numbers within Christianity has varied according to the nature and meaning of the times. The book *Number in Scripture* by the Bible scholar E.W. Bullinger is one example of renewed interest in the late 19th century. This work briefly touched upon the phenomenon of time relating to distance in sacred units, which states that

The Ark (of Noah) was borne by the flood fifteen cubits upwards, Gen. 7:20.

Bethany, where Lazarus was raised, and from whence the Lord ascended was fifteen furlongs from Jerusalem, John 11:18.[4]

In these examples, the number fifteen is associated with resurrection, and the Ark of Noah and linear measure from the city of Jerusalem use the cubit and the furlong, which are values that Newton spent decades investigating. Newton's book *A Dissertation upon the Sacred Cubit of the Jews* was written during his work on gravitation. He believed that the sacred cubit would give him an accurate value of the diameter of the earth, a value needed for his calculations of gravity and calculus that he employed in *Principia.*[5]

The "distance equals time" relationship seems to hinge on the reality of Christ as the "Word of God" made flesh. The Word of God formed all dimension, and manifested in time as well as space. Prophecy, which is also a manifestation of the Word of God, may be reckoned in years from the point of the incarnation of Jesus Christ.

Prophetic events are then axiomatically connected to their distance from the Ark, the shrine of the Word of God in the Temple of Jerusalem. The unit of measurement that binds this relationship as also being part of the Word of God is the Law. This means that the sacred cubit and linear quantities, also part of the Law, are the only measurements that will produce these phenomena. The calibration of years and calibration of units of distance are supernaturally related in this way.

The Sacred Cubit and the Ark

The "time equals distance" phenomenon is dependent on the sacred cubit, and it is therefore necessary to establish its value as precisely as possible.

The Ark of the Covenant was a sacred wooden chest of the ancient Hebrews, which was identified with God and represented Him. Always heavily veiled, according to Exodus 34:35, Moses and the high priest alone could look upon the Ark's uncovered surface. From the mercy seat of the Ark where God spoke to Moses, eternity and heaven merged at one point on Earth in time and space. Those transgressing the laws concerning the handling of the Ark died supernatural deaths. In one circumstance, the act of simply touching it killed instantly (2 Samuel 6:6,7). Due to an unauthorized opening of the Ark by the curious, 50,700 Israelites died (1 Samuel 6:19). Levite priests carried the Ark by staves thrust through rings on its side that were never to be removed. The Levites bore the Ark ahead of the Hebrew army during battles and while it remained under their control, they were always victorious.

Its dimensions and design conveyed profound religious meaning. In Exodus 25, it was described as being constructed of acacia wood and overlaid with gold inside and out, 1½ cubits tall by 1½ cubits wide and 2½ cubits long.

The Ark contained four articles; the first was the Law of God from which it derives its name, "Ark of the Covenant" or "Ark of the Law." These were two tablets of stone on which were inscribed the Ten Commandments, the only text ever written by God's own hand. According to Deuteronomy 31:26, the second article contained in the Ark was the autographed copy of the 613 Laws, written out by Moses and deposited there. This repository of every law of God necessarily created contained the standards of measurement, as stated in Proverbs 20:10: "Divers weights, [and] divers measures, both of them [are] alike abomination to the LORD." According to Deuteronomy 25:14,

> Thou shalt not have in thine house divers measures, a great and a small. [But] thou shalt have a perfect and just weight, a perfect and just measure shalt thou have: that thy days may be lengthened in the land which the LORD thy God giveth thee. For all that do such things, [and] all that do unrighteously, [are] an abomination unto the LORD thy God.[6]

The first mention of the construction of the Holy Ark is found in the book of Exodus, 25:10. The Sacred Cubit was the basis of the Ark's design, which revealed that "Two cubits and a half shall be the length thereof, and a cubit and a half the breadth thereof, and a cubit and a half the height thereof." The description of the construction of the Ark ends in verse 20:

> And the cherubims shall stretch forth [their] wings on high, covering the mercy seat with their wings, and their faces [shall look] one to another; toward the mercy seat shall the faces of the cherubims be.[7]

The biblical chapter and verse of the Ark's construction ending in Exodus 25:20 may not have been by accident. The Israelites' cubit in the time of Moses until Solomon was equal to 25.20 modern inches.[8] This number also follows the pattern of 2,520, the writing on the wall.

The Dominican Cardinal Hugo of St. Cher of France first set the chapters of the Bible in AD 1240. It is highly likely that the French Order of Knights Templar influenced Hugo's understanding of the cubit. In AD 1119, the Templars established themselves in Jerusalem, predating the founding of the Dominican order by 121 years. From the Holy Land, they transferred vast treasures of knowledge and currency to nobles in France. The Templar Knights encountered the teachings of a mystic sect of Jews called the Johanites or Mandaeans, from the name "Manda" which means "secret knowledge." The Mandaeans believed that the future of mankind on the Earth was directed from heaven and preserved in the temple in Jerusalem.[7]

Flanders Petrie, in his extensive study of ancient calibration from the book *Inductive Metrology*, defines the Sacred Cubit of the Hebrews in the time of Moses as being

> The 25-inch cubit…found in ancient Egypt, Assyria, Persia, Syria, and probably in Greece, varying from 25.1 to 25.4. In modern Persia, Arabia, Greece, a *pic* or *braccio* of the same length also [varies] from 25.0 to 25.3. The mean of measurement from ancient structures around Jerusalem is 25.2 + - .1, which is the sacred Hebrew cubit.[8]

This was close to the value Isaac Newton had estimated the cubit to be in British inches, of which he wrote:

> The stature of the human body, according to the Talmudists, contains about 3 cubits from the feet to the head. Now the ordinary stature of men, when they are barefoot,

is greater than 5 Roman feet and less than 6 Roman feet. Take a third part of this and the vulgar cubit will be more than 20 unicae and less than 24 unicae of the Roman foot; and consequently the Sacred Cubit will be more than 24 unicae and less than 28 + (4/5) unicae of the same foot.[9]

The sacred cubit was the principle measurement of the Ark, the Tabernacle of the Exodus, and the Temple of Solomon. Petrie concludes that:

> Dr. Oppert, examining the Assyrian metrology from literary remains [the Senkereh tablet, etc.], comes to the conclusion that besides the main series of Assyrian measures [the cubit of which is, according to him, 21.60 inches] there were other units, clearly not forming part of the regular system; these he values at 25.20 inches and 39.96 inches.[10]

At the close of his extensive study, Petrie explains the sacred cubit (25.20 inches) was the standard for all others as well as modern British measurement:

> This unit was divided by 25 in Egypt and Persia, and also decimally in Greece; in fact, it seems very probable that the 25th (the inch, if I may so call it) was the real basis of the cubit....This is well known as the sacred Hebrew, Royal Persian, and Chaldean cubit, mentioned by Newton, Golius, Kelly, Quiepo, and Oppert....The Sacred Hebrew or Royal Persian cubit is found to have been used in Greece, Mohammedan Persia, and apparently by North American mound-builders....The Assyrian cubit, "great hu" of Oppert is found in Syria, Asia Minor, Sardinia, and Roman Britain, and is very probably the basis of mediaeval English units, including the British inch.[11]

The Sacred Cubit as a fractal of the number of the writing on the wall, 2,520, represented an elemental law in the creation of God. It was the standard of design according to the pattern of heaven shown to Moses on Mount Sinai.

The ancient Jewish sages maintained that time and space were of the same distinction, implying that they mirror each other in shape. Although the universe is infinite, the matter within and time that binds it is not. Therefore time, like matter, has a defined beginning and end. According to this understanding, the division of time into smaller units does not alter its inherent structure, just as the division of physical objects does not alter their structure. The pattern of both, according to the Law of God, is based on the number 2,520 and its fractal in the sacred cubit, 25.20.

It is significant that this number, encoded in the writing of the wall, manifested through the agency of a "hand," maintains the ancient metaphor of the "finger or hand of God" working His will in the material universe.

However, it is the arm that extends the hand and fingers. These work to execute the will, to create, write, and even make war. The cubit was directly representative of these functions, and was the linear standard of all creation. James Strong (1822–1894), professor of biblical literature and exegetical theology at Troy University, further explained this concept:

> In the figurative idiom of the Hebrew its name is characteristically *amah*, which is merely a variation of the word *em*, a *mother* not so much (as the lexicons explain) "because the forearm is the mother of the [entire] arm" (a metaphor not very obvious surely), but because the cubit (or ulna) is the "mother," as it were, of all dimensions whether in the human body or elsewhere.[12]

In ancient Egypt, cubit rods used for architecture and building were divided by the units of "digits," which are primarily a reference to the fingers of the hand.[13] This further connects the number written on the wall as corresponding with the Sacred Cubit, as it is based on the dimension of the arm and is also measured in units of the hand itself. According to Daniel 5:5,

> At that moment (*fingers*) of a man's (*hand*) came out and wrote on the plaster of the wall of the king's palace across from the lampstand. And the king saw the palm of the hand that wrote.[14]

Newton included work on the cubit of the Jews in several manuscripts and books. He explained the relationship of the Sacred Cubit to "palms" of length. In his *Prolegomena* to a Lexicon propheticumhe, Newton lists the Sacred Cubit as 7 palms and the Common Cubit as 6 palms, based on the description of the rod that was used to measure the temple in Ezekiel 40:5.[15]

> The 7-palm cubit would stand out as sacred due to its relation to the number 7.
> Seven is the only cardinal number that does not divide evenly into 360. The sacred number, 2,520, (100 times the sacred cubit) is also the result of 360 x 7.[16]

THE HISTORICAL MEANING OF THE ARK

In light of the central importance the Ark maintained in the religious and civil lives of the Israelites throughout the Scriptures, it is intriguing that its actual Hebrew name, the *Arown*, אֲרוֹן, literally means a chest or box, and was not *transliterated* (i.e., phonetically retained) in later versions of the Bible of common languages. It has been translated "Ark" in every version of the Bible of our age. This variation began with the Vulgate, the most ancient translation of the entire Bible into Latin. The Vulgate uses the word *arca* for both the Ark of Flood of

Noah and the Ark of the Covenant. This Latin translation was created by St. Jerome at the insistence of Pope Damascus I in the 4th Century AD. It has remained the official Bible of the Catholic Church into modern times. Despite the care with which Jerome translated the Hebrew Masoretic text of the Old Testament into Latin, as history records, with the close advice of rabbi scholars, the word "ark" was substituted for *arown*.

The closest match between the three-letters of the Greek word "ark" αρκ (alpha, rho, kappa)and the three letters in Aramaic square script (modern Hebrew) that correspond with it phonetically are: אךר (aleph, resh, koph). These bear a close resemblance to the original Hebrew word *arown*, אךר (aleph, resh nun). The difference between the final (koph) in A R K and the (nun) in *arown* is so minute that these Hebrew words might easily be confused. However, it is more likely that St. Jerome deliberately chose the Latin and Greek "ark," a word that suited the generic meaning of the Hebrew word *arown*, a box. However, the word "ark" does exist in Hebrew; its literal meaning is virtually the same as an "ark" from Greek and Latin.

The Hebrew word *a,r,k,* אךר, can be pronounced seven different ways, and has a variety of meanings:

(1) ark means to draw out, lengthen, prolonged,
(2) awrak means to lengthen, to meet or reach a given point,
(3) arak is a length of time,
(4) awrake is to long, [or be] patient,
(5) ehrek is to long,
(6) awrke means length,
(7) orek means long, length, forever.[17]

Just as the word "ark" in Hebrew has the meaning of "a measure of time and distance," the word in Greek and Latin "arc" embodies these same ideas. From these roots extend a large variety of words in the modern English language, repeating a theme that describes the supernatural property of the Ark itself.

arch: the *arc of a circle*, a curved support in architecture, bow. [L. *arca*, a chest, and *arcus*, a bow].
arch 2: the first of a class, chief in rule, from [Gk. *arc-ein*, to rule].
archaic: ancient [Gk. *arc-aios*].
archer: one who shoots with a bow. [L. *arcus*, a bow].
arcanum: a secret; mystery [L. *arcanum*, secret].[18]

As in the Greek and Latin forms of the name for the Ark of God, the Hebrew word "ark" connotes very similar ideas. Time over the measure of distance, the flight of an arrow from a bow, the length of its flight in an arc, the secrets of the rule of law and measure, the arch of support for the *arch*itecture of creation, and the ancient rule of God in time between two eternities are all conveyed through the history of trade between the ancient Hebrews and Greeks and sheds light on the transfer of words and alphabets.

Early Phoenician and Israelite traders of the Mediterranean shared not only commerce and goods with the rest of the civilized world, but writing and knowledge as well. This consisted of sacred writing on parchment scrolls of Moses from pre-exiletic Israelites. The alphabet used for these earliest works is termed in paleo-Hebrew or Phoenician script. The paleo-Hebrew and early Greek alphabets are nearly identical except for one feature: the early Greeks wrote their letters in mirror image of the Hebrew. A simple reason for this is that Hebrew is written from right to left, and Greek from left to right. The Greeks merely superimposed the sounds of their language into the letters given to them by Israelite and Phoenician traders.

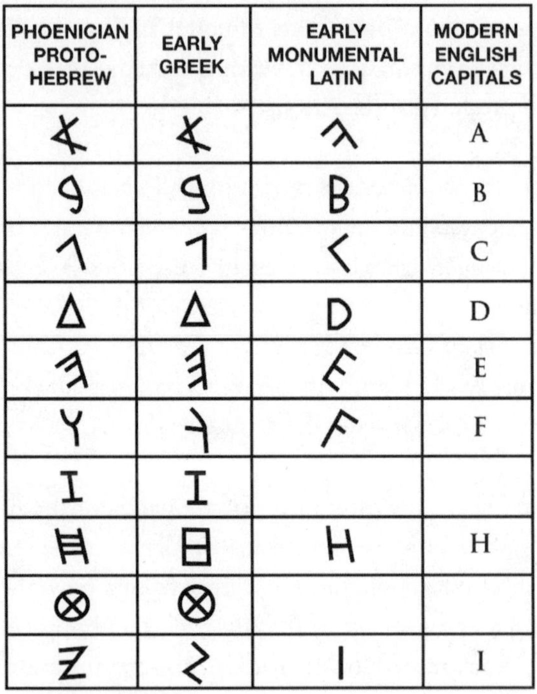

PHOENICIAN PROTO-HEBREW	EARLY GREEK	EARLY MONUMENTAL LATIN	MODERN ENGLISH CAPITALS
𐤀	𐤀	⋏	A
9	9	B	B
↗	⅂	<	C
Δ	Δ	D	D
⋺	⋺	⅀	E
Y	⅂	⅀	F
I	I		
⊟	⊟	H	H
⊗	⊗		
Z	⧘	I	I

Fig. 13. Image reprinted from *Illustrated Bible Dictionary*, Third Edition, M.G. Easton M.A., D.D.,Thomas Nelson, New York 1897.

During the exile of the kingdoms of Judah and Israel in Babylon between 587 BC and 538 BC, the Hebrew alphabet was changed to the Aramaic "square script" still in use today.

The Greeks would have become familiar with the same texts held most valuable by the Hebrews, especially the story of the Exodus. Formulators of the Greek alphabet would have revered the "letters" that made words immortal. They were the words, "by which the heavens and the earth were created."[19] These same words conveyed the supernatural properties of the Ark of God.

It is logical that the Greeks would identify the Ark of the Almighty recorded in the book of Moses with a Hebrew word that most clearly defined the nature of its power.

The most prominent feature of the Ark of the Covenant, as well every "ark" found in the Bible, is its movement over the Earth from one point to another under the navigation of God.

An Ark carried Moses along the Nile to the daughter of Pharaoh. The Ark of Noah navigated the deluge to the dry summit of Mount Ararat. The Ark of the Covenant traveled before the tribes of the Exodus to the Promised Land. All three contained "seeds" for the future of mankind designed for planting at their destinations. All carried or were followed by a portion of humanity under God's protection, leading to a realm of life and promise out of a land of destruction and death.

The movement from one point to another across the earth necessarily produces an arc, as the Earth itself is a sphere. Speed is measured by the length of time it takes to travel over a set distance. These concepts are most commonly defined by the physics of Newton's *Calculus*, which determines instantaneous rates of change, and may be used to find the velocity (rate of change of distance with respect to time) of an object moving through space or the slope of a curve at any given point. Calculus is necessary for finding *arc* length and measuring the area of a region bounded by a curve.

Before the development of calculus by Isaac Newton, mathematics dealt only with static situations, i.e., those that were not in motion. Between 1665 and 1666, Isaac Newton began to develop calculus and formulate the theory of gravitation. It was not until Newton brought forth his work *Principia* and his three laws of motion and universal gravitation that the foundation was laid for a consideration of the relative motions of all bodies.

Motion cannot exist without time. Time does not exist without motion. The laws of space, gravity, and time bind us in our reality. God by definition exists throughout all space and all time, but also outside and apart from them. Having created the laws of the universe, His perspective of time and space is omnipotent and his understanding of them omniscient. It is reasonable that the names used by the ancients for the Ark of the Covenant in Latin, Greek and Hebrew, were addressing these aspects.

The parallels between calculus as a tool for measuring distance over time and the meaning of the word ark in the ancient languages suggest an interrelationship between them. Newton had encountered these relationships in his studies of the ancient Jewish texts.

NOTES

1. Isaac Newton Part 2, Chapter 1 - *Observations upon the Prophecies of Daniel and the Apocalypse of St. John.* Jewish National and University Library, Jerusalem, Yahuda Ms. 1.1 Transcribed by Shelley Innes summer 1998. The Newton Project—University of Sussex, East Sussex London: 2007 www. newtonproject.sussex.ac.uk

2. Augustine, *Confessions,* book IX, vs. II, pg. 90. William Benton, The University of Chicago, Publisher. Encyclopaedia Britannica, Inc. Chicago IL. U.S.A. 1952.

3. Isaac Newton, *Treatise on Revelation,* Jewish National and University Library, Jerusalem, Yahuda Ms. 1.1. The Newton Project—University of Sussex, East Sussex London: 2007 www. newtonproject.sussex.ac.uk

4. Ethelbert W. Bullinger *Number in Scripture: Its Supernatural Design and Spiritual Significance.* PART II, Kregel Publications 1967 Grand Rapids Michigan. Pg. 257.

5. Piazzi Smyth *Life and Work at the Great Pyramid* Edinburgh UK: Edmonston and Douglas. 1867. Pg. 341 books.google.com

6. Deuteronomy25:14 KJV

7. Exodus, 25: 6 KJV

8. The Columbia Encyclopedia, Sixth Edition. Columbia University Press 2001–07. Entry under "Mandaeans".

9. Petrie W. M. Flanders, *Inductive Metrology or, The Recovery of Ancient Measures From The Monuments.* (London UK : Hargrove Suanders,1877).

10. Piazzi Smyth *Life and Work at the Great Pyramid* Edinburgh UK: Edmonston and Douglas. 1867. Pg. 362.

11. Ibid. Petrie W. M. Flanders, *Inductive Metrology.* pg. 67.

12. Ibid. Petrie W. M. Flanders, *Inductive Metrology* pg. 145, writes: "The possibility of this widespread unit having some connection

with the Chinese foot (the double of which is 25.18+ -.04) and with the North American mound builder's foot (1/2 of 25.20 + -.04) should not be disregarded…Don Quiepo also connects with it the Japanese 'inc' 75.21 - i.e., 3 x 25.07.

13. James Strong, *The Tabernacle of Israel* New edition, 1987 Kregel Publications, Grand Rapids MI 49501 page. 118 A. Bockh, Metrologische Untersuchungen (1838) (general) 'Emphasis mine'.

14. Petrie W. M. Flanders, *Inductive Metrology or, The Recovery of Ancient Measures from the Monuments.* London: Hargrove Saunders, 1877.

15. James Strongs Exhaustive Concordance of the Bible. World Bible Publishers, Inc., Iowa Dalls, IA. U.S.A. 1986. Hebrew Lexicon: fingers (estaba) # 677, hand (yad) #3028 palm (pac) # 6447.

16. Isaac Newton *Prolegomena to a Lexicon propheticumhe*, Yahuda mss 14. f. The Newton Project—University of Sussex, East Sussex London: 2007 www.newtonproject.sussex.ac.uk

17. Ibid. Strong's Hebrew and Chaldee dictionary of the Old Testament entry # 748 through #754.

18. Webster's Dictionary. 1987 edition. PSI Associates Miami, Florida.

19. *Babylonian Talmud*, Berakoth, 55a. Translated by Michael L. Rodkinson. New York: New Talmud Pub. Co.1903.

5

A LINE OVER JERUSALEM

A statement found in Zechariah 1 suggests that the distances between the temple and the capitals of nations that oppressed the exiled Israelites were important. It was given to Zechariah in the same year that Cyrus the Great issued Israel's release from Babylon.

Thus saith the LORD of hosts; I am jealous for Jerusalem and for Zion with a great jealousy. And I am very sore displeased with the heathen [that are] at ease: for I was but a little displeased, and they helped forward the affliction. Therefore thus saith the LORD; I am returned to Jerusalem with mercies: my house shall be built in it, saith the LORD of hosts, and a line shall be stretched forth upon Jerusalem.[1]

It is clear from history that the foundation and remains of the temple still existed when the Babylonian exiles returned, and the process of constructing the temple would not have involved extensive land survey to establish the temple's correct location. Additionally the temple lay not over Jerusalem itself, but only on Mount Zion. At the writing of the prophecy, Babylon would soon be overthrown and the Medes and Persians would alternately be in support of Israel and the rebuilding of the temple. Biblical events of antiquity often foreshadow the future fulfillment of God's plans.

The use of a measuring line in building and architecture has been known from greatest antiquity. In the paradigm of God as the geometer of creation, devices of measurement assume a mystical nature, existing not only as tools for building, but as a metaphor of the order in creation. According to Newton, both creation and the biblical cannon bore the stamp of his authorship. This theme is apparent in many prophetic texts of the Old Testament. Zechariah identifies the "nations" as Jerusalem's oppressors. The "measuring line" in this case serves as a device of judicial calibration in the sense that the future nations as well as Babylon would be judged using the standard of God's law concerning their treatment of Jerusalem and especially His temple.

This idea is embellished further in St. John's Revelation 11:2, which states that

A reed like a staff was given to me, and the angel stood, saying rise and measure the temple of God and the altar and those worshiping in it. But the court which is without the temple leave out, and measure it not; for it is given unto the Gentiles [literally, nations].[2]

Here again there is a relationship between the nations of the Earth and their location proximate to the temple. For the "outside court" of the temple, John the revelator uses the Greek pharse *aulen ton exothen*, meaning literally "away toward the winds."[3] This implied the nations of the entire world as scattered to the four winds. Their distance from the temple of God is both a metaphor for the disregard or enmity they have for it, as well as the distance in which they lie away from the temple. According to Isaiah 28:17, "Judgment will I lay to the *line*, and righteousness to the *plummet*." A similar message is conveyed in

Micah 1:2: "Hear, all ye people; hearken, O earth, and all that therein is: and let the Lord GOD be witness against you, the Lord from his holy temple."

Having Zechariah and John's perspective of measuring line (and Newton's belief of a universal standard in the geometry of the temple), we can put a hypothesis that linear measure may relate to or equal years of the Gregorian calendar to the test. In modern times, literal "measuring lines" exist that can calculate precise distances between any two points on the globe, taking into account the slight flattening at the poles. Using modern geo-coordinated satellites fixed in orbit around earth, the distance between terrestrial points can be determined within inches.

The "measuring line of God" has been demonstrated in the distance between Jerusalem and Babylon. Newton paired both cities in chapter five of *Chronologies* by insertion of the geometric study of the temple of Jerusalem after describing the reign and fall of Babylon.

However, Newton also focused extensively on the prophecies of the second advent of Christ. Because the temple in Jerusalem was a focal point of the return of Christ in the writings of both the prophet Daniel and John the Revelator, its reappearance in the future on the temple mount of Jerusalem, either through divine or human means, would herald Christ's return. In his studies of Revelation, Newton had noted that its prophecies concerning the return of Christ contained some reference to the Ark, the temple, or its sacrifices. The link between Jesus Christ, the Ark, and the temple is also a fundamental aspect of the time/distance phenomenon.

The temple that symbolizes Christ as the origin of measure toward the nation and his birth in AD 1 is the origin of the time that calibrates with these measurements.

It could not be built unless the priests from the tribe of Levi were re-established in Jerusalem. According to Mosaic Law, God designated the tribe of Levi as priests to the temple. However, since AD 70, the Diaspora had scattered the Jews across the globe. In Newton's day,

✓

Israel was under Turkish rule. The Jews would not possess Israel as
their homeland for another 220 years.

In addition to the familiar 10 Commandments given to Moses by
God on Mount Sinai, there are 603 more laws recorded in the Old Testament. Of these laws, two-thirds are involved in various degrees with
Temple ritual, sacrifice, feast days, and requirements of a citizen of Israel,
all of which are impossible to keep unless a temple exists in Jerusalem.

Newton clearly understood the Law of Moses. His writings underscored the significance of the law with respect to nature, prophecy,
and the interpretation of both. While living in London as Master of
the Mint and President of the Royal Society, Newton wrote concerning the law of return of the Jews to Jerusalem and the building of the
temple in *Observations upon the Prophecies of Daniel*:

> Since the commandment to return and to build Jerusalem
> precedes the Messiah the Prince by 49 years;[4] it may perhaps
> come forth not from the Jews themselves, but from some other
> kingdom friendly to them, and precede their return from cap-
> tivity, and give occasion to it; and lastly, that this rebuilding of
> Jerusalem and the waste places of Judah is predicted in Micah
> 7:11, Amos 9:11, 14. Ezekiel 36:33, 35, 36, 38. Isaiah 54:3,
> 11, 12, 55:12, 61:4, 65:18, 21, 22; and Tobit 14:5. and that
> the return from captivity and coming of the Messiah and his
> kingdom are described in Daniel 7 Revelation 19…and Acts
> 1 Matthew 24 Joel 3 Ezekiel 36, 37. Isaiah 60, 62. 63, 65. and
> 66:and many other places of scripture. The manner I know
> not. Let time be the Interpreter.[5]

Indeed, time *is* the interpreter, and the temple, as Newton had
long suspected, was the key.

By fixing a point on the site of the temple mount, a measuring line
extended over Jerusalem to the center of London, produces 1,948.40
nautical miles.

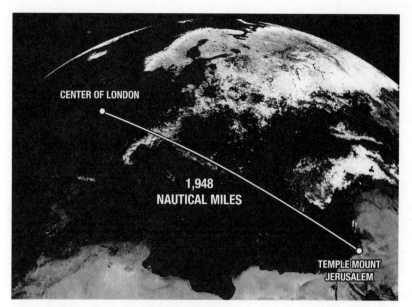

CENTER OF LONDON

1,948
NAUTICAL MILES

TEMPLE MOUNT
JERUSALEM

Fig. 14. Courtesy of NASA World Wind

Recorded in the earth between the temple mount of Jerusalem and the historic center of London is the fulfillment of Newton's own prediction. Israel became a nation again on May 14th, 1948.

Britain was the nation that was "friendly to the Jews" and enabled them to return to Israel over two hundred years after Newton's death. During the time he wrote the *Observations upon the Prophecies of Daniel*, Newton's living quarters were in the Tower of London, while he was employed as Master of the Royal Mint from 1696 to 1727.

The British defeated the Ottoman Turks and became administrators of the land of ancient Israel in 1917. Through mandate after World War I and World War II until 1948, London was the heart of the governing intellect over the region.

London's original location at its founding is an important point in establishing the exact value of distance between it and Jerusalem's temple.

The Romans established Londinium ca. AD 47. It was a civilian

settlement built where the Thames became narrow enough for a bridge
to be built across it, but was still deep enough to admit large ocean vessels. Before the Romans invaded Britain in AD 43, the area of London
was almost certainly open countryside.

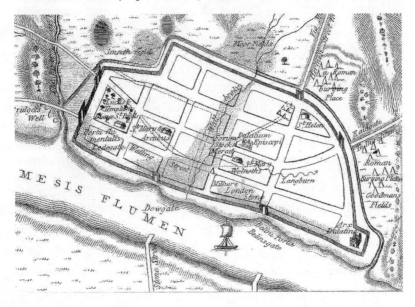

Fig. 15. In this map of ancient "Londinium," the center of the city
is marked by a milestone. This gnomon, known as the "London
stone," is still in existence to this day. Its original location in
the center of Cannon Street has been retained in London's
historical records. Reprinted from George Lawrence Gomme, *The
Governance of London with Maps* (London: T. Fisher Unwin, 1907),
78.

In the 16th century, William Camden believed that the "London
Stone" was a Roman milestone from which all distances were measured in the province. In the 17th century, Christopher Wren was able
to observe the foundations of the London Stone underneath Cannon
Street during the rebuilding of London after the Great Fire.[6] With this
information, it is possible to extend a measuring line from the temple
mount in Jerusalem to the exact center of ancient London.

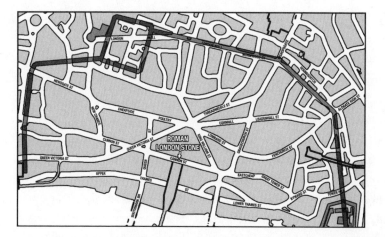

Fig. 16. Image by author based on descriptions of the ancient center of London as defined by Roman settlement boundaries in George Lawrence Gomme, *The Governance of London with Maps* (London: T. Fisher Unwin, 1907), 78.

The origin of a measuring line extended from the center of London at modern day Cannon Street, and ends with its terminus on the temple mount in Jerusalem. The point chosen on the temple mount itself is the location of the foundation stone, the site upon which the Ark of the Covenant rested.

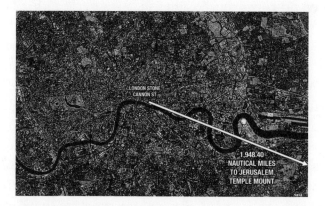

Fig. 17. The ancient center of London, England, 1,948.40 nautical miles from Jerusalem's temple mount. Image courtesy of NASA World Wind.

Of all the numbers that could be represented in miles between the Temple mount of Jerusalem and the historical center of London, statistically speaking, the odds of hitting the exact year of Israel's rebirth as a nation, 1948, in any form of measurement are astronomical. One can calculate distance using many—even arbitrary—systems. However, it is significant that the distance between London's center and Jerusalem's center, the temple mount, reflects the rebirth of Israel in nautical miles. Nautical miles are based on the ratio of degrees in a circle to minutes in an hour. The 360-degree circle and the 60-minute hour have existed from the birth of civilization. Each degree of the great circle of the Earth equals 60 nautical miles. The circumference of the earth is therefore 21,600 miles (360 x 60). This is related to the value of the common cubit, which is 21.60 inches. With the understanding of the etymological connection between the words navy and nautical with Noah, the Ark of the deluge, and the Ark of the Covenant, the nautical mile can be reasonably termed, an "Ark mile" or "temple mile."

In relation to the *prisca theologia* suggested in Newton's research, the nautical mile calibrates to prophetic events occurring *after* the birth of Christ. Alternately, the statute mile seems to relate to events occurring *before* the birth of Christ. Both miles are numerically and symbolically significant with respect to prophecy.

In calculations of distance using the Statute mile, such as between Babylon and Jerusalem, the *priscia theologia* value manifests because the ratio of sacred cubit (25.20 inches) was preserved within the British mile up until Newton's time. The establishment of the statute mile in accord with the Sacred Cubit was a matter of great importance to the British metrologists during the reign of Queen Elizabeth. The full significance of the statute mile will be explored in later chapters.

In addition to the distance between both cities recording the year of Israel's rebirth, 1948 also figures into the dominical number, 2,520. There were 2,486 years between the release of the Jews from Babylon (by Cyrus the great in 538 BC) and the rebirth of Israel in 1948.

These years are counted in 365 solar days. If years are calculated using 360 days (like all prophetic years in the Old Testament) the exact distance in time between both events is 2,520 years, and is as follows:

$$2,486 \times 365 = 907,390 / 360 = 2,520$$

This quantity is also found by adding the year of the *fall* of Babylon with the year of the rebirth of Israel, plus the number 33:

$$1948 + 539 = 2,487 + 33 = 2,520$$

WHY WOULD 33 STAND OUT?

In the Gregorian calendar, AD is an abbreviation of the Latin *Anno Domini*, meaning "in the year of our Lord." Apart from the birth of Christ, on which the modern calendar is based, his resurrection is the most important event in Christianity. Most chronologists assign the age of Christ's death and resurrection to 33 years. Newton also agreed with this chronology and listed the passion of Jesus as having occurred no later than AD 34 in chapter 11 of *Observations upon the Prophecies of Daniel and the Apocalypse of St. John.*[7]

In the system of percent, 1/3 represents 33.33% of 100. Newton was well aware of St. John's incorporation of the number 33 (1/3) throughout Revelation. He believed the number represented a hierarchal division of creation. Its repeated mention in the judgments of Revelation correlated to the rebellion of the angels aligned to the Dragon in Revelation 12. Also according to his studies of the dispensation of the prophecy, time was an inseparable factor.

The universal hour has 60 minutes in the ancient sexagesimal system. In navigational and geodetic measurements, the following calculation converts decimal distances (based on 10) into degrees of minutes and seconds (based on 60):

To find "minutes," the decimal .33 is multiplied by 60:

$$.33 \times 60 = 19.8 \ (19 \text{ minutes})$$

To find "seconds," the decimal .8 is again multiplied by 60:

$$.80 \times 60 = 48 \text{ seconds.}[8]$$

Therefore, the conversion of .33 percent or 1/3 of an hour is exactly 19 minutes, 48 seconds, which is a fractal representation of the year 1948.

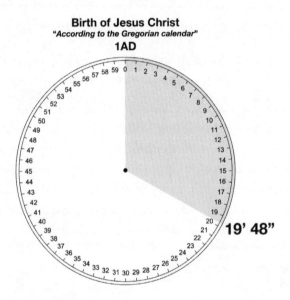

Fig. 18. Image by author

The same two numbers associated with the third *of time* (33 and 1948) also mark the *orientation* of Jerusalem in the land of Israel. Thirty three miles is the shortest distance to the Mediterranean Sea from Jerusalem. The direction of this path generates an azimuth of 19.48 degrees, north of west.

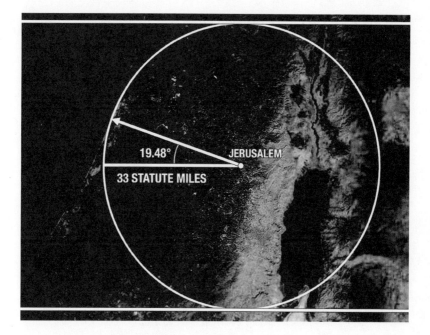

Fig. 19. Courtesy of NASA World Wind

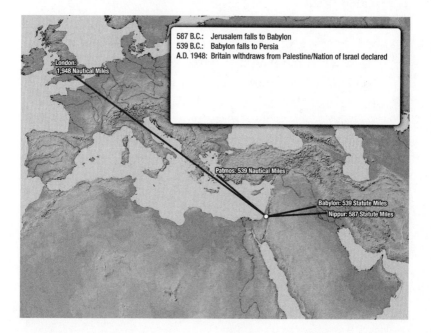

NOTES

1. Zechariah 1:15, 16 KJV Emphasis mine.
2. Revelation 11:2 KJV Emphasis mine.
3. Greek Lexicon entry # 833. in *James Strongs Exhaustive Concordance of the Bible*. World Bible Publishers, Inc., Iowa Dalls, IA. U.S.A. 1986.
4. Author note: Here Newton relied on his chronological view that the end of days was set during the reinstitution of the Western Roman Empire in AD 800 by Charlemagne; his reasons for this are examined in detail in chapter 18.
5. Isaac Newton *Observations upon the Prophecies of Daniel.* Part 1, Chapter 10. The Newton Project—University of Sussex, East Sussex London: 2007 www.newtonproject.sussex.ac.uk
6. Royal Commission on Historical Monuments, Vol 3, Pg. 232. Roman London. Publisher: His Majesty's Stationary Office. London. 1928
7. Isaac Newton, *Observations upon the Prophecies of Daniel and the Apocalypse of St. John Of the Times of the Birth and Passion of Christ,.* Newton Project – University of Sussex, East Sussex London: 2007 www.newtonproject.sussex.ac.uk.
8. United States National Geodetic Survey NADCON decimal conversion program. URL: http://www.ngs.noaa.gov/cgi-bin/nadcon.prl

6

A PREVIOUS ATTEMPT

Though Newton suspected that the temple held the answer to prophetic time because it mathematically incorporated dimensions of the Earth as a literal geometer, also known as "earth measure," he could not define the value of the temple's location in relationship in distance to the nations due to a lack of information. The exact coordinates for many ancient cities and the dimensions of the earth were speculative in Newton's time. Undoubtedly, he would have recorded the connection of time versus distance if he possessed these values.

Newton did not leave any record, so far as has been discovered, that he attempted to measure the exact distance between Jerusalem and London. However, because his writings record his suspicion that a unifying constant existed in prophecy and in the dimensions of the temple of Jerusalem, Newton may have made calculations that have not yet been discovered or have been lost.

The idea that distance could represent significant historical points in Israel's history seems esoteric in the extreme—perhaps so extreme that one would suspect only a mind like Newton's would deem it worthy of investigation. However, it is little known that a London theologian named Samuel Lee attempted to measure the distance between London and Jerusalem in 1659, two years before Isaac Newton was admitted to Trinity College at Cambridge.

In his treatise *Orbis Miraculum, or the Temple of Solomon portrayed in Scriptural light*, Lee explained his reasoning for the London to Jerusalem calculation. In introductory statements in the preface of his book, he addressed the discrepancy in size of the temple of Ezekiel, and compared it to the Temple of Solomon in terms of Messianic symbolism:

> Since the temple limits in the prophetic description do so wonderfully surpass the circuits of the very mountain itself, surely it was to typify the Church of Christ, being the Gospel-Temple, whose great enlargement was signified by that vision: which interpretation seem to be very solid, and may be farther evidenced by the portions set out by the same prophet for the city of Jerusalem, for the priests, for the Prince and the whole land in succeeding chapters; which do all exceedingly transcend the true Geographical limits of the City, or the Holy Land, or any of the other portions.[1]

Lee believed that the dimensions of Ezekiel's temple represented a metaphorical and spiritual message, one transcending the geographic limits of Jerusalem to the church distributed over the earth. In this light, the relationship between Jerusalem and the centers of Christendom scattered across the globe would also have significance. In the writing style of the time, Lee wrote concerning this idea:

> One proemial inquiry more we shall crave leave to exhibit, before we come to the main design, [of the temple] and that is the exact distance (as far as may be deduced of authors) of this famous city *Jerusalem* (Wherein the temple was built) from *London* the metropolis of *England*; That we may know whereabouts in the world our discourse lies.[2]

At the end of chapter one of *Orbis Miraculum,* Lee worked out the distance between London and Jerusalem using "the doctrine of triangles." Unfortunately, he used a coordinate for the latitude of Jerusalem that was in error, listing Jerusalem at 32 degrees, 10 minutes north (its actual latitude is 31 degrees, 46 minutes north). Additionally Lee used the longitudes for both cities calibrated from a "0" meridian located at that time at the Canary Islands according to Ptolemy (the Greenwich meridian was not established until 1881).[3]

After arriving at a number of degrees between each city through the "canon of logarithms," Lee attempted to convert the degrees into statute miles. This was an extremely difficult task. In the 1600s, the number of statute miles for a degree of the Earth had not been accurately calibrated. He relied heavily on the works of the Greek geographers Ptolemy and Eratosthenes for the measurements of 66, 60, and 69 statue miles to one degree of the earth. After calculating for each value, he arrived at three distances: 2,355; 2,579; and 2,717 statute miles between London and Jerusalem. These figures converted to nautical miles are 2,046; 2,240; and 2,360. Though it was an admirable attempt, Lee's calculations were in error of between 122 and 474 statue miles in excess of the actual distance: 2,242 statute miles or 1948.39 nautical miles.

It is evident that Samuel Lee had anticipated some special relationship between his nation's capital and Jerusalem through his studies of the temple proportion. His research followed a long tradition of relating the divine proportion of the sacred building with the proportion of creation.

NOTES

1. Samuel Lee, *Orbis Miraculum*, London. Printed by John Streater for Humphrey Mosley, at Signe of the Prince's Arms in St. Paul's–Church-Yard. MDCLIX Preface.
2. Ibid. *Orbis Miaculum* Chapter 1. page 9.
3. R. Stafforde, *A Geographical and Anthologicall Description of all the Empires and Kingdomes, both of Continent and Islands in this terrestrial Globe* (London, 1634).

7

THE ARK OF TIME

Hast thou perceived the breadth of the earth?
declare if thou knowest it all.

JOB 38:18

T he sacred Ark led the tribes of Israel during the Exodus, navigating a course determined by God. The presence of God abided with Israelites as the pillar of smoke by day and a pillar of fire by night. It guided the Ark and the Israelites, who followed it like a ship through the desert. When the pillar came to rest above the Ark, they set up camp; when the pillar moved from its place above the Ark, they broke camp and followed. This the Israelites did continually during their 40-year journey in the wilderness of the Sinai desert. It was only after Solomon built the temple in Jerusalem that the sacred Ark finally found a permanent resting place. The Ark would remain in the Holy of Holies of the temple as long as the tribes of Israel remained faithful to the covenant of God. The foundation stone in the Holy of Holies of the temple in Jerusalem was the Ark's lawful resting place. As with the Ark, the edifice of the temple and its location on Mount Zion was designed and established by God's wisdom. Both represented the divine standard for measurement of all dimensions. Exodus 31:1–2 explains that God specifically chose a man named Bezaleel for the task of building the Ark, saying,

> See, I have called by name Bezaleel the son of Uri, the son of Hur, of the tribe of Judah: And I have filled him with the spirit of God, in wisdom, and in understanding, and in knowledge, and in all manner of workmanship.

THE ARK AND MERCY SEAT.

Fig. 20. Image reprinted from D. W. Thomson, *Youth's Illustrated Bible History* (NY: Bill Publishers, 1881), 61.

Bezaleel, pronounced B tzel'el, in Hebrew means "under the shadow of God."[1] "Bezaleel, the builder of the Tabernacle in the Wilderness," says the Talmud, "knew how to combine the letters by which the heavens and the earth were created."[2]

> And Bezaleel made the ark [of] shittim wood:...And he overlaid it with pure gold within and without, and made a crown of gold to it round about. And he cast for it four rings of gold, [to be set] by the four corners of it;...And he made staves [of] shittim wood, and overlaid them with gold. And he put the staves into the rings by the sides of the ark, to bear the

ark. And he made the mercy seat [of] pure gold: two cubits and a half [was] the length thereof, and one cubit and a half the breadth thereof. And he made two cherubims [of] gold, beaten out of one piece made he them, on the two ends of the mercy seat.[3]

In Hebrews 9:5 in the New Testament, Paul explained that the tabernacle and the ark were a pattern of heavenly and perfect law "overshadowing" the priests of the temple and that they served as "the copy and shadow of heavenly things." He explained the holiness of the tabernacle furnishings in ascending order, ending with the ark, saying, "And over it the cherubims of glory shadowing the mercyseat; of which we cannot now speak particularly."[4]

The words for shadow, *skia* in Greek and *tzel* in Hebrew, have virtually the same meaning. B tzel'el (under the shadow of God) or B tzel'shadai (under the shadow of the Almighty) is a phrase that appears in the Psalms. In Psalm 91:1, 4, King David, author of the Psalms, was given the pattern of the Temple by God that Solomon later built:

He that dwelleth in the secret place of the most High shall abide under the shadow of the Almighty...He shall cover thee with his feathers, and under his wings shalt thou trust: his truth [shall be thy] shield and buckler.

This refers to the configuration of the cherubim. It is obvious that the Psalmist considered their form and shape extremely significant, for under all the heavens, only between the wings of the cherubim could one access the presence of God.[5] In the time that the ark was with the Israelites, eternity *arced* or *bowed* time from between the cherubim. David implied this intersection of the ark of God from eternity in Psalm 18:9–10, and said,

He bowed the heavens also, and came down: and darkness
[was] under his feet. And he rode upon a cherub, and did fly:
yea, he did fly upon the wings of the wind.

Within this significant context, it is peculiar that no extensive de-
tails of the appearance of the Ark's cherubim exist in the Bible narrative beyond the method for their construction. In Exodus 25:18–20,
we are told that their wings lifted upwards and were outspread so
as to cover the ark, and that they were presented in a posture facing
one another, looking down upon the mercy seat. Throughout history, various designs of the cherubim have been proposed, usually
based on the additional references made to the symbolic creatures
found in the book of Ezekiel. It would seem there is no solution to
this mystery, unless attention is directed to evidence of the close interaction between Israel and Egypt during the reign of Solomon, ca.
970 to 928 BC:[6]

And Solomon made affinity with Pharaoh king of Egypt, and
took Pharaoh's daughter, and brought her into the city of David,
until he had made an end of building his own house, and the
house of the LORD, and the wall of Jerusalem round about.[7]

According to the historian Immanuel Velikovsky, the Egyptians
engaged in trade with Israel from the time of the first temple and
intermittently up until the age of the Greeks.
He also states that,

Solomon was not an obscure prince, as he is often represented.
The riches of his kingdom astounded the Egyptians under
their most magnificent monarch...Jewish artists brought to
Egypt introduced their fine arts and influenced the aesthetic
conceptions of the Egyptians....The architecture and ordi-

nances of the Temple of Solomon were copied in the Temple of Amon [see Figure 21] at Deir El Bahari. The plan of this structure and its terraces can help in the reconstruction of the plan of the Temple of Solomon.[8]

J. STRONG, *THE TABERNACLE OF ISRAEL.* P. 88

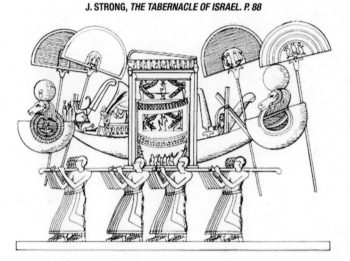

Fig. 21. Cherubim overshadowing the "seat of God," at the temple of Amon. Here, the throne of God as a navigating celestial boat or (barque) is emphasized. Reprinted from James Strong, *The Tabernacle of Israel in the Desert* (Providence: Harris, Jones, 1888), 88.

The Egyptian's reverence for the temple at Jerusalem was also evident in the funerary temple of Ramses III at Menidet Habu, built during the 4th century BC. This structure also imitates the design of the temple of Jerusalem. More importantly, and generally unknown to most biblical researchers, is that this temple displays several images of the Ark of the Covenant carved in relief upon its walls.[9]

F. PETRIE, *EGYPT & ISRAEL* P. 62A

Fig. 22. Relief from the temple at Medinet Habu. The two cherubim are clearly seen with wings in the attitude described in Exodus 25:20: "And the cherubims shall stretch forth [their] wings on high, covering the mercy seat with their wings" (i.e., two wings on high and two wings covering the mercy seat). W. M. Flinders Petrie, ***Egypt and Israel*** (London: A Society for Promoting Christian Knowledge, 1911), 62.

These images may be the closest representation of the cherubim of the Ark, combining the Egyptian artistry familiar to Moses and influences of Jewish settlers living in Egypt during the time of their creation. Velikovsky explained that the Egyptian obsession with the Hebrew God and religion began with the meeting of Queen Hatshepsu (the Queen of Sheba) and King Solomon. The Egyptian "cult of the Hebrews" continued throughout the rise of Babylon and reached a climax during the 4th century, during which time a Jewish military colony was stationed at Elephantine to defend the eastern borders of Egypt under Ramses III. These Jews took part in the defense of the country during the campaign of Alexander the Great.[10]

In his comprehensive study on the tabernacle of the Exodus, the theologian James Strong (1822–1894) described the contents of the Ark of God. Besides the stone tablets of the Ten Commandments,

> The ark also contained an autograph copy of the law, written by Moses and deposited there. These are presumed to have been the complete five scrolls of the Old Testament that were removed at some point later, along with everything except the tablets of the Ten Commandments according to 1 Kings 8:9. The last two objects deposited in the Ark were a golden pot of manna (Exodus 16:33,34) and the rod of Aaron that miraculously budded and grew ripe almonds over the course of one night (Numbers 17:10).[11]

After the forty years of wandering in the Sinai desert came to an end, the Ark led the Israelites into Canaan. The Jordan River marked the boundary between the desert and the Promised Land. As the feet of the priests bearing the Ark touched the Jordan River, its waters "stood and rose up upon a heap." The ark remained in the midst of the riverbed until all the people had crossed to the other side.[12] The first city of conquest by the Israelites was Jericho, which fell after being compassed by the Ark seven days.

There is far more significance to this story. It is a lesson of the divine proportion.

Joshua 6:3 says, "You shall compass the city…and go round about the city once. Thus shalt thou do six days."[13]

The six-fold compassing of Jericho yields an exquisite yet simple equation, and its intrinsic meaning fits the astronomical works and theories of Isaac Newton.

"Jericho," literally translated, means the moon (or Moon city), and is a homonym of the Hebrew word for "thrown down place."[14]

The Ark (in its metaphoric capacity as a standard of dimension) made six circles of 360 degrees around Jericho totaling 2,160 degrees. The 360-degree system used for the circle had existed in Egypt and

Sumer from the beginning of their civilizations. As told in Exodus 12:40, the Israelites, having lived four hundred and thirty years in Egypt before their wandering in the Sinai desert, would have un-doubtedly been acquainted with this system of geometry.

THE MOON'S MEASUREMENT

In circumscribing 2,160 degrees of Jericho with the Ark, the Israelites marked the diameter of the moon in modern statute miles. The cir-cumference (the distance around the moon) is found by multiplying 2,160 by the number 3.14159265. This number is symbolized by the Greek letter π. The value of π, or pi, was clearly in use during the time of Exodus. Its appearance in the architecture of Egypt and Sumer is well documented.

$$3.14159265 \ldots \times 2,160 = 6,785.8401 \text{ miles}$$

Pi is a ratio found in circles and their applications that is an im-portant feature of Pythagorean geometry. It is a universal constant that does not depend on any number system to function and is the only number in existence that defines all circles. It works simply; the distance across any circle *multiplied* by pi gives the distance around the circle. The distance around any circle *divided* by pi gives the distance across the circle. Mathematicians consider pi an existential number because its decimal places extend forever. Use of pi in building and architecture is considered the identifying characteristic of an advanced civilization by historians; in fact, without understanding the value of pi, building and architecture cannot exist.

Additionally, according to Joshua 6:4, the Ark and its circling of Jericho produce far greater evidence of divine standards, stating that on "the seventh day ye shall compass the city seven times." The significance of this sentence goes far beyond the exegetic interpretation usually encountered in modern theology. It contains the unifying proportion that Newton sought, the divine number that according to Daniel would be finally understood in the time of the end.

$$7 \times 360 = 2,520$$

This is the number of the writing on the wall, and the unifying value of creation suggested throughout Newton's works. Two thousand five hundred and twenty is not only a number of the proportion of creation; it also solves Daniel's time-based prophecies. The exploration of this number with respect to all Earth dimensions is now possible with the advent of the high technology of calibration, a possibility that did not exist in Newton's time. These findings are based on the length of the sacred cubit and the sacred inch that were preserved in the statute mile through the influence of geometers of Queen Elizabeth's reign from 1558 to 1603. The particulars of this subject will be explored in following chapters.

THE EARTH'S MEASUREMENT

Using 2,520 and pi, or 3.14159265, the average diameter of the earth is determined.

$$2,520 \times \pi = 7,916.813 \text{ statute miles}$$

The most recent NASA studies list the Earth's average diameter at 7,917.479 statute miles.[15]

This modern measurement is only off by 0.666 of a mile greater than the sacred calculation.

To find average circumference (distance around the earth), 7,916 is multiplied by pi:

7,916.813 x π = 24,871.403 statute miles
7,916.813 + 0.666 = (7,917.479) x π = 24,873.493
(the modern calibration)

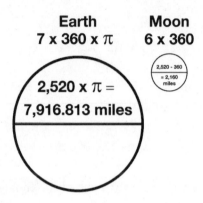

Fig. 23. Image by author

The Greek scholar Eratosthenes (ca. 275–195 BC) was credited with being the first to measure the Earth accurately. The most distinct account, and one of the earliest, is found in the remaining work of Cleomedes.[16] Eratosthenes was told that deep wells in Syene, Egypt were illuminated to the bottom on the day of the summer solstice, and that vertical objects cast no shadows. He concluded that Syene was on the Tropic of Cancer at 23.4 degrees north latitude. In Alexandria, during the summer solstice, an obelisk cast a shadow with an angle of 7.2 degrees, providing Eratosthenes with the number of degrees of a circle between the two cities. He then divided 360 degrees of a circle by the 7.2 degree angle and multiplied this amount by the distance between Syene and Alexandria (5,040 stadia).[17] His result for the circumference of the earth was 250,000 stadia.[18]

The exact length of the stadia that Eratosthenes used has been the subject of controversy for centuries. There were three main stadia that were in use during his age: the Itinerary, Olympic, and Egyptian. The itinerary stadia at 515.09 feet would have produced a circumference of 24,583.9 statute miles. However, this is still 287 miles short of the actual mean circumference of the Earth. Both the Olympic and Egyptian stadia produce figures that are thousands of miles too large.[19]

However, Eratosthenes' figure for the circumference of the earth at 252,000 is 100 times the sacred number 2,520. This suggests that he was acquainted with this number from *some* resource in antiquity, and in fact, there were several *priscia sapientia* works available to Eratosthenes at the time he made his calculation. Besides 2,520, the distance listed between Syene and Alexandria at 5,040 stadia was a sacred number recorded in Plato's *Laws* written ca. 350 BC. Five thousand and forty is a number closely related to the number of the writing on the wall (2,520 + 2,520 = 5,040).

In *Laws*, Plato suggested a design of perfect rule for a hypothetical city called Magnesia in which its citizens numbered 5,040. According to the tenets of Pythagoras, this number related to the greatest order in nature and civilization, because 5,040 represented the greatest order of all numbers. Plato wrote the following concerning the number:

> Let us proceed to another class of laws, beginning with their foundation in religion. And we must first return to the number 5040—the entire number had, and has, a great many convenient divisions....Now every portion should be regarded by us as a sacred gift of Heaven, corresponding to the months and to the revolution of the universe.[20]

In an 1888 translation and analysis of Plato's *Laws*, Benjamin Jowett describes the mystery of the number:

> This is a puzzle almost as great as the Number of the Beast in the Book of Revelation, and though apparently known to Aristotle, is referred to by Cicero as a proverb of obscurity. And some have imagined that there is no answer to the puzzle.... Our hope of understanding the passage depends principally

on an accurate study of the words themselves; on which a
faint light is thrown by the parallel passage in the ninth book.
Another help is the allusion in Aristotle, who makes the important remark that the latter part of the passage describes a
solid figure.[21]

This is the extent of the meaning of 5,040 that Jowett offers. However, within the framework of Newton's *priscia sapientia*, its meaning
is not hard to understand. The solid object to which 5,040 refers is
the Earth. The principle of law that Plato sought in *Laws* was a mirror
of the lawful standard of measurement. The doubling of 2,520 symbolically repeats the perfect measure that defines the proportion of the
Earth and the heavens.

This is why Eratosthenes used 5,040 in his calculations; it is also
why he arrived at the figure 252,000 stadia for the circumference of
the Earth, since both reflect the *perfect* number (2,520) and its fractal,
the Sacred Cubit. Additionally, 5,040 shows up in the most ancient
of all Jewish mystical works, the *Sepher Yetzirah*, (the Book of Formation). Although the oldest printed copy of this work dates from 1680,
several Jewish commentators from the first century AD refer to the
work as extremely ancient. This conclusion is based on its use of Phoenician letters similar to the work of Philo of Byblos, ca. AD 100, who
based his work on even older Greek and Egyptian manuscripts.[22]

The *Sepher Yetzirah* is a primary book of the occult Kabbalah and
is concerned with the process of the formation of the universe by God.
Its basic premise is that because God spoke creation into existence
out of nothing (ex nihilo), the letters of the Word of God given to
Moses retained the same creative force. Through permutation of all
the 22 letters of the ancient Hebrew alphabet, words could be spoken
that would affect reality either positively or negatively. Within the
Sepher Yetzirah, there is particular significance assigned to the number
seven:

With the seven double letters He (God) also designed seven Earths, seven heavens, seven continents, seven seas, seven rivers, seven deserts, seven days, seven weeks (from Passover to Pentecost), and in the midst of them His Holy Palace (the temple of Jerusalem). There is a cycle of seven years and the seventh is the release year, and after seven release years is the Jubilee. For this reason God loves the number seven more than any other thing under the heavens. In this manner God joined the seven double letters together. Two stones build two houses, three stones build six houses, four stones build twenty-four houses, five stones build 120 houses, six stones build 720 houses, and seven stones build 5,040 houses. Make a beginning according to this arrangement and reckon further than the mouth can express or the ear can hear.[23]

Newton realized that the system of sevens was integral to *prophetic time* in the books of Daniel and Revelation. The number seven dominates the creation account in Genesis and the formation of Israel's theological and civil structure in Exodus and Joshua of the Old Testament. Newton would have undoubtedly encountered the *Sepher Yetzirah* because of its premier importance in the works of Jewish mystics. It relates 5,040 as the multiplication of the first seven numbers.

$$1 \times 2 = 2$$
$$1 \times 2 \times 3 = 6$$
$$1 \times 2 \times 3 \times 4 = 24$$
$$1 \times 2 \times 3 \times 4 \times 5 = 120$$
$$1 \times 2 \times 3 \times 4 \times 5 \times 6 = 720$$
$$1 \times 2 \times 3 \times 4 \times 5 \times 6 \times 7 = 5,040.^{24}$$

Works of the mystery of numbers would have been readily accessible to Eratosthenes during his lifetime, as he served as the chief librarian in the most famous book repository of all antiquity, the great library of Alexandria, Egypt. It was there that the written works concerning the pure knowledge of Plato, Pythagoras, and many other great geometers and philosophers were stored.

Ptolemy II Philadelphus had appointed Eratosthenes as Alexandria's chief librarian in ca. 240 BC, during which time the library contained hundreds of thousands of papyrus and parchment scrolls of the greatest intellects from history.[25] These were tragically lost through successive wars with the Romans and disappeared entirely after Alexandria was sacked by the Moslems under Amr ibn al 'Ass, in AD 645.[26]

Eratosthenes was also credited with calculating the size and distance of the sun and the moon.[27] These feats are accomplished through simple arithmetic using the base number 2,520 and variations of 7 and 360. The moon's diameter is determined by subtracting the number of degrees in a circle, 360, from 2,520, equaling 2,160 miles. The *average* distance between the surface of the earth and the moon is found by multiplying 77.77 times pi seven times:

$$77.77 \times \pi \times \pi \times \pi \times \pi \times \pi \times \pi \times \pi = 234{,}888 \text{ statute miles}$$

Modern calculations put the earth-moon mean distance at 234,855 miles.[28] Since the moon orbits the Earth in an elliptical path, its distance varies from greatest distance from the Earth (apogee) to closest (perigee) by 23,600 miles. The moon at apogee emulates the number of *priscia sapentia* at 252,000 statute miles from the Earth (or 2,520 x 100).[29] The mean diameter of the sun is

$$2{,}520 \times 7 \times 7 \times 7 = 864{,}360 + 1{,}260 = 865{,}620 \text{ statute miles.}[30]$$

The moon's circumference, 6,785.8401 miles, subtracted from the Earth's diameter, 7,916.8134 miles, equals 1,130.9733 miles. This number, divided by pi, reveals 360.

In other words, the *physical* dimensions of both the Earth and moon are based on 2,520, pi, and 360:

$$2,520 - 360 = 2,160$$
$$\pi \times 2160 = 6,785.8401, \text{ statute miles (lunar circumference).}$$
$$\pi \times 360 = 1,130.9733.$$
$$1,130.9733 + 6,785.8401 \text{(lunar circumference)} = 7916.8134 \text{ statute miles (diameter of the Earth).}$$

The *temporal* dimensions of the Earth are also based on 2,520, pi, and 360:

$$\pi \times 360 = 1,130$$
$$1,130 + 2,520 = 3650 / 10 = 365, \text{ the solar year of the Earth.}$$

Eratosthenes may have understood the true dimensions of the Earth and other objects in the solar system through his possession of the *prisca sapientia*, but as Newton and other researchers of his age had observed, the simplicity of this knowledge was concealed. In the words of Descartes, "through the use of more ingenious calculations." A much simpler equation for determining the circumference of the earth has been demonstrated using 2,520 x pi x pi; however, the result is in modern statute miles.

It is truly remarkable that the ancient geometers suspected the dimensions of the Earth were based on this number, but more so that its value has been retained in the statute mile of modern times. If this were not so, none of the time/distance relationships in prophecy would appear in statute miles, as has been demonstrated in the distance between Babylon and Jerusalem. The statute mile is so called because of an English "Statue of Parliament" of Queen Elizabeth I in1592 that set the determined length of a mile at 5,280 feet.

The further significance of this unit of measure and its origin will be examined in later chapters.

NOTES

1. Strong's Hebrew Lexicon entry #121
2. In *James Strongs Exhaustive Concordance of the Bible.*World Bible Publishers, Inc., Iowa Dalls, IA. U.S.A. 1986.2. Babylonian Talmud. Berakoth, 55a. Translated by Michael L. Rodkinson. New York: New. Talmud Pub. Co. c1896–c1903.
3. Exodus 37: 1, 6 & 7. KJV
4. Hebrews 9:5 KJV
5. Author note: After the death of Moses and Aaron, only on Yom Kippur (the day of atonement) could the high priest approach the ark in the Holy of Holies.
6. "And Solomon made affinity with Pharaoh king of Egypt, and took Pharaoh's daughter, and brought her into the city of David, until he had made an end of building his own house, and the house of the LORD, and the wall of Jerusalem round about." 1 Kings 3:1 KJV
7. Immanuel Velikovsky *Ages in Chaos.* Chapter 4. Pg. 168. Sidgwick & Jackson, London.1968
8. Flinders Petrie, *Egypt and Israel,* Pg. 65 (*London UK:* Society for Promoting Christian Knowledge, 1911).
9. Ibid. Flinders Petrie, *Egypt and Israel.* Pg. 68.
10. Ibid. Immanuel Velikovsky, *Ages in Chaos.*
11. James Strong, *The Tabernacle of Israel,*1888. 1987 reprint, Grand Rapids Kregel, Inc. Grand Rapids MI., pg. 91.
12. Joshua 3:14–17 KJV
13. Joshua 6:3 KJV
14. Ibid. Strong's Exhaustive Concordance. Jericho from 'yereach' moon Hebrew Lexicon entry # 3394.
15. Helmut Moritz and Bernhard Hofmann, *Physical Geodesy.* (New York: Springer, Wien, 2005).

16. *Dictionary of Greek and Roman Biography and Mythology.* Vol 2. page 45.William Smith Editor. Taylor and Walton. London 1846

17. The "Stadia" was an ancient Greek measure of distance, based on the length of a Stadia course on which foot races were held in ancient Greece and equal to about 515.09 feet. From Greek "stadion" perhaps alteration (influenced by stadios, *firm*) of spadion, *racetrack,* from sp n, *to pull.*] *The American Heritage Dictionary of the English Language,* Fourth Edition. Houghton Mifflin Company. New York 2000

18. Ibid. *A Dictionary of Greek and Roman Biography and Mythology,* Vol. 2. Page 45.

19. Fred Hoyle, *Astronomy,* (London: Rathbone Books Limited, 1962).20. *The Dialogues of Plato.* 2 vols. Translated by Benjamin Jowett. New York, Random House, 1937.21. Ibid.

20. Plato, "The Timaeus" Translated by Benjamin Jowett, Charles Scribner Sons. New York 1907. vol 4, pg 292

21. Plato, "The Timaeus" Translated by Benjamin Jowett, Oxford, Clarendon press, UK. 1888, pg. 130.

22. *Jewish Encyclopedia*: Entry, YETZIRAH, SEFER Online version of the 1901–1906 www.jewishencyclopedia.com

23. Phineas Mordell *The Origin of Letters & Numerals According to the Sepher Yetzirah,* chapter 4. Published by Samuel Weiser, Inc. York Beach, ME 1975.

24. The decimal points of any number that divides unequally by seven are .1428571428571… (360 divided by 7.1428571 = 50.40) This number times 100 equals the number of Plato's Magnesia from the *Laws.*

25. *The Columbia Encyclopedia,* 6th ed.Pg. 666. (Columbia University Press, New York 2007).

26. Ibid. *The Columbia Encyclopedia.*

27. Ibid. *Dictionary of Greek and Roman Biography and Mythology.* Vol 2. page 46.William Smith Editor. Taylor and Walton.

London 1846. Plutarch and Macrobius both credit Eratosthenes with these calculations.

28. Figures courtesy NASA's National Space Science Data Center (NSSDC). nssdc.gsfc.nasa.gov

29. Ibid.

30. Ibid.

8

THE LOCATION OF THE ARK
OF THE COVENANT

Most researchers consider the Ark lost from view after the narrative of Solomon's temple in the Bible, and various theories have been proposed as to the Ark's fate through history. Many historians speculate that because Babylon destroyed the Temple of Solomon, it also removed the Ark to Babylon. There it is said the Ark was eventually destroyed along with the other artifacts from the temple, the gold melted down and set into coins for their treasury. It is difficult to imagine that the Babylonians would have destroyed it however, if they'd even captured it at all.

The Book of Daniel makes specific mention of the golden menorah from the temple of Jerusalem in the palace of Belshazzar. The Babylonian king had preserved it, a major artifact from the Jewish temple, in an attempt to demonstrate the superiority of Babylonia's gods to the God of the Hebrews. That the menorah was set on display in this manner underscores how unlikely the Babylon's would have been to destroy the Ark, the greatest symbol of the God of the Hebrews. It would have been considered an ultimate statement of the superiority of the Babylonians if it had been obtained. The Bible documents the menorah having remained intact until the last night of Babylonian rule. Its light illuminated the scene of the writing on the wall in the book of Daniel. After the fall of Babylon, the Medes and Persians were friendly to the Jews and allowed them to rebuild the temple. It is most likely that the menorah was returned along with the other furnishings and vessels that had been captured by Nebuchadnezzar. However, the Ark was mentioned as *not* existing in the second temple of Zerubbabel, the raised foundation stone was the only feature inside the Holy of Holies.[1]

Certain tracts of the Midot in the Jewish Talmud dealing with temple laws, practices, and rituals allude to the creation of more than one Ark; the second made as a decoy to protect the original. It claims that certain articles of the temple furnishings, including the true Ark, remain in a secret vault underneath the temple mount in Jerusalem.[2] However, it seems highly unlikely that the Ark would have been left to fate under the temple mount, open to any treasure hunter with the motivation to merely dig. It is difficult to explain how the location could remain secret, as Jerusalem remained open for excavation and plundering for hundreds of years after its fall to the Romans in AD 70. Motivated treasure seekers over the ensuing centuries have had ample time to excavate the area underneath the temple.

The recovery of temple treasure of Solomon was the highest goal of the Knights Templar that established their center on the temple mount during the crusades. The fact was documented in 1884, when the British conducted an ordinance survey of Jerusalem and discovered Templar artifacts, left in extensive tunneling beneath the temple mount.[3] As to the extent of the underground features, a later publication of the British survey explained:

> Jerusalem, as is well known, is honeycombed with excavated caves, natural caverns, cisterns cut in the rock, subterranean passages and aqueducts….In its underground chambers and catacombs it is richer than any known city.[4]

Various Judaic sects of Ethiopia believe that the Ark has been guarded and kept in the city of Axum in their country for thousands of years.[5] The legend claims that it was brought to Axum by the son of King Solomon and the Queen of Sheba, Prince Menelik I. It has been said that Menelik removed the Ark from the temple at the behest of his father in order that it be kept safe after the division of his kingdom (into Judah and Israel), because Solomon knew that the dissolution of his kingdom was inevitable after his death. 1 Kings 11:9–12 says that the Lord Himself told Solomon that the LORD was angry with Solomon, because his heart was turned from the LORD God of Israel, which had appeared unto him twice....Wherefore the LORD said unto Solomon, Forasmuch as this is done of thee, and thou hast not kept my covenant and my statutes, which I have commanded thee, I will surely rend the kingdom from thee, and will give it to thy servant. Notwithstanding in thy days I will not do it for David thy father's sake: [but] I will rend it out of the hand of thy son.[6]

Though intriguing, the legend of Menelik I is not consistent with the biblical record, as will be shown in this chapter. If the Ark was not moved to Ethiopia, it is speculated that after the division of the Kingdom of Solomon, Rehoboam, King of Judah, gave the Ark to the Egyptian Pharaoh Shisak (Sheshonk I, ca. 929 or 924 BC) to avoid the destruction of Jerusalem by his armies, ca. 940 BC.

So Shishak King of Egypt came up against Jerusalem, and took away the treasures of the house of the LORD, and the treasures of the king's house; he took all.[7]

Some historians believe that the Egyptians took the ark and hid it underground in the city of Tanis, Egypt, the seat of Shishak's dynasty. The location was lost over the course of history.[8] Because it was written that Shishak "took all" the articles of the temple, many researchers conclude that the Ark was among the spoils taken to Egypt. However, after Judah's conflict with Shishak, the temple was ransacked again seventy years later by Jehoash, King of Israel. At that time, the temple treasures were removed to Samaria. [9] In this instance, as with the encounter with Shishak, the Bible again uses the phrase, "All the temple treasures were removed." Despite these two accounts, the Ark appears again in the biblical narrative when King Josiah ordered the return of the Ark of the Covenant to the temple.[10] This occurred over two hundred years after the pillage of the temple by Jehoash, and three hundred years after the pillage of Shishak.

> And [Josiah] said unto the Levites that taught all Israel, which were holy unto the LORD, Put the holy ark in the house which Solomon the son of David king of Israel did build; [it shall] not [be] a burden upon [your] shoulders.[11]

This one biblical passage renders the legends of the Ark's present location in Axum, Ethiopia, or in Tanis, Egypt completely impossible, as both theories place the hiding of the Ark several hundred years before the reign of King Josiah. It was a central feature of the temple of Jerusalem and reinstitution of worship during the reign of Josiah.

It is noteworthy, also, that the Bible is extremely detailed concerning the only account of the Ark's capture by the foremost enemy of Israel, the Philistines. After it had been captured by the Philistines, their entire country was afflicted by God. The judgment was so great that the people begged their lords to find a respectful way to transport the Ark back to its rightful place, and it was returned. It is illogical that the same judgments would not have befallen any other country that removed the Ark from the Israelites. Although God allowed its capture by the Philistines due to the idolatry of Israel, the pagan Philistines were certainly not able to abide its presence. For that matter, neither Babylon—the epitome of world idolatry—or Egypt would survive the Ark's presence. Certainly, if one of these countries had captured it, the account would be as notable as the removal by the Philistines. Yet, no scriptural record of such an event exists.

Robert Jamieson's biblical commentary explains the Ark's location before its return to the temple in the reign of Josiah, King of Judah is that:

> Some think that it had been ignominiously put away from the sanctuary by order of some idolatrous king, probably Manasseh, who set a carved image in the house of God (2 Chronicles 33:7), or Amon; while others are of opinion that it had been temporarily removed by Josiah himself into some adjoining chamber, during the repairs on the temple. In replacing it, the Levites had evidently carried it upon their shoulders, deeming that still to be the duty, which the law imposed on them. But Josiah reminded them of the change of circumstances. As the service of God was now performed in a fixed and permanent temple, they were not required to be bearers of the ark any longer; and, being released from the service, they should address themselves with the greater alacrity to the discharge of other functions.[12]

An amazing story follows the reinstitution of the Ark to the temple of God in the account of Josiah's death:

> After all this, when Josiah had prepared the temple, Necho king of Egypt came up to fight against Carchemish by Euphrates: and Josiah went out against him. But he sent ambassadors to him, saying, what have I to do with thee, thou king of Judah? [I come] not against thee this day, but against the house wherewith I have war: for God commanded me to make haste: forbear thee from [meddling with] God, who [is] with me, that he destroy thee not. Nevertheless Josiah would not turn his face

from him, but disguised himself, that he might fight with him, and hearkened not unto the words of Necho from the mouth of God, and came to fight in the valley of Megiddo.[13]

This supports Velikovsky's claim that the Egyptian pharaohs revered the God of Abraham in the time of the Kings of Israel and Judah. Although King Josiah and the people of Judah had a strong bias for alliance with Egypt during the reign of Manasseh, the country had become a vassal of Assyria. Josiah thought himself bound to support the interests of Assyria. Therefore, when "Necho King of Egypt" came up to fight Carchemish, Josiah went out against him. Bible commentators are not agreed whether Necho had been given a divine commission by the God of Israel, or whether he merely used the name of God as an authority that Josiah would not refuse to obey.[14] However, it appears likely that God *was* a benefactor to the pharaoh as the bible records Josiah's death by Necho's archers.[15]

Jeremiah the prophet lamented the death of Josiah when his body was returned after the battle. In 2 Chronicles 35:25, Jeremiah had been a major force in Josiah's restitution of the Ark to the Temple of Solomon. He was also the main player in the most well documented *and biblical* account of the fate of the Ark and theory of its present location.

The Mountain of the Ark

The book of 2 Maccabees 2:4 explains that before the destruction of Solomon's temple by the Babylonians in 587 BC, the Ark was hidden by the prophet Jeremiah in a cave at the base of Mount Nebo in the Pisgah range of Jordan. 2 Maccabees, as well as other Apocryphal works, are retained in modern Catholic bibles as well as the Septuagint and Vulgate.[17] It is found in the records

> …that Jeremy the prophet, being warned of God, commanded the tabernacle and the ark to go with him, as he went forth

into the mountain, where Moses climbed up, and saw the heritage of God. And when Jeremy came thither, he found an hollow cave, wherein he laid the tabernacle, and the ark, and the altar of incense, and so stopped the door.

And some of those that followed him came to mark the way, but they could not find it. Which when Jeremy perceived, he blamed them, saying, As for that place, it shall be unknown until the time that God gather his people again together, and receive them unto mercy. Then shall the Lord show them these things, and the glory of the Lord shall appear, and the cloud also, as it was showed under Moses, and as when Solomon desired that the place might be honourably sanctified.[18]

This account of the Ark from 2 Maccabees is also mentioned in the Jewish Talmud, in Huriot 12A and Tractate Yoma 72a. These texts explain that the Ark's location would not be recovered until the Jews were brought back to Israel following the Diaspora, an event that miraculously *did* occur in 1948. The pseudepigraphic book 2 Baruch, written near the 1st century, repeats the prophetic age in which the Ark would be recovered:

> Oh earth…guard them [the temple vessels and the Ark] until the last times, So that, when thou art ordered, thou mayst restore them, So that strangers may not get possession of them. For the time comes when Jerusalem also will be delivered for a time, until it is said, that it is again restored for ever.[19]

According to prophecy, the Jews of the end time would return to Israel from all the nations of the Earth. Isaiah 11:11–12 explains that Israel would be populated by exiles that formerly lived in every part of the world. This has been the situation since 1948, and is not related to the first return of Jews to Israel after the Babylonian exile:

And it shall come to pass in that day, that the LORD shall set his hand again the second time to recover the remnant of his people....And he shall set up an ensign for the nations, and shall assemble the outcasts of Israel, and gather together the dispersed of Judah from the four corners of the earth.

Amos 9:14–15 declares that after the second return of the exiles, they would never again go into dispersion: "And I will plant them upon their land, and they shall no more be pulled up out of their land which I have given them, saith the LORD thy God."

The legendary accounts of Jeremiah and the Ark provide a hidden clue to its location at Mount Nebo. This is a symbolic link that exists between the names of the Babylonian king that threatened to destroy the Ark, and the mountain where it was hidden by Jeremiah. Both Nebuchadnezzar and Nebo stem from the Semitic root *nebu*, meaning the god Mercury. This was also intimated in the prophecies of Ezekiel condemning Jerusalem (chapter 2). The name Nebuchadnezzar means "the prince of the god Merucury."[20] The Hebrew word *nebo* is from the root *neba* ("to prophesy" and also "a prophet").[21] In the same role as the prophets of the God of Israel, Nebo was worshiped as the celestial scribe of the Assyrians, the "interpreter of the gods, and declarer of their will."[22]

According to the Bible, the greatest prophet of all time was Moses, which states, "And there arose not a prophet [*neba*] since in Israel like unto Moses, whom the LORD knew face to face."[23] Ironically, Mount Nebo was the site of the death of Moses:

And Moses went up from the plains of Moab unto the mountain of Nebo, to the top of Pisgah, that [is] over against Jericho. And the LORD shewed him all the land of Gilead, unto Dan....And the LORD said unto him, This [is] the land which I sware unto Abraham, unto Isaac, and unto Jacob, saying, I will give it unto thy seed: I have caused thee to see [it] with thine eyes, but thou shalt not go over thither. So Moses the servant of the LORD died there in the land of Moab, according to the word of the LORD.[24]

The Hebrew words *nobe*, meaning "high place," and *nabab*, meaning "to hollow out," "gate," or "pupil of the eye," also correlate with the location for the resting place of the ark in a "hollow cave" on Mount Nebo, described in 2 Maccabees.[25]

The Talmud explains that the tower of Babel was dedicated to Nebo, son of Marduk (Greek Jupiter) and that its destruction coincided with the confusion of languages and forgetfulness of knowledge.[26] The emblem of Mercury, a snake entwined on a pole, was first recorded in Exodus, which was the brazen serpent on a pole lifted by Moses to cure the rebellious Israelites of a plague of snakes (Numbers 21:9). [27]

The serpent on the pole was used as a Messianic symbol, and was illustrated by Christ himself, as told in John 3:14: "And as Moses lifted up the serpent in the wilderness, even so must the Son of man be lifted up." However, this object was preserved and later worshiped as Mercury—Nebo by the Israelites—until being destroyed by King Hezekiah ca. 725 BC, when "he broke into pieces the bronze serpent that Moses had made, for until those days the people of Israel had burned incense to it; it was called Nehushtan."[28]

It is fitting with the cryptic name of Mount Nebo that a modern sculpture in metal of a serpent on a pole stands at its summit near the Church of Moses.[29] If the Ark was hidden in Mount Nebo, it was to remain forgotten until the end of days. This prophecy has remarkable similarities to the theme of Mercury as god of knowledge and forgetfulness. Its recovery sometime before the return of Christ fits the prophetic scheme of Newton wherein a rebuilt temple, the Ark, and a world rule by "Babylon the Great" predominate.

Although Babylon's power over Israel resulted in the loss of the Ark and the destruction of the temple, the resurgence of Babylon as a spiritual force that governs the world at the end of days will accompany the rebuilding of the temple and the discovery of the Ark. In conformity with these prophecies, the Earth itself is connected to Babylon through *prisca sapientia* geometry. For example:

$$2,520 \times \pi = 7,916.\,813 \text{ (Earth's mean diameter)}$$

$$7,916.813 \times 360° \text{ in a circle} = 2,850,052.$$

If 2,850,052 is divided by 5,280 (feet in a statute mile), the result is 539, the year of the writing on the wall and the fall of Babylon.

Moses was associated with two of the three Arks mentioned in the Bible, i.e., the Ark of the Bulrushes, in which he floated on the Nile, and the Ark of the Covenant. Mount Nebo was also the site of many symbolic events that connect the Church age with the second coming of Christ. Jesus Christ died on Mount Golgotha, and Moses died on Mount Nebo, exactly to the east of Jerusalem. Both the locations were known, although their burial places were unknown; the location of Jesus' tomb is more the place of his resurrection than the site for his resting place. Jude 1:9 explains that the Archangel Michael took Moses' body. This assumption is reinforced in the Gospel with Moses' appearance on the transfiguration mount with Elijah. In connection with this idea, some eschatologists theorize that the witnesses of Revelation 11 shall be Moses and Elijah. Remarkably, the last act of the two witnesses mentioned in the book is the physical resurrection from the dead and ascension into heaven. The judgments of the witnesses described in Revelation match the plagues of Egypt heralded by Moses and those of Elijah, holding rain and causing fire to fall from heaven. Both prophets received their commission while on Mt Sinai[30] (Moses, Exodus 3:1; Elijah, 1 Kings 19:7). Additionally, the description of the death of Moses by Flavius Josephus parallels many aspects of the crucifixion:

Now as he [Moses] went thence to the place where he was to vanish out of their sight, they all followed after him weeping; but Moses beckoned with his hand to those that were remote from him, and bade them stay behind in quiet, while he exhorted those that were near to him that they would not render his departure so lamentable. As he was still discoursing with them, a cloud stood over him on the sudden, and he disappeared in a certain valley, although he wrote in the holy books that he died, which was done out of fear, lest they should venture to say that, because of his extraordinary virtue, he went to God.[31]

This is similar in the manner of Jesus' ascent to the mount of his crucifixion.

And there followed him [Jesus] a great company of people, and of women, which also bewailed and lamented him. But Jesus turning unto them said, Daughters of Jerusalem, weep not for me, but weep for yourselves, and for your children.[32]

The most important point of these associations is that the Ark itself represented Jesus Christ. Many theological works from history have expanded this theme. In the story of the Exodus only Moses, the greatest prophet, and his brother Aaron, the first high priest of Israel,[33] were allowed access to the presence of God at the mercy seat between the cherubim on the Ark.[34] In contrast, mankind has been given access to the presence of God through Jesus Christ, the ultimate high priest and the author of prophecy.

As Moses viewed the land of promise from Mount Nebo, but was prevented from entering, the Ark's location upon Mount Nebo is seen, but not yet been obtained. However, according to prophecy, Moses will walk in Jerusalem in the end times, having finally gained access to the land viewed from atop Mount Nebo. As he waits for his designated time to enter the Promised Land, the Ark waits until the hour chosen by God.

The Bible records that the "Glory of the Lord" moved into the Holy of Holies at the first installation of the Ark in Solomon's temple.[35] Ezekiel, the prophet that warned of the destruction of Solomon's temple, while exiled in Nippur, Babylonia, had witnessed the glory of the Lord move away from the temple to the east, directly in line with Mount Nebo. This was in reference to God abandoning the temple to its enemies, and is stated in Ezekiel 11:23: "And the glory of the LORD went up from the midst of the city, and stood upon the mountain which [is] on the east side of the city."[36] Later, Ezekiel was shown the vision of the restored temple of the future in which the glory of the Lord *returned* from the east, stated in Ezekiel 43:4: "And the glory of the LORD came into the temple by the way of the gate whose prospect [is] toward the east."[37]

The "Glory of the Lord" was a distinct feature of the Ark between the cherubim. Translated, "glory" is *shekinah* in Hebrew, meaning "presence." This presence of God was in form of a pillar of fire by night, and a pillar of smoke by day during the travel of the Israelites in the desert. Whenever the glory of the Lord moved from the tabernacle in the wilderness, the people followed. As the pillar of fire or smoke stood above the Ark, the Israelites stopped and set up camp. The glory of the Lord stood in a vertical column extending from heaven to the surface of the Ark. The book of Exodus records that the Holy of Holies in the tabernacle had no lamps, largely because none was needed due to the intense glow of the Ark itself. In fact, when Moses went into the Holy of Holies to speak to God at the mercy seat, his face glowed so intensely that the Israelites were afraid to come near him unless he wore a veil.[38] These descriptions associate the Ark with the glory of the Lord. When the Philistines captured the Ark and removed it from Israel, the daughter-in-law of Eli, the high priest, referred to the Ark as the glory of the Lord, itself saying, "The glory is departed from Israel: for the ark of God is taken."[39]

The Apocalypse of 2 Baruch provides the direction in which the Ark may lie in relation to the temple. While the Babylonians began their siege of Jerusalem in 587 BC, Jeremiah the prophet threw the keys of the temple and its sanctuary towards the sun:

> But taking the keys of the temple, Jeremiah went outside the city and threw them away in the presence of the sun, saying: I say to you, Sun, take the keys of the temple of God and guard them until the day in which the Lord asks you for them. For we have not been found worthy to keep them, for we have become unfaithful guardians.[40]

This legend is found with variations in the Jewish Talmud, and pertains to the destruction of the first and second temples.[41] As the sun rises in the east, throwing the keys of the temple to the sun implies this direction. It is remarkable that the story of the keys and the hiding of the Ark are both connected to Jeremiah. This story is also significant metaphorically. The "keys" of the temple represent both the stewardship of the priests of God, and the sacred knowledge embodied by the temple and its rituals. In the Talmud versions, the Levites or the high priest climbed to the temple roof and threw the keys into heaven, from whence a divine hand caught them and disappeared into a cloud.[42]

Jewish mystics believe that this act represented the loss of the correct pronunciation of the name of God, or the knowledge of Solomon. When viewed from this perspective, the "lost key" story represents the *priscia theologia* of the temple of God as a divine receptacle of pure knowledge. It is a line of reasoning that Newton certainly had perused.

The Ark, representing the whole of the law, was designed using the Sacred Cubit. Because the 25.20-inch Sacred Cubit is a ratio of the Earth, being a fractal of 2,520 (and 2,520 x pi is Earth's diameter), the Ark reflects this *geo-metry* (literally, earth-measure). The solution for determining its present location might be found in the very word used for the divinely chosen resting place of the Ark, the *naus* or *navis*, the origin of the word "navigation," which is the skill of measuring the Earth. As an expert in the Law, Jeremiah may have reasoned that if the Ark could not dwell in the temple that was designed as its permanent resting place, it might at least remain in alignment with it, which suggests a specific navigational process for locating the Ark.

A measuring line extended *directly towards the east* from the foundation stone of the temple mount must remain on the latitude of the foundation stone where the Ark rested in the Holy of Holies, which is north 31 degrees, 46 minutes, and 43 seconds. Its length must also be related to the Sacred Cubit, which is exactly 25.20 nautical miles. The result at the end of the measuring line touches the north slope of Mount Nebo less than a mile from its summit.

Fig. 24. Image by author

That 2,520 is a constant is incredible. The terminus of this measuring line touches a point on the north slope of Mount Nebo 1,260 feet above sea level, which is half of 2,520, and the temple mount in

Jerusalem rests on a hill 2,520 feet above sea level.[43] In fitting with the altitude of the location of the Ark on Mount Nebo, the letters of the name of Solomon in Greek, Σολομον, equal 1,260; it is revealed that *it was* he who built the first temple and established the Ark in the Holy of Holies.

These values are consistent with Newton's scheme of the temple's *prisca theologia*, based on 25.20 of the Sacred Cubit and 2,520 of time recorded in the books of Daniel and Revelation. This numeric signature of prophecy and law is redundantly apparent in the proposed location of the Ark, situated in an area corresponding to the *only* description found in the biblical texts of its hiding place. Current satellite maps of the area reveal no modern settlements or excavations. In addition, the geology of the area is similar to the Qumran region of the Dead Sea, in which many caves exist. It would have been an extremely favorable location to deposit the Ark and furnishings of the Temple of Solomon.

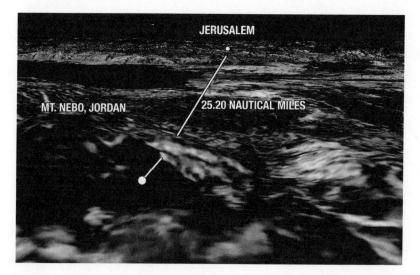

Fig. 25. Courtesy of NASA World Wind

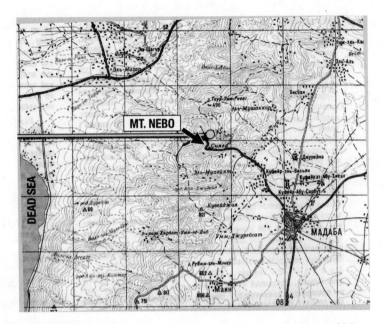

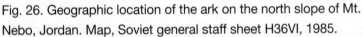

Fig. 26. Geographic location of the ark on the north slope of Mt. Nebo, Jordan. Map, Soviet general staff sheet H36VI, 1985.

There are questions that arise concerning the exposure of the location of the Ark, if this calculation is accurate. Is it wise to uncover it? Will it fall into the wrong hands? Will the Ark be present in the rebuilt temple of the end times?

It is reasonable that God would not provide information to find the Ark unless it was part of His divine plan. Although the acacia wood comprising it may have disintegrated, the gold overlaid around it, as well the solid gold of the mercy seat and cherubim, would have certainly withstood the effects of time. Its recovery would follow the precise design of God from the beginning. If the Ark's location has been revealed, then it is God's intention that it be discovered in this age. One specific detail must be worked out however. The site of Ark of the Covenant on Mount Nebo is dependent on the exact location of the foundation stone on the temple mount. There are several theories concerning this question, the most promising of these is significantly, linked to the Eastern Gate of the temple.

NOTES

1. Talmud Yoma v. 2. Translated by Michael L. Rodkinson. New York: New Talmud Pub. Co.1903.

2. *Mishnah*, in Tractate Shkalim, it is written: "A priest in the Second Temple saw a section the floor which was different from the other floors and he understood that in this place there was an entrance to an underground tunnel and he came and shared it with his friend. Before he could finish sharing what he had seen with his friends, he died. They then knew very clearly that that was the place where the Ark of the Covenant was hidden." According to Maimonides, Solomon knew that the Temple would be destroyed in the future and prepared a repository for the Ark underneath the Temple mount. Later King Josiah hid the Ark in Solomon's secret vault. Maimonides, The Book of Temple Service, 17. also Hilchot Beit HaBecheirah 4:1 and Tractate Yoma, 53b. Translated by Michael L. Rodkinson. New York: New Talmud Pub. Co.1903.

3. Captain Charles W. Wilson, *Ordinance Survey of Jerusalem.* Published by Palestine Exploration Fund. London 1884.

4. Major Condor, *Our work in Palestine;, Palestine Exploration Fund,* London 1866.

5. Kebra Nagast: The Glory of Kings. Pg. 4

6. Miguel F. Brooks, Ed. Lawrenceville, N.J.: Red Sea Press. 1966. 1 Kings 11: 9–12 KJV

7. II Chron.12:9 KJV

8. *Columbia Encyclopedia,* 3rd ed. Pg. 453. New York: Columbia University, 1963).

9. Robert Jamieson, A.R.Fausset, and David Brown. *Commentary Critical and Explanatory on the Whole Bible.*1871. Hendrickson Publishers; New Ed edition (March 1, 1997)

10. 2 Chronicles 26: 24. KJV

11. 2 Chronicles 35:3 KJV
12. Ibid. *Commentary Critical and Explanatory on the Whole Bible*
13. 2 Chronicles 35: 20 KJV
14. Ibid. *Commentary Critical and Explanatory on the Whole Bible*
15. 2 Chronicles 35: 22–24. KJV
16. 2 Chronicles 35: 25. KJV
17. Ibid. Columbia encyclopedia. Pg. 213.The Apocryphal books were considered historically valuable enough to be included in the King James Bible from its formation in 1611 until 1885. Later these 14 books were officially removed from the English printings of the King James bible by the Archbishop of Canterbury in 1885.
18. II Macabees 2 :4 Bishop Challoner's 18th century revision of the Douay Rheims version Catholic Public Domain Version. 2005 Ronald L. Conte Jr., translator and editor. www.sacredbible.org
19. R. H. Charles *The Apocrypha and Pseudepigrapha of the Old Testament*, Vol. 2, 2 Baruch 6 Oxford Press. Oxford, UK 1913
20. James *Strong's Exhaustive Concordance of the bible, Hebrew Dictionary, Hebrew Lexicon # 5015* World Bible Publishers, Inc., Iowa Falls, IA. U.S.A. 1986.
21. Ibid. Strong's Hebrew Dictionary entry # 5013.
22. Ibid. Strong's Hebrew Dictionary entry # 5011.
23. Deuteronomy 34: 10 KJV
24. Deuteronomy 34: 5 KJV
25. Ibid. Strong's Hebrew Dictionary entry # 5014
26. Ibid. Talmud (Sanhedrin XI. 109a) (Cf. Obermeyer, pp. 314, 327, 346). Translated by Michael L. Rodkinson. New York: New Talmud Pub. Co. c1896–c1903.
27. Numbers 21:9 KJV
28. 2 Kings 18:24 KJV
29. The sculpture of the serpent on the pole was created by Italian artist, Giovanni Fantoni. Wikipedia Mount Nebo. www.wikipedia.org

30. Moses, in Exodus 3:1, Elijah, in I Kings 19: 7.

31. Flavius Josephus. *Antiquities of the Jews* - Book IV. chapter 8, Pg. 48 William Whiston translator. Kregel. Grand Rapids, Michigan;. 1999

32. Luke 23:27–28 KJV

33. Exodus 28:1 KJV

34. Exodus. 25:16, 21–22; Numbers. 17:4 KJV

35. 1 Kings 8:10 KJV

36. Ezekiel 11:23 KJV

37. Ezekiel 43: 4 KJV

38. Exodus. 34:35 KJV

39. 1 Samuel 4:22 KJV

40. R. H. Charles, *The Apocrypha and Pseudepigrapha of the Old Testament*, Vol. 2,Talmud 2 Baruch 6 Oxford Press. Oxford, UK 1913.

41. Ibid. R. H. Charles, *The Apocrypha and Pseudepigrapha of the Old Testament* Talmud. Ta'anit 29a and in Pesikta Rabbati 26:6.

42. Ibid. Talmud. Jalkut Shekalim 50a and B. on Isa. xxi.

43. Ibid. Columbia encyclopedia.Pg. 1080.

9

THE DOME OF THE SPIRITS

"Son of man, describe the temple to the house of Israel,
that they may be ashamed of their iniquities;
and let them measure the pattern."
—EZEKIEL 43:10

For centuries, Christian theologians and Jewish scholars have de-
bated the site of the foundation stone on the temple. This was,
and still is, a matter of great importance to the Jewish sages because the foundation stone lay directly beneath the Ark of the Covenant. Without knowing the precise location, a temple cannot be built
according to the Law of Moses. As it is said in Ezra 5:15, "Let the
House of Yahweh be rebuilt on its original site."

> The most established place (of the Temple) is that of the altar,
> and it must never be changed for all eternity.... There is a tra-
> dition in the hands of all that the place where (Kings) David
> and Solomon built the altar is the very place where Abraham

erected the altar upon which he bound Isaac....It was likewise
(the altar) built by Noah when he emerged from the ark; it
was the altar upon which Cain and Abel offered their sacrifice
when he was created, and from there (its dust) was he (Adam)
created.[1]

The most popular belief is that the stone exists in the center of
the Islamic shrine the Dome of the Rock or "Qubbat Al-Sakhra"
constructed in AD 687 by Caliph Abd al-Malik. Moslems believe
that this shrine was built over the place where Mohamed made his
"Night Journey" into the heavens and back to Mecca. This is according to the Koran chapter 17, verse 1, although the passage does not
describe the Temple mount in Jerusalem as the location for this event
specifically.

In the 1st century BC, Herod the Great expanded the temple
mount enclosure during his renovations of the temple. Further expan-
sion and reconstruction of the temple mount walls were undertaken
by the builder of the Dome of the Rock, Abd al-Malik, and later by
the Sultan Suleiman the Magnificent (1537–1541) after the Ottoman conquest of Israel.[2] However, the eastern wall and its single gate
were left in place due to its location on the edge of the Kidron Valley.
In order to extend the temple mount to the east, the valley would
have been filled and leveled. This was never undertaken because of
the great architectural problems it presented and, more importantly,
because the Kidron Valley was necessary for the Levitical rituals of the
temple.

First-century historian Flavius Josephus researched and wrote on
history of the Jewish Wars, and explained that the wall east of the temple was the only one that Herod did not rebuild.[3] In 1983, the Hebrew
University physicist Dr. Asher S. Kaufman published a theory that
the First Temple and Herod's Second Temple were aligned along an
east-to-west axis sighted through the Eastern Gate.[4] Kaufman's theory

followed the opinion of the great rabbi, Maimonides, who explained
that a line running from the Eastern Gate in the wall of the old city
of Jerusalem to the west would cross the center of the temple and the
Holy of Holies above the foundation stone.[5]

Fig. 27. Reprinted from Charles Chipiez, *La Temple de Jérusalem et
la Maison du Bois-Liban restitués d'après Ezechiel et le Livre des
Rois,* With plates. (New York: Chapman & Hall, 1890), 44. Addition
of orientation line by author.

In addition, Kaufman's theory was based on archaeological evidence collected from the temple platform area and the Talmud's book
of measurement called the Mishnah Tractate or Middot. According
to these sources, the true foundation stone lies under a cupola named
the Dome of the Jinn, Spirits, or Dome of the Tablets, located on
the northwest edge of the temple mount. Both the former and latter
names allude to the Ark of the Covenant as the oracle of God containing the stone tablets of the Ten Commandments. The Ark would have
rested in Holy of Holies situated furthest to the west in the temple.
Further verifying this theory, the Dome of the Tablets is the only place
where exposed bedrock exists on the temple mount as the rest of the
platform is paved. Not only does this bedrock have the exact dimensions of the foundation stone as recorded in the Talmud, but also

several drilled holes spaced according to the Sacred Cubit used only in the construction of the temple.[6]

LOCATION OF THE HOLY OF HOLIES

Fig. 28. Photo by author

In 1969, James Flemming, a graduate student of biblical archaeology at the American Institute of Holy Land Studies, was examining the Eastern Gate of the temple mount when he fell into a mass grave at its base. The ground had been saturated with rain during the night, and a hole left from a mortar round from the 6-day war two years before had reopened. Beneath the visible level, he discovered an arch belonging to the original ancient gate of the First and Second temples. He took pictures of the structure before the hole was later filled in and a fence was erected around the grave.

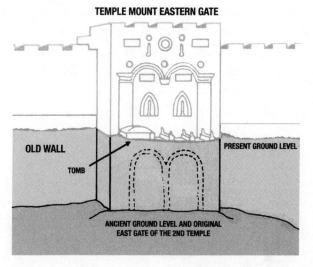

Fig. 29. Image by author

The discovery of the original location of the Eastern Gate provides archaeological proof of the true location of the foundation stone according to the historical accounts.[7]

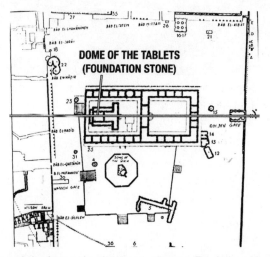

Fig. 30. The original temple site according to Dr. Asher Kaufman and Maimonides. Reprinted from British Ordinance survey map (Warren map), 1886.

With the knowledge of the exact location of the ancient foundation stone of the temple, calculations of distance between it and various points on the globe can be resolved to an extremely fine degree. This also suggests that on Mount Nebo, 25.20 nautical miles away, the Ark of the Covenant rests precisely on the same east-west line as the Dome of the Tablets and the Eastern Gate.

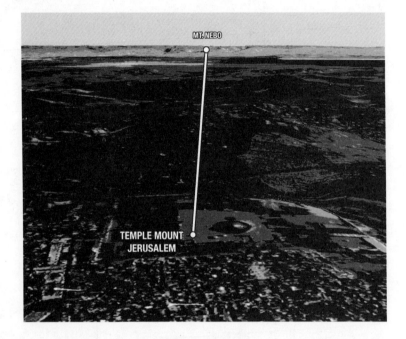

Fig. 31. Down range view of the Ark's location, through the eastern gate on the temple mount, Jerusalem. Courtesy of NASA World Wind.

NOTES

1. Maimonides, *Laws of the Chosen House*, 2:1,2. Mishna Torah. Published by Maznaim New York: 1986.
2. Encyclopaedia Judaica, Isidore Singer and Cyrus Alder, et al eds. New York: Funk and Wagnalls, 1906 "Jerusalem, History, Under Ottoman Rule (1517–1917) Suleiman The Magnificent And His Work".
3. Flavius Josephus, *The Jewish War V*, 184–189 [v. 1]. (Author), Betty Radice (Author), E. Mary Smallwood (Editor), G. A. Williamson (Introduction, Translator) Penguin Classics (February 7, 1984)
4. Dr. Asher S. Kaufman "Where the Ancient Temple of Jerusalem Stood; Extant 'Foundation Stone' for the Ark of the Covenant Is Identified." *Biblical Archaeology Review*, 9, no. 2, (1983): 40–58.
5. Ibid. Encyclopaedia Judaica, "Temple Mount"; Mishnah, Middot 2:1.
6. Ibid. Kaufman "Where the Ancient Temple of Jerusalem Stood, Extant 'Foundation Stone' for the Ark of the Covenant Is Identified.":p. 70–73.
7. Ibid. Kaufman "Where the Ancient Temple of Jerusalem Stood, Extant "Foundation Stone" for the Ark of the Covenant Is Identified." 179–183 & 70–73.

10

EXPERIMENTUM CRUCIS

When Old Testament texts were translated into English, the complex analogy, metaphor, and symbolism of the Hebrew language was sometimes lost. The ancient Hebrew sages understood that the divine hand had left certain knowledge obscured. Revealing prophecy, especially, was reserved for future men and kingdoms, as God himself set the times and seasons. Newton believed that his understanding of the natural world had been granted in this context, and that his scientific accomplishments were manifest by the providence of God. The Jewish mystical works from antiquity inspired him to seek scientific truth that upheld and verified scripture, impelling him to focus his analytical and powerful intellect equally between the scientific and the spiritual realms.

Newton's theory of the properties of light, *Optics* (1704), contains many symbolic aspects of the foremost Jewish mystical work on the same subject, the Book of Light or the Zohar. It explains that creation emanated from the stone set in the temple mount of Jerusalem, and that the point at which it dwells is the center of the universe. It also

focuses on universality of the temple of Jerusalem and more importantly, its link between dimensions.

Newton began researching the Zohar and other books of Judaic
mystical thought in the 1670s, twenty years before he developed his
Corpuscular Theory of Light, which explained that light was transmitted by particles, through experiments he performed at Cambridge.
As a fundamental text of Jewish mysticism, Newton read the Zohar
from cover to cover. In the Jewish Book of Light, the rainbow is linked
with the foundation stone and Noah's covenant with God. The Hebrew word for the foundation stone is the "Eben Shetiyah" (stone of
drawing forth)[1] and is considered the hidden source of the water of life
from which the world drinks.

> When the Holy One, blessed be He, was about to create the
> world, He detached one precious stone from underneath His
> throne of glory and plunged it into the abyss; one end of
> it remained fastened therein, while the other end stood out
> above. Out of the latter the world started, spreading itself to
> the right and left and into all directions.[2]...This alludes to the
> foundation stone, which is the central point of the universe
> and on which stands the Holy of Holies.[3]

In the Talmud, the ancient Jewish sages explained that this stone
was called shetiyah, which in Hebrew also means "drinking," because
it is hidden the source of all the springs and fountains from which the
world drinks its water.[4] This was based on the belief that the world was
created from the stone located in the Holy of Holies of the Temple
in Jerusalem, thus forming the center of the world. It goes on to say
that the "eben shetiyyah," on which the Ineffable Name of God is
inscribed, serves as a capstone that seals the waters of the abyss and
prevents them from welling up and overwhelming the world.[5] These
concepts are based on several texts from the Old Testament. Because

the Word of God produced the universe, the "foundation" of His creation was both a symbol of the Word and the stone underlying the temple. Scripture uses the phrases, "the Word of God" and "the foundation stone" to signify Jesus Christ (Isaiah 28:16, John 1:1–3,14).[6] The Bible also identifies the Word of God as the source for all "living waters."[7]

The progression of creation in Genesis describes, first, darkness over water; second, the creation of light; and third, the separation of the waters of the world from the waters of heaven. The Zohar explains that the water of heaven and the throne of God are of the same essence:

> The three primary colours and the one compounded of them, (the rainbow) which we mentioned before, are all one symbol, and they all show themselves in the cloud. "And above the firmament that was over their heads was the likeness of a throne, as the appearance of a sapphire stone." This alludes to the "foundation stone," which is the central point of the universe and on which stands the Holy of Holies.[8]

Exodus 24:10 also describes the same firmament as blue and transparent, as "they saw the God of Israel: and [there was] under his feet as it were a paved work of a sapphire, and as it were the body of heaven in its clearness." [9]

In both the Zohar and biblical texts, the word used for sapphire is *cephar*, meaning "to score with a mark," "number," "count," "reckon," "declare," "write," or "to count exactly or accurately."[10] A "cephar" is also used throughout the Bible to represent a book or a scroll, as were the books of Law given to Moses. The pavement in Exodus 24:10 is "libna" in Hebrew, meaning "whiteness or transparency."[11] This idea of transparency is reinforced further by the description of the sapphire, "as it were the body of heaven in its *clearness*."[12]

Metaphorically, in the same way the sapphire pavement—or firmament—of heaven is the source for rain and presents light through it in colors of the rainbow, the foundation stone, in the view of the ancient sages, should divide light. As the sun's light from heaven is transmitted through the sky, heaven is transmitted to the temple on Earth through the foundation stone. In the Zohar, this stone is akin to a dimensional doorway. Newton also understood this, since the ancient Hebrew symbol for door was also the fourth letter in their alphabet, *dalet*, which was in the shape of a triangle.

Fig. 32. Image by author

This is the shape of the prism; metaphorically, the sapphire stone is associated with the fourth day of creation when the dry land of Earth was formed. Newton called his use of a prism in separating light an, "experimentum crucis" (crucial experiment) proving that the prism was not "coloring" the light, but separating it. Newton described his process for dividing the constituent colors from the light of the sun in a letter to the publisher of Royal Society of London for the Improvement of Natural Knowledge, February 6, 1671:

> SIR,
>   To perform my late promise to you, I shall without further ceremony acquaint you, that in the beginning of the Year 1666 (at which time I applied my self to the grinding of Optick glasses of other figures than Spherical,) I procured me a Triangular glass-Prisme, to try therewith the celebrated Phænomena of Colours. And in order thereto having dark-

ened my chamber, and made a small hole in my window-
shuts, to let in a convenient quantity of the Sun's light, I
placed my Prisme at his entrance, that it might be thereby
refracted to the opposite wall.[13]

For Newton, the use of a triangular prism in his "crucial experiment" was a realization of supernal with the ordinary, the spiritual
dimension manifesting in the terrestrial.

Knowing the literal Hebrew meaning of the foundation stone as
"a number or a mathematical formula" and "a book," i.e. scripture itself, Newton was compelled to understand its properties. For Newton,
the stamp of God's authorship was evident in both the material creation and the words written in the Bible. Both reflected the same divine intelligence. It should come as no surprise that the sacred number
of the *prisca sapienta,* 2,520, appears in the physics of light through
water. This phenomenon is best described in the biblical account of
the rainbow, a symbol of God's covenant with Noah:

> I do set my bow in the cloud. And it shall be for a token of
> a covenant between me and the earth: And it shall come to
> pass, when I bring a cloud over the earth, that the bow shall be
> seen in the cloud: And I will remember my covenant, which is
> between me and you and every living creature of all flesh; and
> the waters shall no more become a flood to destroy all flesh.[14]

The Hebrew word *qesheth,* meaning to bend or a bow, is used
for the covenant of the rainbow in this passage. As a covenant, the
rainbow is analogous in meaning to the word *arcas,* a bow also used
for the Ark of the Covenant of Moses in Latin translations of Genesis.
Although Aristotle was the earliest to devote serious study to the rainbow, his mistaken explanation misled thinkers for centuries. Newton
was the first to correctly describe the phenomena in *Optics.*

FIGURES FROM ISAAC NEWTON'S "OPTICS."
BOOK I, PART II, TAB IV

THE CRITICAL ANGLE OF REFRACTION OF LIGHT
IN WATER DROPLETS OF A RAINBOW

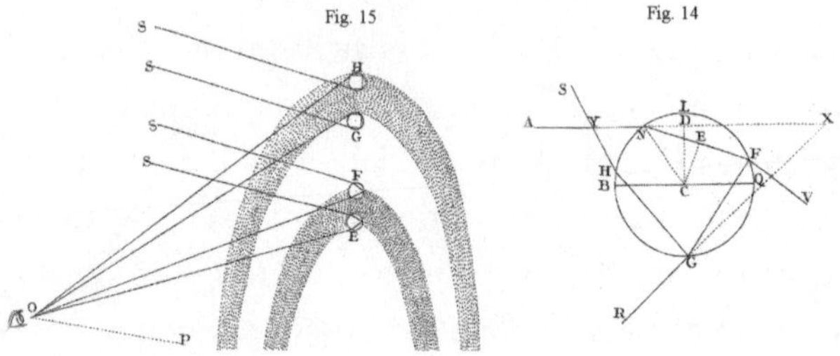

Fig. 33. Author's rendition of figures from Isaac Newton's *Optics,*
book I. Dover Publications Mineola, NY 1952 page 33.

A rainbow is caused by the refraction and reflection of the rays of
the sun through raindrops. Light is refracted as it enters the sphere of
the raindrop, is reflected from the drop's opposite side, and is again
refracted as it leaves the drop and passes to the observer's eye. A rainbow will reflect back towards a viewer only at a certain angle. This is
known as the "critical angle of reflection," which, for water is about 49
degrees, or seven times seven.[15] Light that travels at an angle of inci-
dence more than 49 degrees will not leave a droplet of water; however,
light with angles less than 49 degrees will leave the water. This is why
rainbows do not appear if the sun is too high in the sky. This critical
reflection angle is based on 360 and 7.

$$2,520 / 49 = 51.428571$$
$$51.428571 \times 7 = 360$$
$$360 \times 7 = 2,520$$

$$51.428571 \times 49 = 2,520.$$
The reflection of this equation is:

$$2,520 / 49 = 51.428571$$

The smallest number that can be expressed as product of two reversible numbers in two different ways is 2,520:

$$2520 = 120 \times 021 = 210 \times 012$$

and

$$12 \times 21 \times 10 = 2520$$

Mathematically, 2,520 possesses a mirror-like quality. These same numbers are found in the seventh day of 360-degree revolutions of the Earth when God *rested* from His creation, a similar metaphor existing in the name Noah. Noah is also the etymological root of the words "navy," "navigation," and the Greek *naus*, the holy place of the temple of Jerusalem.[16] The physics of light and water agree with the arithmetic of the circling of Jericho, the writing on the wall of Daniel, and the Sacred Cubit.

NOTES

1. Talmud (Yoma 53b). Translated by Michael L. Rodkinson. New York: New Talmud Pub. Co.1903.

2. Zohar II, 1867, p. 222; III, p. 131. Pritzker 1 Edition, Daniel C. Matt (Translator) Stanford University Press; 2003

3. Ibid. Zohar. Soncino Zohar, Bereshith, Section 1, Page 71b

4. Ibid. Zohar II, 1867, p. 222; III, p. 131. Yerushalmi, Pesahim 4:1; Ta'anit 1:6.

5. Ibid. Talmud (Bavli, Sanhedrin 26b.) Psalms 1:3. J. Caro, Shulkhan Arukh: Orah Haim 551:8.

6. Isaiah 28:16, John 1:1–3,14 KJV.

7. Jeremiah 17:13 Zechariah 14: 8 & Revelation 7: 17 KJV.

8. Ibid. Zohar, Soncino, Bereshith, Section 1, Page 71b.

9. Exodus 24:10 KJV

10. Strong's Hebrew Dictionary # 5608Strongs Exhaustive Concordance of the Bible. AMG Publishers edition, World Bible Publishers, Inc. 1986 Iowa Falls, Ia.

11. Ibid. Strong's Hebrew Dictionary # 3840.

12. Ibid. Strong's Hebrew Dictionary # 2891.

13. Isaac Newton, A Letter containing his New Theory about Light and Colors': Philosophical Transactions of the Royal Society No.80, published 19 Feb. 1671 / 72. facsimile reproduction in Cohen, I. B., and Scofield, R. E., *Isaac Newton's Papers and Letters in Natural Philosophy*, 2nd ed., Cambridge, Mass., and London, 1 1978, pp. 47–59.

14. Genesis 9:13–15 KJV

15. Henry Semat, Ph.D. *Fundamentals of Physics*. Rinehart & Company, Inc. Publishers. New York. 1945. pg. 447.

16. Ibid. Strong's Hebrew Dictionary #s 5116 through 5118.

Chapter Eleven

THE CITY OF LIGHT

*In the Bourrienne Memoirs, there is an account of Napoleon's
conversation on religion with the savants on board l' Orient when
bound for Egypt; how, after exhausting their armory of atheistical
arguments, he pointed to the starry sky and said:
"Very ingenious, Messieurs; but who made all that?"*
—JOHN HOLLAND ROSE, *The Life of Napoleon I*

Napoleon Bonaparte began his conquest of Palestine in 1798 with
and attack on the port city of Acre. Even before moving his
troops north from Egypt, he had already prepared a proclamation making Palestine an independent Jewish state. With the capture
of Acre, Napoleon planned to reinforce his troops with supplies. He
envisioned a triumphal entry into Jerusalem after Acre was secured, at
which time he would issue his proclamation. Napoleon had realized
early in his conquest of Europe that attending to the religious ideals of
his enemies and his willing subjects was key to his success. As a military and political strategist, Napoleon had few equals. His design for

governing the nations was shrewd and in some cases, opportunistic.
Several years after the battle of Acre, Napoleon wrote,

> My policy consists in governing men as the greatest number
> wish to be governed. That, I think, is the way of recognizing
> the sovereignty of the people. By becoming a Catholic I have
> ended the Vendeau War; by becoming a Moslem I gained
> a footing in Egypt; by becoming Ultramontane I won over
> public opinion in Italy. If I governed Jews, I would rebuild
> the temple of Solomon.[1]

Napoleon had previously encountered the prophecies of the Old
Testament in the Jewish community of Malta that he liberated under
French law in 1798. For hundreds of years, the Knights Hospitalier of
Saint John of Jerusalem had oppressed the Jews by enslaving them and
preventing open worship. One of Napoleon's first acts after banishing
the Knights was to allow the Jews to build a synagogue, and the com-
munity of Jews on Malta welcomed Napoleon as a conqueror equal to
Cyrus the Great. They believed that their liberation by a "king of the
North" was fulfillment of the prophecy in Daniel 11:

> He shall enter also into the glorious land, and many [coun-
> tries] shall be overthrown: but these shall escape out of his
> hand, [even] Edom, and Moab, and the chief of the children
> of Ammon. He shall stretch forth his hand also upon the
> countries: and the land of Egypt shall not escape. He shall
> have power over the treasures of gold and of silver, and over all
> the precious things of Egypt: and the Libyans and the Ethio-
> pians [shall be] at his steps.
>   The king of the north will come storming against the
> king of the south with chariots, cavalry and many ships. The
> king of the north will overrun land after land, sweeping over

them like a flood...Amongst them the fairest of all lands, and tens of thousands will fall victims. Yet all these lands (including Edom and Moab and the remnant of the Ammonites) will survive the attack. The king of the north will reach out to land after land, and Egypt will not escape. He will gain control of her hidden stores of gold, silver and all of her treasures; Libyans and Cushites will follow in his train. Then rumors from east and north will alarm him, and he will depart in a rage to destroy and to exterminate many. He will pitch his royal pavilion between the sea and the holy hill, [Jerusalem's temple mount] the fairest of all hills, and he will meet his end with no one to help him.[2]

The Jewish community in Malta conferred this knowledge to Napoleon during his negotiations with them, and the spectacular naval force of 400 ships and 25,000 troops, cavalry, and artillery confirmed their belief that Napoleon was the conqueror of Daniel 11:40. Even before his invasion of Palestine, Napoleon wrote the following statement to the Moslems after quelling an insurrection at Cairo in 1798:

Sherifs, ulamas, preachers in the mosques...Is there a man so blind as not to see that destiny itself guides all my operations?...Let the people know that, from the creation of the world, it is written that after destroying the enemies of Islam and beating down the cross, I was to come from the confines of the Occident to accomplish my appointed task. Show the people that in more than twenty passages of the holy Qur'an, what has happened has been foretold, and what shall happen has been explained....the day will come when all men shall see beyond all doubt that I am guided by orders from above and that all human efforts avail naught against me. Blessed are they who, in good faith, are the first to choose my side.[3]

On the first day of Passover, April 20, 1799, Napoleon issued his proclamation of a Jewish state of Palestine. On May 22, 1799, the Paris newspaper, *Moniteur Universel,* announced:

> Bonaparte has published a proclamation in which he invites all the Jews of Asia and Africa to gather under his flag in order to re-establish the ancient Jerusalem. He has already given arms to a great number, and their battalions threaten Aleppo.[4]

Although the proclamation did not come to fruition, it increased a drive for Jews worldwide to pursue a sovereign state in Israel. Napoleon's ideas were also embraced by many who viewed them as a fulfillment of ancient prophecy, even some belonging to the Protestant Church of England.

Letter to the Jewish Nation from the French Commander-in-Chief Buonaparte (translated from the Original, 1799)

General Headquarters, Jerusalem 1st Floreal, April 20, 1799, in the year of 7 of the French Republic

BUONAPARTE, COMMANDER-IN-CHIEF OF THE ARMIES OF THE FRENCH REPUBLIC IN AFRICA AND ASIA, TO THE RIGHTFUL HEIRS OF PALESTINE.

Israelites, unique nation, whom, in thousands of years, lust of conquest and tyranny have been able to be deprived of their ancestral lands, but not of name and national existence!

Attentive and impartial observers of the destinies of nations, even though not endowed with the gifts of seers like Isaiah and Joel, have long since also felt what these, with beautiful and uplifting faith, have foretold when they saw the approaching destruction of their kingdom and fatherland: And the ransomed of the Lord shall return, and come to Zion with songs and everlasting joy upon their heads; they shall obtain joy and gladness and sorrow and sighing shall flee away.

Arise then, with gladness, ye exiled! A war unexampled In the annals of history, waged in self-defense by a nation whose hereditary lands were regarded by its enemies as plunder to be divided, arbitrarily and at their convenience, by a stroke of the pen of Cabinets, avenges its own shame and the shame of the remotest nations, long forgotten under the yoke of slavery, and also, the almost two-thousand-year-old ignominy put upon you; and, while time and circumstances would seem to be least favourable to a restatement of your claims or even to their expression, and indeed to be compelling their complete abandonment, it offers to you at this very time, and contrary to all expectations, Israel's patrimony!

The young army with which Providence has sent me hither, let by justice and accompanied by victory, has made Jerusalem my headquarters and will, within a few days, transfer them to Damascus, a proximity which is no longer terrifying to David's city.

Rightful heirs of Palestine!

The great nation which does not trade in men and countries as did those which sold your ancestors unto all people[2] herewith calls on you not indeed to conquer your patrimony; nay, only to take over that which has been conquered and, with that nation's warranty and support, to remain master of it to maintain it against all comers.

Arise! Show that the former overwhelming might of your oppressors has but repressed the courage of the descendants of those heroes who alliance of brothers would have done honour even to Sparta and Rome[3] but that the two thousand years of treatment as slaves have not succeeded in stifling it.

Hasten! Now is the moment, which may not return
for thousands of years, to claim the restoration of civic
rights among the population of the universe which had
been shamefully withheld from you for thousands of
years, your political existence as a nation among the
nations, and the unlimited natural right to worship Je-
hovah in accordance with your faith, publicly and most
probably forever.[5]

The map in Figure 34 displays the Roman age of Paris, the city
center can be seen at the northwest point of the Île de la Cité (Island
of the City) in the Seine River. Paris was named after the Parisii, a
Celtic people who settled on this central island in the 3rd century BC.
The city later spread outward from this point along the banks of the
Seine River.

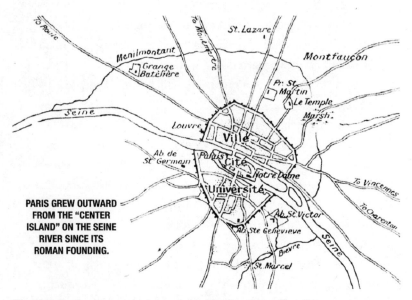

Fig. 34. Author's image based on Anville, Jean-Baptiste
Bourguignon d' (1697–17), Wikimedia Commons, "Plan de Paris
Lutece2," http://commons.wikimedia.org/wiki/Image:Plan_de_Paris_
Lutece2_BNF07710745.png.

This island is considered the birthplace of Paris and was the site of the city's earliest settlements. It was home to the French Kings from AD 400 to AD 1300. The royal palace and parliament were located on the western side of the island. A measuring line extended from this historical center of Paris to the temple mount shows the distance in nautical miles, 1,799.

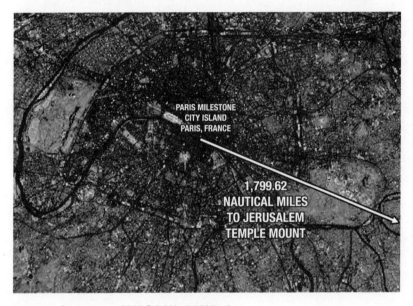

Fig. 35. Courtesy of NASA World Wind

The terminus of this line is fixed on the "0" point marker set in the pavement facing the entrance of the Cathedral of Notre Dame. This is the point from which all distances of French cities are measured from Paris.[6]

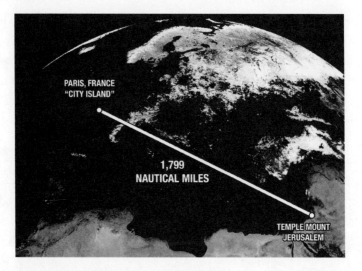

Fig. 36. Courtesy of NASA World Wind

The date of the proclamations of Israel's independence by Napoleon, 1799, displays a curious *priscia sapientia* with respect to 2,520.
It fits the mathematical harmony seen in the relationships of the earth
with the moon as well.

$$2,159 \text{ moon } (2160)$$
$$\underline{- 1,799}$$
$$= 360 \text{ circle}$$

$$1,799$$
$$\underline{- 1260 \text{ (half 2,520)}}$$
$$= 539, \text{ the year of the fall of Babylon}$$
$$1799 \times 3$$
$$\underline{+ 2,520}$$
$$= 7,917, \text{ Earth's mean diameter}$$

Napoleon may have realized that his ambitions for Palestine,
though not without prophetic significance, were premature in the

timeline of God. Although he may even have anticipated the prediction that the King of the North would meet with defeat "between the
sea and the holy hill" in his failure to take Acre, Napoleon was still
resolute in his plan to create a Jewish state. In February 1807, through
Napoleon's aid, the ancient Sanhedrin was opened.[7] This judicial body
had not been in existence since the destruction of Jerusalem in AD
70. The purpose was to set into motion the eventual framework of a
Jewish State with Napoleon's aid from within Europe. However, there
were some scholars of the ancient prophets that saw folly in this venture. The former minister of the interior, Count Chaptal, wrote in his
memoir, *Souvenirs,* that he witnessed an argument at a dinner he was
attending with Napoleon, Cardinal Joseph Fesch, and the Archbishop
of Lyons. The Cardinal was also Napoleon's maternal uncle.

> At the time that Napoleon had brought together the Jews for
> the Sanhédrin in Paris, I attended one day at his dinner where
> I was witness to an astounding exchange. Cardinal Fesch
> rushed into the room with a very worried air about him that
> struck the Emperor. "What is the matter?" he said. "What I
> have is easy to understand," said the Cardinal. "And why?"
> retorted the Emperor. "Do you not know," answered the Car-
> dinal, "that the Scriptures foretell the end of the world when
> the Jews are recognized as constituting a nation?" I and the
> guests were inclined to laugh; But the Emperor changed tone
> and he seemed worried. He rose from the table, went into his
> study with the Cardinal, where he remained conversing for
> over an hour. The next day the Sanhédrin was dissolved.[8]

Despites Napoleon's failings in the campaign of the Holy Land in
the 18th century, many scientists and archaeologists were able to gain
access to the region. In 1798, the French founded Institut de l'Égypte
in Cairo. A year later, the French Army engineer Captain Pierre-Fran-
çois Bouchard discovered the Rosetta Stone, providing the means by

which historians could decode Egyptian hieroglyphs. When Egypt fell to the British in 1801, the Stone was brought to England. Its translation by Jean-François Champollion inspired archaeologists to explore the land of the Pharaohs with the hope of gathering the secrets of antiquity.[9] The greatest mystery of Egypt, and the most inviting to the European intellects of the new 19th century, was the Great Pyramid of Giza.

THE GREAT PYRAMID

In 1721, the researcher Nicolas Shaw explored and measured the Great Pyramid of Giza. He discovered that the granite coffer, the only furnishing in the pyramid, equaled the exact volume of the Ark of the Covenant. This volume was also one-fiftieth the capacity of the Molten Sea of Solomon's temple. The chamber in which the coffer rested was equal to the full volume of the Molten Sea. Both the Ark of the Covenant and the granite coffer of the Great Pyramid were equal to four British quarters, the established standard for grain in England.[10] These two objects additionally furnished the measures of capacity of the earliest Greek and Hebrew nations. The word "coffer" is etymologically based on the Hebrew word for the "mercy seat" of the Ark of the Covenant, *kophereth* from *kopher* meaning "to cover, pardon or make atonement."[11]

According to Jewish scholars, the Exodus of Israel from Egypt was the most powerful manifestation of God's power. It forms the core of the Old Testament narrative and is central to the spiritual and religious identity of the Jews. Fixing the exact date of the Exodus has been the topic of speculation for historians and theologians for centuries. However, the Bible assigns the year of Israel's release from Egyptian slavery backwards from the year of the building of the Temple of Solomon:

> And it came to pass in the four hundred and eightieth year
> after the children of Israel were come out of the land of Egypt,

in the fourth year of Solomon's reign over Israel, in the month
Zif, which [is] the second month, that he began to build the
house of the LORD.[12]

The year Solomon began building the temple was 961 BC, according to the great majority of biblical scholars; delving one level
deeper would place the date of the Exodus at 1,441 BC, or 480 years
prior. As units of length, these numbers have an interesting relationship as well. Four hundred and eighty yards is also 1,441 feet. No
conversion of modern lengths that are relevant to the timing of the
Exodus exists between the numbers 1,441 and 480, except in inches
to yards. The Bible seems to indicate what unit of measurement to
use. The distance between the northeast corner of the Great Pyramid
and the Temple of Jerusalem is 480,000 yards. This relates to the same
number in years between the Exodus and the building of Solomon's
temple, 480 multiplied by 100, which converts to 1,444,100 feet.

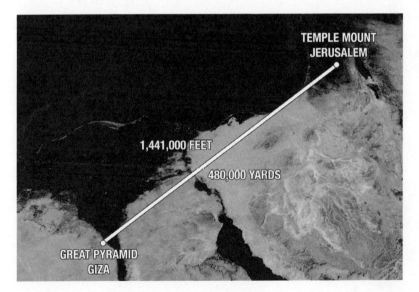

Fig. 37. Courtesy of NASA World Wind

The multiple for both numbers seems at first to be an anomaly, yet once again the time-distance correlation of the temple remains, despite the decimal place incongruity. The year of the Exodus and the year of the temple's construction correlate to the distances between the Great Pyramid and the temple of Jerusalem. The slope of the sides of the pyramid is 51°50', which converts to 51.836275. Twice this number is 103.672557 or pi times 33.

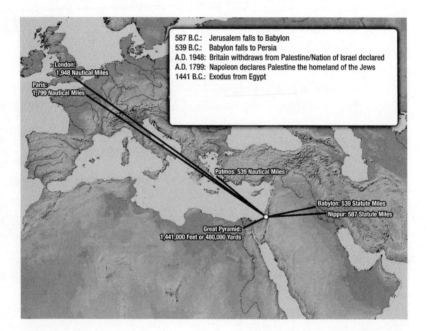

NOTES

1. John. Holland Rose, *The Personality of Napoleon*, pg.16. G. P. Putnams Sons, London UK 1912
2. Daniel 11:41–43 KJV
3. John Holland Rose, *The Life of Napoleon* I, trans. A.S. Kline, (Volumes, 1 and 2) G. Bell and Sons, London UK. 2006.
4. Simon Schwarzfuchs, *Napoleon, The Jews, and the Sanhedrin* Pg. 24. Oxford University Press, USA; New Ed edition, 1984.
5. Ben Weider *Napoleonic Scholarship: The Journal of the The International Napoleonic Society*, Vol.1, No. 2, (1998).
6. Paris "0" point coordinates: 48.85341° N 2.34880° E.
7. Isidore Singer and Cyrus Alder, et al eds. *The Jewish Encyclopedia* (New York: Funk and Wagnalls, 1906).
8. Ibid. John Holland Rose, *The Personality of Napoleon*, pg. 243
9. Don Cameron Allen, "The Predecessors of Champollion," *Proceedings of the American Philosophical Society*, Vol. 144, no. 5. (1960), 527–547.
10. Joseph A. Seiss, *The Great Pyramid: A miracle in stone*, rev. ed (1877; repr., New York: Steiner books, 1989), Pg 167.
11. James Strong *Exhaustive Concordance of the Bible*. AMG Publishers edition, World Bible Publishers, Inc. 1986 Iowa Falls, Ia. Hebrew dictionary # 3727 & 3722.
12. 1 Kings 6:1 KJV

12

BRITISH SACRED MEASUREMENT

The establishment of the statute mile in England was one of the most important, yet often unrecognized factors in its ascension to an Empire. Its establishment by Queen Elizabeth I in 1592 was part of a recovery of ancient measurement standards that enabled Britain to build strength through its navy.[1]

When Elizabeth became Queen in 1558, religious strife, a huge government debt, and failures in the war with France had brought England's fortunes to low ebb. At her death in 1603, England had passed through one of the greatest periods in history—a 45-year period that produced Shakespeare, Francis Bacon, Walter Raleigh, Francis Drake, and many other notable British figures; it was a period that saw England, united as a nation, become a first-rate world power in Europe. Historians credit these advancements to Elizabeth's political skill and cunning. However, none of her designs for Britain would have manifested without the power and skill of her navy. This was the direct result of the advancements made in the science of navigation. The calibration of correct distance of the globe enabled Britain to dominate the seas for nearly 200 years.

Queen Elizabeth did not focus on the improvement of navigational science purely through divine providence, but with mathematical inspiration and tutoring from one of the most influential occult
philosophers of the 16th century, Dr. John Dee.

Dee was born in London in July 13, 1527. His published texts
included studies of mathematics, Hebrew mysticism and Kabbalah,
alchemy, hermeticism, and ancient languages. John Dee was the first
to translate the *Elements* into English. The *Elements*, a work of the
Greek mathematician Euclid, combined all the geometric knowledge
of its time, around 300 BC, and is still used in the modern teaching
of mathematics. Dee knew more about the dimensions of the Earth
than any man in Queen Elizabeth's court. He became the leading
geographical adviser to the Queen and was a strong force behind
the concept of a British Empire. Dee believed that maritime dominance was the key to England's control of Spain and ultimate growth
as a nation. With advice and direction from Dee, Queen Elizabeth
gave increased powers to Trinity House, a guild created in 1514 for
the piloting of ships and the regulating of British navigation. Dee
published *General and Rare Memorials pertayning to the Perfect Arte
of Navigation* in 1577, which emphasized Britain's need for advancements of accurate navigation. He believed that such advancements
would enable the British navy to establish the country as a dominant
world power. These changes were implemented through Dee's influence with the Queen and were so successful that in 1580, Dee presented *Brytanici Imperij Limites* (The Limits of the British Empire),
to the Queen and her ministers. This was an assessment of the progress made by the navy, and outlined Queen Elizabeth's power over
most of the oceans and great expanses of territory in the northern
hemisphere.

Both these works followed his book, *Propaedeumata Aphoristica de
praestantiorbus quibusdam naturae virtutibus* (Aphoristic Introduction
to certain especially important virtues of nature), which was published
in 1568. It was one of the first that he'd dedicated to Queen Elizabeth

that covered the knowledge of the ancients amassed through his collection of over 4,000 books from his personal library at his house in Mortlake. It was the largest library in Britain and became famous as a popular center for learning outside of universities.

Although Elizabeth was already superiorly educated, having learned from tutors such as William Grindal and Roger Ascham, Dee was obliged to teach the Queen the mathematical concepts of *Propaedeumata* and his earlier work, *Monas Hieroglyphia* (The One Sacred Writing), a text that explored the origin of knowledge that was published in 1564. The subject of these books went beyond the numerical skills of the time, and contained ancient concepts of Earth's dimension that Dee had gained through association with one of the greatest cartographers in history, Gerard Mercator.

Mercator, the great Flemish cartographer, born on March 5, 1512, was the first to use the term "atlas" for a album of maps. He had amassed various navigational texts that had been newly translated into Latin. He also collected apparatus from his travels that were not available in England.

Dee met Mercator in 1548 while a student at Louvain University. They worked closely for three years, and along with developing a close friendship, they produced superior methods for navigating the seas. Dee actually dedicated *Propaedeumata Aphoristica* to Mercator. Such was the friendship between the two that Dee wrote:

> It was the custom of our mutual friendship and intimacy that, during three whole years, neither of us lacked the other's presence for as much as three whole days; and such was the eagerness of both for learning and philosophizing that, after we had come together, we scarcely left off the investigation of difficult and useful problems for three minutes of an hour.[2]

Dee's gratitude towards Mercator for helping him publish his first works compelled him to return the favor:

It remains now for me to beg you earnestly to entrust to the
public studies of men... your own remarkable discoveries
both in that excellent branch of philosophy which is called
physics and also in geometry and geography; for thus, certainly, you will greatly enlarge the Republic of letters with
your most useful and fresh inventions.[3]

John Dee was not only the royal cartographer and naval authority
to Queen Elizabeth; he was also her personal astrologer. Dee was considered the most adept mystic in Europe in his day and is still revered
by occultists in modern times. His work in alchemy and mysticism was
born out of the ancient manuscripts that he had in his extensive library.
Most of these manuscripts were not available in Latin or English any-
where in the world. Through his tutorial influences, Elizabeth learned
of the sacred mysteries of Pythagoras and the laws of his school.

The Greek Pythagorean College viewed the universe in relationship to pure geometry and number. These ideas were similar to those
of the mystery schools of Egypt. According to Plato and his *Dialogues*,
the five tenets of Pythagoras were:

That at its deepest level, reality is mathematical in nature,
That philosophy can be used for spiritual perfection,
That the soul can rise to union with the divine,
That certain symbols have mystical significance,
All members of the order should observe strict loyalty and
    secrecy.[4]

According to Dee, these beliefs had been retained throughout
history within ritual and symbol. The ancient science of reckoning
time, movement, and location on the Earth were linked to the mystery schools of Egypt. Geometry, literally the "measure of the earth"
remained foremost in the symbolic transfer of scared knowledge in
ancient Greek thought as well. Like Pythagoras, Dee believed that

everything was composed of number. In this regard, he combined the high Kabbalistic tenet that God spoke numbers to create the universe. Conversely, he reasoned that man could exercise divine power through mathematics.[5]

Dee also produced one of the most influential occult works in modern history, *Liber Loagaeth*, or "Book of Speech from God." This was his account of an angelic language that he termed "Angelical," supposedly used by God to form the universe. Dee learned the language and wrote it down in personal journals that were left unpublished at his death.[6] The term "Enochian" was later assigned to this language by occultists observing Dee's belief that the antediluvian patriarch Enoch was the last mortal to possess the language. The form of the *Liber Loageeth* was based on the number seven. In it, Dee produced Angelic "letter tables" of 49 x 49 squares.[7] This deliberate use of seven in the Angelic system was consistent with the geometric theological works of Dee, especially in his calculations of the dimensions of the Earth and the formulation of the statute mile.

The Bible records that Enoch had walked with God and was later translated into heaven. The pseudepigraphic book of Enoch gives a detailed account, visions, and coded knowledge that Enoch received while in the company of the host of God, i.e. the Tzabaoth (Hosts of the oath).[8] This work is quoted in the letter of Jude 14:15 in the New Testament.

Occult mystics like Dee referred to themselves as "initiates" of the ancient sciences. As mentioned in chapter one, the Hebrew name Enoch meant "initiated," "experienced," or "to dedicate."[9] Dee also knew the significance of the name Enoch as the basis of the word Chanukah, the Jewish feast of initiation or dedication of the temple of Jerusalem. The name Enoch, literally pronounced (Chanuk), contains mystical geometry. Its Hebrew letters, (cheth, nun, vav and koph,) equal one hundred and sixty four. This number corresponds to the actual year 164 BC of the origin of Chanuk-ah, the "Feast of Dedication."

Chanuka was instituted by Judas Maccabeus and his brothers in 164/5 BC to celebrate the new altar of the temple at Jerusalem. Three years earlier in 167/8 BC, the Syrian ruler Antiochus Epiphanes had profaned the temple by entering the Holy of Holies and sacrificing a pig on the altar in the manner of the words of Daniel and later, Christ, "setting up abominations that make desolate" in the holy place of the temple.

Enoch was the seventh from Adam from the line of Seth and lived for 365 years. These numbers and the date of the first Chanuka, 164 BC, work together mathematically to represent both the circle and the Earth's solar year.

$$164 \times 7 = 1{,}148 \ (\pi \times 365.41)$$

The name Jerusalem has the sum of its letters at 1,146 (365 x π).

The *second* temple of Jerusalem, as dedicated (Chanuk) to God, was of central importance to the geometry of dimension. The Feast of Dedication was the high point in the struggle between the Maccabees and Antiochus Epiphanes, a figure distinct as a prototype of the future Antichrist. In Newton's investigation of the time-based prophecies of Daniel and John, the culminating event was the reinstitution of the future *third* temple of Jerusalem. There, according to Newton, the prophetic events of past, present, and future were connected. These prophecies *initiated* from the temple in location and in time. In the book of Daniel, the last 2,520 days before the return of the Messiah would be *initiated* through the treaty reinstating temple sacrifice in Jerusalem. This treaty would be broken in its midst 1,260 days later by the interruption of the sacrifice and the setting up of the "abomination that makes desolate" by the Antichrist.[10]

Christ's description concerning this future event in Matthew 24 was around 198 years after the event of Chanuka. He was referring to a future person, similar in manner to Antiochus, but whose identity was clarified in the Revelation of John and the letters of St. Paul.

When the Romans besieged Jerusalem in AD 70, the general Titus actually tried to save the temple. Additionally, no profanation of its interior of precincts occurred in the time prior to this destruction according to the historical accounts.[11]

The prophecies of Daniel 11 lead through history from Persia to Antiochus. After describing his acts towards the Jews and the Temple of Jerusalem, Daniel's prophecy jumps to the time of the end. From this point, the type of Antiochus is retained symbolically as the "little horn" from chapter 7, as "the king who will come," or the "Beast" mentioned in the Revelation of John. Newton focused intensely on all of these topics in *Observations*.

Chanuka is *Enochian* in the etymological sense. The geometric and symbolic information given to Enoch was similar to the numeric prophecies of Daniel (based on the number 7). Within the books of Daniel and Enoch are examples of the long-sought universal language of which the key to interpretation is the temple of Jerusalem. Obtaining this seven-based language was the main objective of John Dee. However, it must be said that his means and goals were in contradiction to the Law of Moses, and more akin to the occult workings of the Babylonian sages.

The name Elizabeth actually plays part in the mathematical vision of John Dee. The origin of her name is the Hebrew, Eli-shaba.[12] This translates to "God of the oath." However, the word *shaba* means literally "the number seven."[13] *Shaba* is the root for the Hebrew *shabat*, the seventh day of rest. These words tie into the spectrum of the pure knowledge of navigation, Noah (rest), and the work that John Dee transmitted to the Queen during her reign.

The significance of seven was connected to the highest power in creation (7 x 360) and therefore, the greatest oath was "to seven oneself" (to repeat a declaration seven times). The sevenfold oath (Hebrew *shibathaim*)[14] is found seven times in the Old Testament.[15]

The statute mile of Queen Elizabeth, 5,280 feet, can be calculated using pi and the number 7:

$$3.14159265 \times 7 \times 7 \times 7 \times 7 \times 7 = 52{,}800$$
or:
$$0.314159265 \times 7 \times 7 \times 7 \times 7 \times 7 = 5{,}280.$$

It also seems based on permutations of the number seven:

$$7 \times 360 = 2{,}520$$
$$360 \,/\, 25.20 = 14.2857142857\ldots$$
$$25.142857142857 \times 2{,}520 = 63{,}360$$
$$63{,}360 \,/\, 12 \text{ feet} = 5{,}280 \text{ feet}.$$

This means that it is probable that Dee formulated the statute mile believing the Sacred Cubit was equal to 25.1428 inches.

Nevertheless, this estimated value of the Sacred Cubit based on 7 was multiplied by 2,520, which resulted in 5,280 feet. Because the ratio was maintained, the statute mile is fundamentally valid in "time equals distance" calculations. Because the statute mile is also related to pi, it produces the correct dimensions of the Earth in the equation, $2{,}520 \times \pi$. However, the full explanation of *why* it works is difficult to establish. It would require an exact history and record of the communications between John Dee and Queen Elizabeth, as well as the mathematics and ancient sources used to set the matter to rest. We can only draw conclusions from what is generally evident from history.

As for the supernatural phenomena of statue miles equaling years in which prophecy has been fulfilled, or distance in statute miles numerically embellishing scripture, these would not exist except through God's Omnipresence, Omniscience, and Omnipotence.

It *is* certain that the search for a geometric value of unity in nature was the preoccupation of nearly every intellect associated with Elizabeth's reign. The search also continued afterwards, and Newton inherited the works of Dee, Mercator, and the adjustments in calibration by Queen Elizabeth with which he continued his quest for the *prisca sapientia*.

Britain is alone in its work in the advancement of civilization and Western thought. The sun truly did not set on the Empire for a time, and the intellects that it produced within its universities, 100 years from Elizabeth's reign, advanced science and thought to levels left unchallenged to this day. It was there that enlightened groups of natural philosophers remained centered while searching for the same ultimate unity in number, whether it was hidden in the works of the Greeks or Egyptians, or coded in architecture of antiquity. However, a structure that encoded the *priscia sapientia* over 6,000 years ago, still the most ancient work done to help civilization understand the Earth, lay under their British feet at the Avebury circle in Wiltshire England.

NOTES

1. Sir Charles Close: "Old English Mile": *Geographical Journal:* vol.76: pp.338–342. 1930 This is from "An Acte againste newe Buyldinges," 35 Elizabeth I. Chapter 6, 1593 which forbade building within 3 miles of the gates of London, and included a definition of this mile.

2. William Howard Sherman, *The Politics of Reading and Writing in the English Renaissance.* Page 6. (Amherst publishers: University of Massachusetts, 1995).

3. Ibid.

4. Bullfinch's *Mythology, The age of fable*, Chapter 34, Pythagoras, Egyptian deities, Oracles. Modern Library publishers. New York NY 1998

5. John Dee. *Propaedeumata Aphoristica* (1558 and 1568) Latin and English. ed. and trans. by Wayne Shumaker (Berkeley: University of California Press, 1978).

6. Méric Casaubon. *A True and Faithful Relation of What Passed for many Yeers Between Dr. John Dee, (A Mathematician of Great Fame in Q. Eliz. and King James their Reignes) and some spirits.* (1659) repr. Published by Magickal Childe, New York 1992.

7. Dr. John Dee *Mysteriorum Liber Sextus et Sanctus [Liber Loagaeth]* Edited by Joseph H. Peterson. 1954 British Library MS Sloane 3189.

8. Isaiah 6:3 KJV.

9. James Strongs *Exhaustive Concordance of the Bible.* Hebrew dictionary # 2596.AMG Publishers edition, World Bible Publishers, Inc. Iowa Falls, IA 1986.

10. Dan 9:27 KJV

11. Flavius Josephus, *War of the Jews.* E. Mary Smallwood (Editor), G. A. Williamson (Introduction, Translator) Penguin Classics NY USA 1984

12. Ibid. Strong's Hebrew dictionary # 472.
13. Ibid. Strong's Hebrew dictionary # 7650 & 7651.
14. Ibid. Strong's Hebrew dictionary # 5659.
15. E.W. Bullinger, *Number in Scripture*. Pg. 158 (Grand Rapids: Kregel Publications, 1967).

13

THE SACRED CUBIT RECORDED
IN THE EARTH

Geometry primarily concerns the study of space. Of the geometric numbers used in calculating dimension, two stand above all others. The greatest of these is pi, or 3.14159265. Pi is a ratio based on the circle, a geometric shape. A circle is always a circle no matter what size or calibration is used in its measure. Because of this property, the value of pi is always the same. The second most important number, especially in regard to the geometry of antiquity, is the number 360. This is the system of "degrees" of a circle or division of the whole into logical parts. It was known from the beginning of Sumer and Egypt, the first civilizations. There is speculation that the number 360 was the count of days in one year in Earth's primeval past and that during some world cataclysm, the year grew to 365 days. Both numbers are universally understood to relate to circles and time.

The Avebury Circle in Wiltshire England is the largest and oldest megalithic structure in Europe. The extreme age of the 30-foot-deep earthwork ditch has left researchers unsure of the identity of its builders. Julius Caesar wrote of the Druids, ostensibly connected to the knowledge of the constructers of Avebury Circle:

> They also discuss and impart to their young many things con-cerning the heavenly bodies and their movements, the size of the world and our earth, natural sciences, and the influence and power of the immortal gods.[1]

The historian Ammianus Marcellus also mentioned the superior metrology of the Druids in the 4th century AD.

> The Druids are men of penetrating and subtle spirit, and ac-quired the highest renown by their speculations, which were at once subtle and profound. Both Caesar and Mela plainly inti-mate that they were conversant with most sublime speculations in geometry and in measuring the magnitude of the earth.[2]

The location of the Avebury Circle is quite amazing. It has been delib-erately and precisely located over the latitude 51.428571428571, which exactly equals 360 divided by seven. If it is converted to minutes and seconds, it yields 51 degrees, 25 minutes, 42 seconds. As seen in many nu-merically symbolic stories in the Bible, the number 2,520 is represented in latitude of Avebury circle, i.e., 360 multiplied by 7 equals 2,520. The diameter of the Avebury enclosure is 1,260 feet or half of 2,520.[3]

These quantities have existed in the Avebury Circle for thousands of years; as long as the Earth has rotated on the same axis, its latitude has remained constant on the globe. They are a geometric representa-tion of the same numbers encrypted in Daniel's writing on the wall. The latitude of the Avebury Circle, was established with such preci-sion that it underscores the importance of '2,520' as key to the circle's intended *message*. Two thousand, five hundred and twenty, used in concert with three hundred and sixty, the value of pi and the number seven, reveal many things.

7 x 360 = 2,520 x π = 7.916, the diameter of the Earth x π again, the circumference of the Earth.

This value is also found in a more simple way:

$$7 \times \pi \times 360 = 7,916.$$

The angle of a line extending from the center of the Avebury Circle to Jerusalem's temple mount lies 21.60 degrees south of true East. This azimuth represents the common cubit of the Hebrews in inches, and is a fractal of the diameter of the moon, 2,160. It is also the number of years of one zodiacal age in the precession of the equinoxes. Because 2,160 is also 360 less than 2,520, the entire system of the *prisca sapientia* is presented in Avebury's geomantic arrangement. These numbers are inherently astronomical, representing precession and dimension of the Earth-moon system. All function together in our calibrations of years and ages.

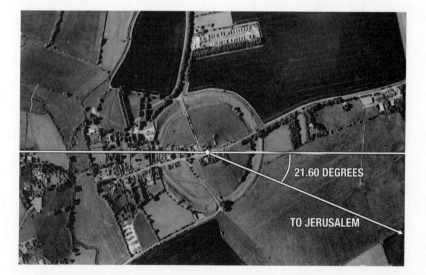

Fig. 38. Image by author

The precision with which the builders set the location suggests that it was designed to withstand the effects of time, up until our present age. All the geometry of the complex seems to indicate a certain point in the future. If this is indeed the case, there should be some key within the structure itself that explains what time frame it indicates.

The numbers that appear redundantly in Avebury seem to be the most important part of its message, which are seven and thirty-three. The distance between the center of Avebury Circle and the foundation stone on the temple mount in Jerusalem is 2,310 statute miles.

$$77 \times 33 - 7 \times 33 = 2{,}310$$
$$77 \times 30 = 2{,}310$$
$$33 \times 70 = 2{,}310$$

If 2,520 years are counted forward from the fall of Babylon in 539 BC, and the 33 years that Christ walked the Earth are subtracted, the year is AD 1948, the rebirth of Israel.

$$2{,}520 - 33 - 539 = 1948$$

In the Gregorian calendar, Babylon fell 7 x 77 years before the birth of Christ, and 7 x 77 + 33 before the resurrection of Christ.

The numbers 70 and 33 correspond to significant years in Israel's history, and both years are closely associated with the temple of Jerusalem.

Jesus Christ defined the temple as an *arch*itectural representation of himself:

What sign do you show to us, since you do these things? Jesus said to them, Destroy this temple, and in three days I will raise it up. Then the Jews said, This temple was forty-six years being built, and do you raise it up in three days? But he spoke about the temple of his body. Then when he was raised from the dead, His disciples recalled that he said this to them. (John 2: 19–22)

Jesus died and rose from the dead at 33 years old, which corresponds to AD 33 in the Gregorian calendar. In this year the temple, represented by his resurrected body was rebuilt. In AD 70 the Romans burned the temple of Jerusalem and leveled it to the ground. The number 33 is written "gl" in Hebrew, pronounced "gal." This word is the closest Hebrew word identifying the Avebury Circle, and means a "round thing," "wheels," and "circle." Analogous to our pursuit of the underlying message of Avebury, a closely related form of "gal," which is "gal-ah," means "to reveal."[4]

The appearance of 33 in chapter and verse of the Bible oftentimes addresses the subject of knowledge within the text. This is seen in the books of Jeremiah, Job, and Ephesians:

Call unto me, and I will answer thee, and shew thee great and mighty things, which thou knowest not. (Jeremiah 33:3)

My words [shall be of] the uprightness of my heart: and my lips shall utter knowledge clearly. (Job 33.3)

If not, hearken unto me: hold thy peace, and I shall teach thee wisdom. (Job 33.33)

How that by revelation he made known unto me the mystery; as I wrote afore in few words. (Ephesians 3:3)

Christ's 33-year ministry was centered in Galilee, north of Jerusalem. Galilee lies within a circular geologic depression, surrounded by mountains and hills, crossed by the 33rd parallel. In the Gospel narrative, the northern extent of Jesus' ministry extended to the port city of Sidon in Canaan situated exactly at 33 degrees, 33 minutes, 33 seconds north latitude.[6]

This pairing of 33 with resurrection from death is found throughout the Gospel. Jesus was crucified on Golgotha, from the same Hebrew root, *gal.* The city Capernaum on the north coast of the Sea of Galilee was the center of Jesus' ministry—its name means "village of compassion"—and was the site of more miracles of Jesus than any other town of Israel. Matthew explains that Jesus began His ministry in Capernuam in order to fulfill Old Testament prophecy:

> And leaving Nazareth, He came and dwelt in Capernaum, which is by the sea, in the regions of Zebulun and Naphtali, that it might be fulfilled which was spoken by Isaiah the prophet, saying: "The land of Zebulun and the land of Naphtali, the way of the sea, beyond the Jordan, Galilee of the Gentiles: the people who sat in darkness saw a great light, and upon those who sat in the region and shadow of death light has dawned."[7]

The site of Galilee was the specific meeting place of the resurrected Christ:

> And the angel answered and said unto the women, Fear not ye: for I know that ye seek Jesus, which was crucified. He is not here: for *he is risen,* as he said. Come, see the place where the Lord lay. And go quickly, and tell his disciples that *he is risen from the dead; and, behold, he goeth before you into Galilee,* there shall ye see him: lo, I have told you. And they departed quickly from the sepulcher with fear and great joy; and did run to bring his disciples word. And as they went to tell his disciples, behold, Jesus met them, saying, All hail. And they came and held him by the feet, and worshipped him. Then said Jesus unto them, Be not afraid: *go tell my brethren that they go into Galilee, and there shall they see me.*[8] (Emphasis mine)

The theme of the *gal* is further embellished in the geographic location of Jesus' birthplace. The traditional site at the Church of the Nativity in Bethlehem is approximately 540 yards from north latitude 31 degrees, 41 minutes, 59 seconds. This is a fractal of pi, the universal value for all circles.

> But thou, Bethlehem Ephratah, [though] thou be little among the thousands of Judah, [yet] out of thee shall he come forth unto me [that is] to be ruler in Israel; whose goings forth [have been] from of old, from everlasting.[9]

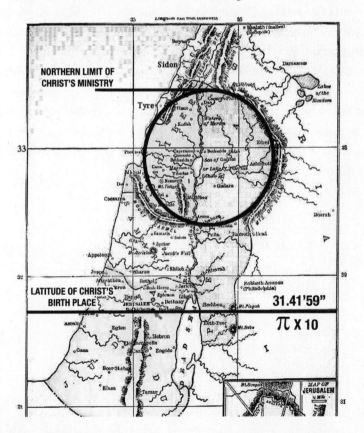

Fig. 39. Image by author. Map reprinted from *Oxford Cyclopedic Concordance* (New York: Oxford University Press, 1947), 125.

The English translation of the book of Genesis mentions God thirty-three times. Jesus Christ began his three-year ministry at age 30, according to Luke 3:23, during which time it is said that Jesus performed 33 miracles.

These values were laid in the earth at Avebury thousands of years before the birth of Christ. Thirty-three, the most prevalent numeric feature of Avebury, is superimposed over values of astronomical time, 2,160 and 7. In the Bible, it symbolizes spiritual transition to a perfected state from ignorance to understanding, from death to life, and from the desolation of Israel to its rebirth, as the year 1948 reflects 33 percent of an hour at 19 minutes, 48 seconds. In the Bible, Revelation focuses exclusively on the culmination of the present age, the return of Christ, and the establishment of rule by God on Earth. Thirty-three is mentioned more times in Revelation within this context more than any book of the Bible. The numbers of astronomical time are imbedded redundantly throughout its prophecies, where the highest order of astronomical time is manifested in the precession of the zodiac. Using these parallels, the ultimate message of the Avebury Circle in Wiltshire can be deciphered.

NOTES

1. Julius Caesar (*On the Druids, Gallic Wars*) H. J. Edwards
   (Translator) Loeb Classical Library, Harvard University Press.
   Cambridge, Massachusetts, U.S 1917.
2. Ammianus Marcellus *Res Gestae* Libri XXXI 15.9. English
   translation (by J.C. Rolfe) Loeb Classical Library, Harvard
   University Press. Cambridge, Massachusetts, U.S 1940
3. Charles Philip Kains-Jackson. *Our Ancient Monuments and
   the Land around them.* Pg. 51. London, UK. Elliot Stock 62.
   PaterNoster Row 1880.
4. John 2: 19–22 KJV
5. Strong's Hebrew dictionary # 1541, Strongs Exhaustive
   Concordance of the Bible. AMG Publishers edition, World Bible
   Publishers, Inc. 1986 Iowa Falls, Ia.
6. Matthew 15:21 & Mark. 7:24 KJV
7. Matthew 4:13–16 KJV
8. Matthew 28:5–10 KJV
9. Micah 5: 2 KJV

14

A THIRD OF TIME

Concerning the clear interpretation of prophecy, the apostle Paul wrote, "For now we see through a glass, darkly."[1] Bible scholars know that many prophetic verses in scripture remain obscured until their fulfillment, and most prophecy seems to contain multiple levels of meaning. A prime example of the challenge for full interpretation of prophecy is found in 1 Corinthians 13:12. In Revelation 12:4, one third of the stars of heaven are thrown to the Earth by a dragon: "And his tail drew the third part of the stars of heaven, and did cast them to the Earth."

Bible commentaries dealing with this passage unanimously assume that the "stars" represent one-third of the angels in heaven that aligned with the dragon, Satan or the devil. However, the same chapter explains that the dragon and his angels war with Michael and his angels in heaven. This presents a contradiction. If the rebellious angels under Satan are thrown to the earth, they would not therefore exist in heaven to engage in a war in heaven.

Daniel 12 also reinforces that the archangel Michael expels the angels of Satan to the earth. This is separate from the vision of the dragon whose tail sweeps a third of the stars to earth. It figuratively represents the exact mechanism of precession. John's vision of the Dragon is a cryptograph of time. The word used in this passage for tail is *ora*, the same lexical Greek root for Heavens, *oranos*, and hour, *hora*.[2]

True north is represented by the axis of Earth's rotation. In the northern sky, this point is now closest to the star known as Polaris that belongs to the constellation Ursa Minor. However, Polaris wasn't always the location of celestial north. The northern axis of the Earth is in constant motion. Over the course of 25,920 years it traces a circle around the largest and most northern constellation known as Draco, the dragon. Its configuration within the precessional circle of the north is such that one-third of the 25,920 years circuit lies directly along Draco's tail.

For observers on the ground, the stars of heaven rise and fall to the Earth while rotating the celestial North Pole. For the last third of the precessional cycle of nearly 8,640 years, the pole has been anchored to the *dragon*.

$$25,920 = 8,640 + 8,640 + 8,640.$$

And there appeared another wonder in heaven; and behold a great red dragon...

And his tail drew the third part of the stars of heaven, and did cast them to the earth.

Revelation 12:3-4

Fig. 40. Image by author

The full text of Revelation 12:4 reveals another time-based clue to its meaning that incorporates the same numeric design found in Avebury Circle:

[A]nd the dragon stood before the woman which was ready to be delivered, for to devour her child as soon as it was born. And she brought forth a man child, who was to rule all nations with a rod of iron: *and her child was caught up unto God, and [to] his throne.*[3] (Emphasis mine)

Using the Gregorian calendar, the year that Jesus Christ rose from the dead, or was "caught up to God, and [to] his throne," was AD 33.

Since one full revolution of the precessional circuit is also 100 percent of its duration, 33 percent represents one-third of the circuit. Within the tenets of Christianity, the resurrection of Jesus Christ from the dead marked the end of Satan's power over mankind. The Messiah's crucifixion fulfilled the payment for sin and ended subjection to the author of sin, the devil or the dragon. In this context, AD 33 is the anchor year from which the one-third of the precession can be calculated. Additionally, the future resurrection of the Christian saints is explained in Revelation as occurring at the time of the throwing down of the dragon and his angels:

And I heard a loud voice saying in heaven, Now is come salvation, and strength, and the kingdom of our God, and the power of his Christ: for the accuser of our brethren is cast down, which accused them before our God day and night. *Therefore rejoice, [ye] heavens, and ye that dwell in them.* Woe to the inhabitors of the earth and of the sea! for the devil is come down unto you, having great wrath, because he knoweth that he hath but a short time.[4]

At the point when Earth's northern axis leaves the tail of Draco, mankind will realize its full independence from the control of Satan with the resurrection of the saints. But the question is, how is the one-third of the precession (8,640 years) anchored to the Gregorian calendar?

Six hundred and sixty-six, "the mark of the beast," is found in Revelation 13:18. This beast, also known as the Antichrist, is given full authority of the dragon during 1,260 days. It is a fractal repetition of one-third of precessional time leading to the resurrection of Christ. At the end of the Antichrist's three-and-a-half-year rule, the full expression of 33 will occur through the resurrection of the saints. Since AD 33 represented the end of Satan's "full authority" over mankind, it is reasonable that a form of this number should appear before AD 33.

If 6,660 years ended in AD 33, the complete cycle of a third of the precession would require an additional 1,980 years to be completed (which would equal 8,640 years).

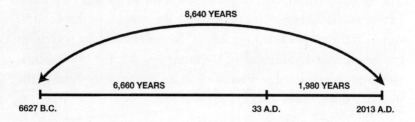

Fig. 41. Image by author

In navigation, 33 degrees of the circle of the Earth has 1,980 nautical miles. This is found by multiplying 60 minutes in an hour times 33. One thousand nine hundred eighty years needs 6,660 years more to equal 8,640 years, and is the exact number of minutes in 33 hours, as well as nautical miles in 33 degrees of the great circle of the Earth. The majority of Draco's tail lies along 6,660 years of the precessional circuit. The number 2013 is the number of minutes in 33 hours + 33 minutes and the number of nautical miles in 33.33 degrees of the great circle of the Earth.

The image below shows the circuit that the northern axis of the earth travels due to precession and its location around the constellation Draco.

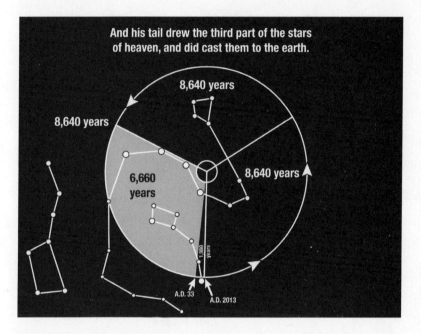

Fig. 42. Image by author

The same time scheme of a third revealed in the precession through Draco is also demonstrated between the proportion of the moon with respect to the Earth.

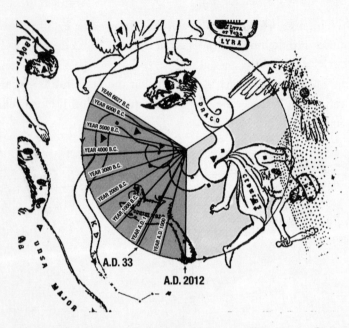

Fig. 43. Image by author based on Alexander Jamieson, *Celestial Atlas Plate II* (London: G. & W. B. Whittaker, 1822), 14.

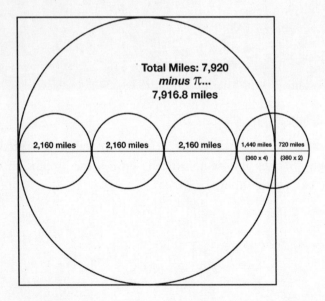

Fig. 44. Image by author

In Figure 45, the portion in which the moon overlaps the silhouette of the Earth is a third of the moon's diameter. The total number of miles of four moon diameters is 8,640, equaling the number of years of a third of the precessional circuit.

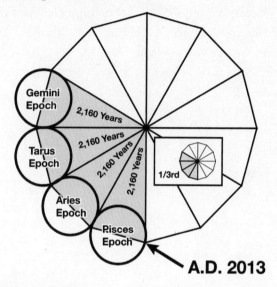

Fig. 45. Image by author

This repeats the time frame paradigm of the end of time anchored to the resurrection. The time after the resurrection of Christ is 1980 years. The remaining third of the moon overlapping the Earth is 720 miles. The number of days from the beginning of the temple sacrifice until its interruption by the Antichrist is found in the following equation:

$$1,980 - 720 = 1,260.$$

When the portion of the Earth's diameter, 7920 miles, is subtracted from 1,260, the result is 6,660.

NOTES

1. 1Corinthians 13: 12 KJV
2. Strong's Greek Lexicon # 3769. James Strong Exhaustive Concordance of the Bible. AMG Publishers edition, World Bible Publishers, Inc. 1986 Iowa Falls, IA. USA
3. Revelation 12:4 KJV
4. Revelation 12: 10 KJV

√

15

SIX HUNDRED, THREE SCORE AND SIX

Much speculation exists concerning the full meaning of the "number of the name of the beast" found in Revelation. Many corollaries between "it" and names of rulers throughout history have been suggested. However, names rendered in Arabic letters of English are not numeric in the manner of Greek and Hebrew and do not have bearing in the computation of names.

Many theologians have speculated that St. John may have encoded the name of the Roman ruler of his day. For example, the calculation of the name "Nero Caesar" in Hebrew letters equals 666 (spelled, nun resh vav nun, qoph samech resh). With respect to the pure theology and science of the Renaissance intellectuals, the distance/year phenomenon may offer additional information for the unraveling of this ancient riddle. Because Newton was convinced that the books of Daniel and St. John concerning the "end of days" were the most time-oriented and numerical of all prophecy, the number (of the beast) should be represented in both.

The Bible mentions the city of Susa in Babylon mainly in Esther and also once each in Nehemiah and Daniel. Both Daniel and

Nehemiah lived in Susa during the Babylonian captivity of Judah. In the story of Purim, Esther became queen there, and saved the Jews from genocide. The tomb of Daniel is thought to be located in the area known as Shush-Daniel. Susa was an ancient city of the Elamite, Persian, and Parthian empires of Iran, and was located about 150 miles east of the Tigris River.

Susa was the scene of one of the most significant time-based prophecies of the Old Testament. It occurred during the Babylonian exile to the Prophet Daniel:

> In the third year of the reign of king Belshazzar a vision appeared unto me, [even unto] me Daniel, after that which appeared unto me at the first. And I saw in a vision; and it came to pass, when I saw, that I [was] at Shushan [in] the palace, which [is] in the province of Elam; and I saw in a vision, and I was by the river of Ulai.[1]

Though Daniel was living in Babylon at the time, he was, for some significant reason, placed near Susa between the banks of the river Ulai during the scene of the prophecy of the Kingdoms of the world. This subject of world rule by the nations is repeated by John in Revelation 16, ending with the "Beast" that rises immediately preceding Christ's return. Daniel was greatly distressed by the visions he had been given and sought the meaning:

> I Daniel had seen the vision, then I sought meaning. And, behold the form of a man stood before me. And I heard a man's voice between *the banks of* Ulai, which called and said, Gabriel, make this man to understand the vision.[2]

The italicized words, "between the banks," found in this passage in English translations are inferred, although the actual Hebrew text literally reads, "And I heard a man's voice between Ulai."

This point is enigmatic if read without geographic knowledge of the area. Eastman's Bible dictionary from 1897 explains that the Ulai river is the divided branch of the river Choasper that runs on the east and west sides of Susa. Without the topographic information that the river is *two* rivers on either side of Susa, it would seem that the voice speaking to Gabriel came in the middle of the river itself. It is another matter entirely if the voice, axiomatically (of prophetic explanation), came from between the two rivers of Ulai.

It is truly remarkable that Bible commentators have missed the riddle of Ulai. The Hebrew name Ulai literally means to be "perverse" or "silly" and can be pronounced, either *oo-lah'ee* or *ev-ee-lee*.[1] Its root, *ev-eel*,[2] is the ancient source for the English word "evil." When a point is made equidistant between the two forks of Ulai near Susa and extended to the foundation stone of the temple mount in Jerusalem, the distance is exactly 666 nautical miles.

Fig. 46. Here, the ruins of Susa are seen with a measuring line extending from Jerusalem's temple mount touching a central canal between the Ulai rivers, 666 nautical miles away. Modern Shush, coordinates: 32.18922° N 48.25778° E. Courtesy of NASA World Wind.

The name Shushan, (spelled shin, shin, nun) or Shush (shin, shin) is related to the Hebrew word for the number six, *shesh-aw*. Hebrew for the number 666 is "shesh (hundred) sheshim, v'shesh."

The prophecy of Daniel chapter 8 is a reiteration of Nebuchadnezzar's dream of world kingdoms in the form of a statue with a head of gold, chest of silver, waist of brass, legs of iron, and feet of iron mixed with clay. Daniel had interpreted the dream as the last world kingdoms, Babylon, Persia, Greece, Rome, and the final empire of a revived Rome of ten nations. This was the prophecy that the Fifth Monarchists of Newton's day believed referenced their age. Their theology and interpretation of the year 1666 was a major factor in development of Newton's early works.

The Hebrew sages often decipher the mystical meaning of words with a method called "atbash" or the transfer of letters from their placement from their opposite order in the Hebrew alphabet. This process is explained in the word itself. *Atbash* is spelled with first, last, second, and second to last letters of the Hebrew alphabet. The ancient sages maintained that "Shishak," the name of the Egyptian pharaoh that invaded Israel during Solomon's reign, has a symbolic meaning that can be revealed in this way. The names "Shushan" and "Shishak" are very similar. Using atbash, the name Shishak (literally, SHSHK) becomes BBL (Babel), the Hebrew spelling for Babylon. Babel also is synonymous with the word *balal*, (BLL) meaning "to mix," or "confuse." This play on words figures conceptually in the code of atbash itself. The name Shushan is not only a reference to the value 666; it has a reverse message as well, becoming BBN or *ba-ben*, meaning "the mixing or confusing of nations."[3]

Susa was also the setting for the struggle of Purim in which the Persian Haman, a figure consistently assigned by theologians as a type of the Antichrist, sought to destroy the Jews. The Hebrew word *purim* means "lots," or the casting of dice in order to determine a future between two possible outcomes. The Messianic symbolism of Purim is found in the Gospel narrative, described by John the Revelator:

Then the soldiers, when they had crucified Jesus, took his garments, and they made four parts, to every soldier a part: and also they took his cloak: now the cloak was without seam, woven from the top throughout. They said therefore among themselves, let us not rend it but cast lots for it, whose it shall be: that the scripture might be fulfilled Psalms 22:18 which saith, "They parted my raiment among them, and for my vesture they did cast lots."[4]

Jesus explained the spiritual importance of a cloak before the crucifixion in the Gospel of John:

If the world hate you, ye know that it hated me before it hated you…if they have persecuted me, they will also persecute you; if they have kept my saying, they will keep yours also….If I had not come and spoken unto them, they had not had sin: but now *they have no cloak for their sin.*[5] (Emphasis mine)

Haman had cast lots to fix the date in which he would exterminate the Jews. This scenario mirrors the satanic plot to eliminate Jesus Christ at the crucifixion, which was ultimately thwarted by his resurrection.

With the intercession of the Jewess Esther (Greek *aster*, "a star") through gaining favor with King Ahasuerus, the evil Haman was killed, along with everyone that conspired against the Jewish race.

Let it be written to reverse the letters devised by Haman… which he wrote to destroy the Jews which are in all the king's provinces. (Esther 8:5)

And the decree [that the Jews should avenge themselves on their enemies] was given at Shushan [modern Susa] the palace.[6]

The name Esther, or "a star," represents one of the most significant symbols of Jesus, "a star that would rise out of Jacob."[7] Jesus came from the lineage of Jacob (later changed to Israel) through Joseph, the husband of Mary, as stated in Matthew 1:16. John expands the meaning of the star in Revelation 2:26, 28, saying,

> And he that overcomes, and keeps my works until the end, to him will I give power over the nations…And I will give him the morning star.

The authors of the Gospel understood the star of Israel as a symbol of Jesus Christ as well. Peter writes:

> We have also a more sure word of prophecy; whereunto ye do well that ye take heed, as unto a light that shines in a dark place, until the day dawn, and the day star arise in your hearts.[8]

The majority of biblical scholars believe that the words of Isaiah 14:12 are addressed to Satan. The King James Version reads, "How you have fallen from heaven, Lucifer, star of the morning." Those relying on this translation have oftentimes struggled to understand why the identity of Jesus as the true "morning star" would be in any way associated with Satan, which is a complete distortion of the translation, however. There is no etymological connection between Christ and Satan as the morning star. The confusion was due to the substitution of the English word "star" for the Hebrew *halel* meaning "bright sounding."

The full sentence in Hebrew is *Halel ben shaker*, which literally translates to "Bright one, son of the dawn." St. Jerome, the author of the Vulgate, rendered *halel* as "Luciferon," or "light bearing." This was close to the Greek Septuagint translation "phosphoros." This was later rendered "morning star" in the King James. Nowhere in the Old Testament is the word *halel* found, except Isaiah 14. In addition, the Hebrew word for star is consistently *kochab*, and not *halel*.

It is a great possibility that the word "hell" in English has its etymological root in *halel*, as the spelling in Hebrew without pronunciation points is HYLL. The influence of this mistranslation has, throughout time, fallen in line with the counterfeiting nature of the one addressed in the very passage. God has permitted this being to wield power over the Earth and men to the point of counterfeiting Christ. In the same chapter of Isaiah where the "star" error occurs in some Bible translations, Satan declares his goals directly:

> I will ascend to heaven, I will exalt my throne above the stars of God; I will sit also upon the mount of congregation, in the sides of the north: I will ascend above the heights of the clouds; I will be like the most High.[9]

Within the end time prophecies, the greatest counterfeit of Satan's design in rebellion against God will take place in the temple of God in Jerusalem, as stated in Daniel 9:27:

> And he shall confirm the covenant with many for one week: and in the midst of the week he shall cause the sacrifice and the oblation to cease, and for the overspreading of abominations he shall make it desolate, even until the consummation, and that determined shall be poured upon the desolate.[10]

The expression of abominations occurs three times in the prophecies of Daniel. The reference is to the "Beast," or "man of sin," who is the cause of the abominations. This is seen in 2 Thessalonians 2:3–4, in Daniel 9:27 and 12:11, and in Matthew 24:15:

> When ye therefore shall see the abomination of desolation, spoken of by Daniel the prophet, stand in the holy place, (whoso readeth, let him understand)…for then shall be great tribulation, such as was not since the beginning of the world to this time, no, nor ever shall be.[11]

As Antiochus Epiphanes was clearly an early type of the Antichrist, slaughtering a pig on the altar of the temple and setting up an idol, he was not the ultimate subject of these prophecies. The words of Christ in AD 33 make it impossible for Anitochus of 165 BC to have been the fulfillment of Daniel's "man of sin." Newton clearly saw the Revelation of John connected with the prophecies of Daniel, about which he wrote:

> This Prophecy is called the Revelation, with respect to the scripture of truth, which Daniel was commanded to shut up and seal, till the time of the end. Daniel sealed it until the time of the end; and until that time comes…these Prophecies of Daniel and John should not be understood till the time of the end: but then some should prophesy out of them in an afflicted and mournful state for a long time, and that but darkly, so as to convert but few. But in the very end, the Prophecy should be so far interpreted as to convince many. Then, saith Daniel, many shall run to and fro, and knowledge shall be encreased.[12]

There is also a fascinating relationship between the letterform of the mark of the Antichrist, which is six hundred, sixty, and six, written in Greek

χξς

Fig. 47. Image by author

and the first act of rebellion of mankind, manifested in the fall of Adam and Eve.

As investigated earlier, the Greeks inherited the letters for their language from the Phoenician and Israelite traders from the texts of the Old Testament. The earliest versions of the Old Testament used this same phonetic "pictographic" script. The first letter, *chi* (*x*), equaling 600, was a Greek transformation of the Phoenician letter *tav* (*x*), a symbol of a tree or crossed sticks which meant "a mark" *Xi*

Fig. 48. Image by author

symbolized a branch and equals 60. The final letter, *stigma*

Fig. 49. Image by author

actually meaning "a mark" is a later Greek addition to the Phonetic alphabet. It symbolizes a serpent and was used to represent the number six. The pictographic meaning in Greek of the number 666 is, then, *a serpent on the branch of a tree*, exactly the scene of Genesis 3:1.

The archaeological remains of a memorial to the event of Luke, chapter 8 stands on the eastern coast of the Sea of Galilee:

And they arrived at the country of the Gadarenes, which is over against Galilee. And when he went forth to land, there met him out of the city a certain man, which had devils long time, and ware no clothes, neither abode in [any] house, but in the tombs. When he saw Jesus, he cried out, and fell down before him, and with a loud voice said, What have I to do with thee, Jesus, [thou] Son of God most high? I beseech thee, torment me not....And Jesus asked him, saying, What is thy name? And he said, Legion: because many devils were entered into him.

And they besought him that he would not command them to go out into the deep. And there was a herd of many swine feeding on the mountain: and they besought him that he would suffer them to enter into them. And he suffered them. Then went the devils out of the man, and entered into the swine: and the herd ran violently down a steep place into the lake, and was choked.[13]

Frederic William Farrar explained the location of the event in his book *The Gospel According to St. Luke*, which was published in 1881:

[T]he herd ran violently [down a steep place] into the lake. Rather, down the precipice. Near Kherza is the only spot on the entire lake where a steep slope sweeps down to within a few yards of the sea, into which the herd would certainly have plunged if hurried by any violent impulse down the hill.[14]

This location was verified in 1967, when a bulldozer struck the remains of the Byzantine monastery of Kherza (Kursi) during the construction of a road along the eastern shore of the Sea of Galilee. In the 5th century AD, the monastery of the Miracle of the Swine was established at this site, which had previously been abandoned due to fire, and in subsequent years was covered over with silt.

In 1980, a small chapel was discovered in a cave adjacent to the monastery. Christian tradition ties this cave with the place the possessed man revealed himself to Jesus and where Jesus cleansed him.[15] According to many historical references, a legion was a chief subdivision of the Roman army, which contained about 6,000 infantry.[16] From the cave chapel of Kursi, to the foundation stone of the temple mount, there are 66.06 nautical miles.

In an article published in September 1983 of *Smithsonian* magazine, the archaeologist Juris Zarins reported the discovery of four rivers described in the book of Genesis describing the location of the Garden of Eden through the use of LANDSAT photographs.

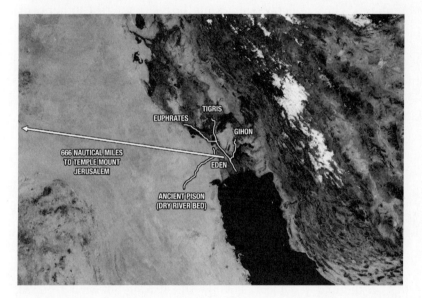

Fig. 50. Courtesy of NASA World Wind

The straightforward logic of the article is intriguing. If Eden had existed as a literal feature on the Earth, it could also exhibit some symbolic relationship in distance between itself and the temple of Jerusalem, which is supported by these findings. Between each location is exactly 666 nautical miles. Both the distances between the legendary site of Eden or the known location of Susa from the location of the foundation stone on the temple mount are 666 nautical miles, and the *modern* latitude and longitude coordinates temple site itself lies at latitude 31 degrees, 14 minutes north, and longitude 35 degrees, 46 minutes east. Added together, these values equal 66.60.

At first glance, the number 666 does not seem related to the Garden of Eden or the temple of Jerusalem. These places seem unconnected with the mark of the beast in Revelation 13:18. However, with this mark, this future ruler will set up a worldwide system of trade. The Latin word for trade is *mercury*. Here again the Roman version of the Babylonian god Nebo and Egyptian, Thoth, surfaces in context with prophecy. The number 666 represents the full counterfeit authority of Satan over mankind. The Antichrist will usurp the symbols of Christ, and distort them to fit the same pagan corruptions from antiquity. He will be accepted as the true messiah by the inhabitants of the earth and set himself in the temple of God claiming to be God. Similarly, as the Hebrew root *nebo* represents a prophet, the false prophet of revelation will uphold the Antichrist's rule over the earth. This underscores the significance of the Ark's location at Mount Nebo, and its function as the oracle of God. In the single case where the Ark was placed in a heathen temple of the Philistines (of the god Dagon) the result was judgment with plague and death. It may be that when the Ark is found and replaced in the temple of Jerusalem under the Antichrist, the entire world will be judged, as the Bible explains that all the world will be his kingdom.

In the Old Testament, 1 Kings 10:14, King Solomon acquired 666 talents of gold in one year for the construction of his palace. This he built while also constructing the temple of God. This number is also found connected with the census of the priests that rebuilt the temple after the exile in Babylon. Besides Revelation, these are the only other places in the Bible that mention the number, yet both connect it with the temple's construction. Six hundred sixty-six also shows up in the chronology of the first and second temples and the empires that oppressed Israel. The Assyrian empire lasted 666 years before it was conquered by Babylon. The Roman Empire occupied

Jerusalem for 666 years between the battle of Actium in 31 BC to the Saracen conquest in AD 636.[17]

The Temple of Solomon was destroyed by the Babylonians in 587 BC and the second, built by Zerubbabel, was destroyed in AD 70 by the Romans. Both temples fell on the same day of the Hebrew calendar, the 9th of Av. The number of years between each temple's demise measured in 360-day biblical years is 666 years.

$$587 \text{ BC (temple's destruction by Babylon)} + 70$$
$$(\text{temple's destruction by Rome})$$
$$= 657 \text{ solar years}$$
$$657 \times 365 = 239{,}805 \text{ solar days.}$$
$$239{,}805 / 360 = 666$$

The number "of the beast" consistently appears in relationship to the temple, and opposition or corruption of it points to the prototype of spiritual and governmental rebellion in Babylonian. The religious authority of the end of days will be Babylon the Great, according to Revelation. As the number 666 reveals the design of Babylon, the design of God's plan in response to Babylon incorporated the number of the writing on the wall (2,520). This number reveals the Sacred Cubit, the proportions of the temple and of prophetic time. In the investigation of the number 666, there is one other significant connection that exists. Beyond the construction of the temple in Jerusalem and the rebirth of Israel as a nation, the rise of enemies of the Jews is an unfortunate prophetic fulfillment. In modern times, the greatest of these is militant Islam.

The researcher Altaf Simon, has suggested that the Greek morphology of letters is related to a unique Islamic phrase, *bism Allah*, meaning in Arabic, "in the name of Allah." This is used extensively in Islam on documents.[18] According to Simon, who was once himself Moslem, the Arabic words closely match the Greek for 666. These appear as a mirror image of the stigma and *Xi* in the words "in the name of Allah," followed by the x, *chi* in Greek, as the crossed swords of Islam. This phrase is spoken before the sacrifice of animals in Allah's name while facing the direction of Mecca, Saudi Arabia, the holiest site in Islam.

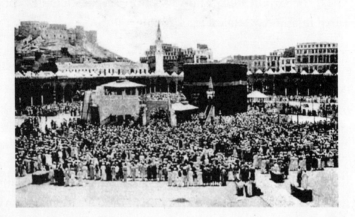

Fig. 51. The Kabbah shrine in Mecca, Saudi Arabia, the holiest site of Islam. Reprinted from Emily Ruete, *Memoirs of an Arabian Princess,* trans. Lionel Strachey (New York: Doubleday, Page & Co., 1907), 44.

This association by itself is intriguing, however, with the addition of the linear significance of the "ultimate science" and the importance placed on the direction Moslems face towards Mecca during worship, the connection is astonishing. Both Jews and Moslems have an ancient tradition of facing their most holy sites when praying. In Islam, this direction is called the *Qibla*, and is related to the Hebrew word *qibal* (to aquire or stand in front of something).[19] The Hebrew word *Khabal* (measuring line)[20] is also closely related to *Qibla*.

The Old Testament records a practice of the Jews to face Jerusalem while praying. (1 Kings 8:29, 34, 44, 48; 2 Chronicles 6:21,34; Daniel 6:10). This was predominantly practiced during the times of exile. The synagogues that coexisted with the temple in Jerusalem during the first century were not built in a specific orientation to the temple. After the Temple was destroyed in AD 70, many synagogues were built with both entrances and windows facing the temple.[21] The Talmud explains:

> If [one in the Diaspora] was riding on an ass, he should dismount [to say *tefillah*, i.e., the eighteen benedictions] If he cannot dismount, he should turn his face towards Jerusalem. If he cannot turn his face, he should direct his heart toward the holy of holies. If he was journeying on a ship or a wagon, or a raft, he should direct his heart toward the holy of holies.[22]

The comments of this passage, located in the Midrashim, Tosefta, and the Palestinian and Babylonian Talmuds, explain the requirements in greater detail:

> They who stand in prayer outside the land [of Israel] turn their faces towards land of Israel and pray, as it is said, "when they pray to You in the direction of their land." [23]

> They who stand in the Land of Israel turn their faces toward Jerusalem and as is said: "and they pray towards this house." (2 Chronicles 6:32).

> They who stand in the Temple direct their hearts toward the Holy of Holies and pray, as is said "and then they pray toward this place."[24]

While in Babylon, Daniel prayed toward the temple three times a day through the windows of his upper room.[25] These were prayers of supplication for the reinstatement of the Jews to their land as well as the rebuilding of the temple itself. The temple's orientation from Babylon and the relationship of distance with the year of the fall of Babylon manifest supernaturally within the book of Daniel.

During the rise of Islam in the 6ᵗʰ century AD, the Jews continued to face the temple from their location in countries of dispersion.
Muhammad followed the same tradition at the beginning of the formation of Islam from AD 622 until AD 624.[26] Later, the direction of
praying towards Jerusalem was changed for Muslims to the Kab'ah
stone in Mecca in Arabia. The Qur'an states:

The fools among the people will say: "What hath turned
them from the Qibla to which they were used?" Say: To God
belong both east and West: He guideth whom He will to a
Way that is straight. Thus, have We made of you an Ummat
justly balanced, that ye might be witnesses over the nations,
and the Apostle a witness over yourselves; and We appointed
the Qibla to which thou wast used, only to test those who
followed the Apostle from those who would turn on their
heels (From the Faith). Indeed it was (A change) momentous,
except to those guided by God. And never would God Make
your faith of no effect. For God is to all people Most surely
full of kindness, Most Merciful. We see the turning of thy face
(for guidance) to the heavens: now Shall We turn thee to a
Qiblat that shall please thee. Turn then Thy face in the direction of the sacred Mosque: Wherever ye are, turn your faces
in that direction. The people of the Book know well that that
is the truth from their Lord. Nor is God unmindful of what
they do. Even if thou wert to bring to the people of the Book
all the Signs (together), they would not follow Thy Qibla;
nor art thou going to follow their Qibla; nor indeed will they
follow each other's Qibla. If thou after the knowledge hath
reached thee, Wert to follow their (vain) desires—then wert
thou Indeed (clearly) in the wrong.[27]

In this passage, Mohammad was condemning the Jews, calling
them "the people of the Book," i.e., the Old Testament, for ques-

tioning the reversal of the direction of prayer towards the temple of
Jerusalem to the Kab'ah in Mecca. The rescission of facing Jerusalem
was in complete opposition to words of "the book." God appointed
the temple of Jerusalem as His sacred residence for eternity, saying
to Solomon, "I have hallowed this house that you have built to put
My name there forever; and My eyes and My heart shall be there
forever."[28]

At the temple's completion, King Solomon reiterated God's promise concerning the direction of prayer towards His dwelling place on
earth:

> For Your eyes are open to this house night and day, toward the
> place of which You have said, My name shall be there; to lis-
> ten to the prayer which Your servant prays toward this place.
> And you shall listen to the supplication of Your servant, and
> of Your people Israel, when they shall pray toward this place;
> yea, you shall listen in your dwelling place, in Heaven; and
> You shall hear and shall forgive.[29]

A provision of blessing to nations that prayed towards the temple
of Jerusalem was included in the prayer of Solomon, which is a blessing that Muhammad rejected:

> And also, to the stranger who is not of Your people Israel, and
> has come from a land afar off for your name's sake—for they
> shall hear of Your great name, and of Your strong hand, and
> of Your out-stretched arm—and he shall have come in and
> prayed towards this house. You shall hear in Heaven, Your
> dwelling place, and shall do according to all that the stranger
> call to You for, so that all the peoples of the earth may know
> Your name, to fear You as do Your people Israel, and to know
> that your name has been called on this house which I have
> built.[30]

The practice of facing Mecca is included in every religious ritual of Islam. In a mosque, the *mihrab* or niche in the wall indicates the direction of Mecca. All Moslem cemeteries are aligned towards the *qibla* with the heads of the interred facing Mecca. Animals are sacrificed in this direction and many activities of regular life are also performed towards the qibla. Moslems believe that any task performed in this direction determines whether the outcome is good or useless.

In the early history of Islam, Moslems invented the qibla indicator along with the astrolabe establishing a religious connection with the navigation of the Earth. The earliest version of the qibla may have been a line connecting Jerusalem and Mecca. This proposes a moral and religious contrast between these religious centers. With respect to their distance apart from each other, this contrast is even more remarkable. The distance between the Kab'ah stone in Mecca to the temple mount is 666 nautical miles, which is accurate to the foot.

Fig. 52. Reprint of postcard with drawing from Charles Hamilton Smith Victoria and Albert Museum, London 1807.

Mecca is the focus of the religious world of Islam. Every Moslem tries to make at least one *hajj* (pilgrimage) to Mecca during his or her lifetime. While in the city, the pilgrims make a *twaf,* a circling of the

Kab'ah seven times. This act represents the seven heavens and humanity's interaction between the spiritual and terrestrial planes. Through the enactment of these rituals at Mecca, the Moslem draws to the center of a faith at enmity with Judaism. The claim of ownership the Jews maintain over Jerusalem and the temple mount is in diametric opposition to Islam's religious primacy. Moslems believe that Jerusalem was visited by Mohammad and made it their chief shrine after Mecca in AD 637. The mosque of Omar, better known as the Dome of the Rock, was built over the place where legend claims Mohammad leapt to heaven on his steed.[31] Mohammad's life has been enshrouded by a mass of legends and traditions (contained in the Hadith). Mohammad firmly believed in his position as the last of the prophets and a successor of Jesus Christ, and he is considered to have been sinless by most Moslems.

The book of Islam, the Qur'an, has various spellings (Quran, Koran), in Arabic it means "to recite," or "that which is spoken." The Hebrew words that are phonetically equivalent have very different meanings. The word, *keh-ren* means (a horn),[32] and the word *khaw-rone* means, a burning of anger, sore displeasure, fierce, fury and wrath.[33]

The Arabic and Hebrew languages descended from a common Semitic origin.[34] The word *Moslem* in Arabic means, "one who submits himself to god" and the word *Meshulam* in Hebrew means "allied."[35] In Hebrew, the word similar to the name Mohammad is *mehoomaw* and means "confusion" or "uproar," "destruction," "discomfiture," "trouble," "tumult," "vexation," and "vexed."[36]

מְהוּמָה f. (from the root הוּם), *commotion, disturbance*, Isa. 22:5; Deut. 7:23; 2 Chron. 15:5. מְהוּמַת־מָוֶת deadly disturbance, 1 Sa. 5:9, 11. Used of the irregular and voluptuous life of a rich man, Pro. 15:16.

Fig. 53. Reprinted from Wilhelm Gesenius, *Hebrew and Chaldee Lexicon to the Old Testament Scriptures*, trans. and ed. S. P. Tregelles (Grand Rapids, Michigan: Baker, 1979), 101.

The Hebrew word *Arab*, (spelled ayin, resh, beth) means "to mix," " to grow dark," or "sterile," as related to the desert country of Arabia.[37] However, when spelled aleph, resh, beth, the word means "to lurk," "lie in ambush," or "lie in wait."[38]

Some Islamic scholars have suggested that the name Allah is the same as the Hebrew name *Elohim*. This fallacious etymology is a source of confusion for many Moslems that neither read the Old Testament nor understand Hebrew. The Arabic letters of Allah correspond only to the Hebrew *el-o-ah* or *aw-law* in the analysis of Thayer's Lexicon:

אֱלוֹהַּ (with prefix and suffix לֶאֱלֹהַּ Dan. 11:38; לֶאֱלֹהוֹ Hab. 1:11), m. *God* (Arab. اللّٰه, الٰه, with art. اللّٰه of the true God; Syr. ܐܰܠܳܗܳܐ; Chald. אֱלָהּ).

Fig. 54. Reprinted from Wilhelm Gesenius, *Hebrew and Chaldee Lexicon to the Old Testament Scriptures*, Translated and edited by S. P. Tregelles (**Grand Rapids, Michigan: Baker, 1979**), 200.

The Arabic pronunciation "al-lah" or "el-o-ah" is dissimilar to the pronunciation of the Hebrew "el-aw" or "el-ohim" meaning "God Almighty."[39] The former has two meanings that correspond to Hebrew, *aw-law* means "to curse", "swear," or "execration"[40] and *el-o-ah* means "any god."[41] The word *el-o-ah* is found in Daniel 11:37–39, 2 Chronicles 32:15, and Nehemiah 9:17, of which the Thayer's Hebrew lexicon has this entry:

There is a proverbial expression (that uses the form *el-o-ah* for god) Habakkuk 1:11, of an obstinate self-confident man, "whose strength is as his god," i.e., who despises every god and confides in his own strong hand and sword. This is similar to the use of the word in Job 12:6 "who bears his god in his hand."[42]

The word *mecca* in Hebrew has many applications.[43]

מַכָּה f. (from the root נָכָה) pl. מַכּוֹת, more rarely מַכִּים 2 Ki. 8:29; 9:15.

(1) *a smiting, striking*, Deut. 25:3; 2 Ch. 2:9, חִטִּים מַכּוֹת commonly taken to be for חִטֵּי מַכּוֹת *wheat beaten out*, or *threshed*, but perhaps the reading is corrupted from חִטִּים מַכֹּלֶת 1Ki. 5:25. Especially used of *plagues*, i. e. calamities inflicted by God, Lev. 26:21; Deu. 28:59, 61; 29:21.

(2) *a wound*, 1 Ki. 22:35; Isa. 1:6.

(3) *slaughter* in battle, Josh. 10:10, 20; Jud. 11:33; 15:8; or wrought by God, 1 Sa. 6:19.

Fig. 55. Reprinted from Wilhelm Gesenius, *Hebrew and Chaldee Lexicon to the Old Testament Scriptures,* trans. and ed. S. P. Tregelles (Grand Rapids, Michigan: Baker, 1979), 78.

The word for the holy shrine in Mecca also has meaning in Hebrew. A *khabaw* is a primary root meaning "to hide or to do secretly."[44]

חָבָא unused in Kal, i.q. חָבָה TO HIDE, compare the kindred roots חָפָא, חָפַף. Arab. خَبِئ, Æth. ኀብአ: to hide; also خَمَا for خَمُو to put out fire, properly to hide; Conj. X. to hide oneself.

Fig. 56. Reprinted from Wilhelm Gesenius, *Hebrew and Chaldee Lexicon to the Old Testamament Scriptures,* trans. and ed. S. P. Tregelles (Grand Rapids, Michigan: Baker, 1979), 166.

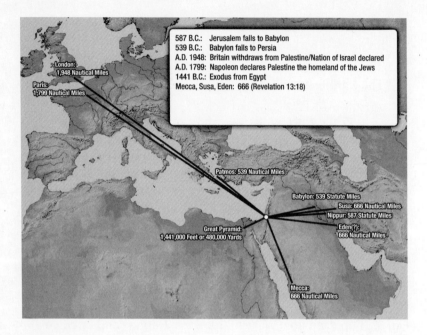

587 B.C.:   Jerusalem falls to Babylon
539 B.C.:   Babylon falls to Persia
A.D. 1948:   Britain withdraws from Palestine/Nation of Israel declared
A.D. 1799:   Napoleon declares Palestine the homeland of the Jews
1441 B.C.:   Exodus from Egypt
Mecca, Susa, Eden: 666 (Revelation 13:18)

London:
1,948 Nautical Miles

Paris:
1,799 Nautical Miles

Patmos: 539 Nautical Miles

Babylon: 539 Statute Miles
Susa: 666 Nautical Miles
Nippur: 587 Statute Miles

Great Pyramid:
1,441,000 Feet or 480,000 Yards

Eden(?):
666 Nautical Miles

Mecca:
666 Nautical Miles

NOTES

1. Daniel 8:1, 2. KJV
2. Daniel 8:16 KJV
3. Strong's Hebrew dictionary # 894. *James Strong Exhaustive Concordance of the Bible*. AMG Publishers edition, World Bible Publishers, Inc. 1986 Iowa Falls, Ia.
4. John 1: 23, 24 KJV
5. John 15:18–22 KJV
6. Esther 8:13,14 KJV
7. Numbers 24:17 KJV
8. II Peter 1:19 KJV
9. Isaiah 14:13–14 KJV
10. Daniel 9: 27 KJV
11. Matthew 24:15, 21 KJV
12. Isaac Newton, *Observations upon the Prophecies of Daniel, and the Apocalypse of St. John* Part II, Chapter I, (London: 1733). Professor Rob Iliffe., Newton Papers Project University of Sussex, East Sussex. UK.2007 www.newtonproject.sussex.ac.uk
13. Luke 8:26–37 KJV
14. Farrar, D.D. Archdeacon of Westminster, *The Gospel According to St. Luke*. edited for the syndics of the University Press. © (London UK : University Press, 1891).
15. Vassilios Tzaferis, *The Excavations of Kursi-Gergesa*. Volume I Pg.16 (English Series). Publishers. c.Atiqot. Israel 1983
16. William Smith. *Smith's Bible Dictionary*. Hendrickson Publishers; Rev Sub edition 1990 Peabody, Massachusetts, U.S.A.
17. Ethelbert Bullinger, *Number in Scripture* (Kregel, Grand Rapids, MI 1967).
18. Altaf Simon,"Peace or beast"Abrahamic-Faith LondonWC1N 3XX England (UK).

19. Ibid. Strong's Hebrew dictionary # 6903.
20. Ibid. Strong's Hebrew Dictionary # 2256.
21. Joan R. Branham., *Sacred Space under Erasure in Ancient Synagogues and Early Church. The Art Bulletin*, Vol. 74, No. 3 (Sep., 1992), pp. 375–394 Duke University. Durham, NC
22. Talmud. Berakot 4:5–6. Translated by Michael L. Rodkinson. New York: New Talmud Pub. Co. 1903.
23. 1 Kings 8:48 KJV
24. Israel Finkelstien. and N. A. Silberman, *The Bible Unearthed: Archaeology's New Vision of Ancient Israel and the Origin of Its Sacred Texts.* Sifre to Deuteronomy Pg. 47 New York USA: Free Press, 2001.
25. Daniel 6: 11 KJV
26. Columbia Encyclopedia, Pg. 1106.Edited by William Bridgewater. Columbia Universty Press, London, UK. 1963
27. Qur'an, Surah 2:144. Sayed A. A. Razwy (Editor), Abdullah Yusuf Ali (Translator) Published by Tahrike Tarsile, New York 1999
28. 1 Kings 9:3 KJV
29. I Kings 8:29 KJV
30. I Kings 8:41–43Hendrickson's Interlinear bible. Jay P. Green (Editor, Translator) Hendrickson Publishers Inc.,U.S 2005
31. Qur'an, Surah 17:1 Sayed A. A. Razwy (Editor), Abdullah Yusuf Ali (Translator) Published by Tahrike Tarsile, New York 1999
32. Ibid. Strong's Hebrew Dictionary # 7161.
33. Ibid, Strong's Hebrew Dictionary #2740.
34. *Ethnologue: Languages of the World*, Fifteenth edition. Raymond G Gordon, Jr. (ed.), Dallas, Tex.: SIL International. 2005.
35. Ibid. Strong's Hebrew Dictionary # 4918.
36. Ibid. Strong's Hebrew Dictionary # 4103.
37. Ibid. Strong's Hebrew Dictionary # 6152.
38. Ibid. Strong's Hebrew Dictionary # 693.
39. Ibid. Strong's Hebrew Dictionary # 426, 430.

40. Ibid. Strong's Hebrew Dictionary # 422.
41. Ibid. Strong's Hebrew Dictionary # 433.
42. Ibid.
43. Ibid. Strong's Hebrew Dictionary # 4229, 4347, from the root "naka" to smite # 5217.
44. Ibid. Strong's Hebrew Dictionary # 2244.

16

ROME

Newton believed that a revived Rome would be the prominent ruling force during biblical end time events. He was well acquainted with the havoc of intermittent Catholic rule in his own country and Europe as well, as biblical interpretation of both Revelation and the book of Daniel in his day. Many early church scholars shared his views of the dominance of Rome in the end times. Hippolytus of Rome from the 3rd century AD wrote:

> A fourth beast, dreadful and terrible; it had iron teeth and claws of brass. And who are these but the Romans? Which (kingdom) is meant by the iron—the kingdom which is now established; for the legs of that (image) were of iron. And after this, what remains, beloved, but the toes of the feet of the image, in which part is iron and part clay, mixed together?[1]

St. Cyril of Jerusalem (ca. 315–386) wrote:

But this aforesaid Antichrist is to come when the times of the Roman Empire shall have been fulfilled, and the end of the world is now drawing near. There shall rise up together ten kings of the Romans, reigning in different parts perhaps, but all about the same time; and after these an eleventh, the Antichrist, who by his magical craft shall seize upon the Roman power; and of the kings who reigned before him, three he shall humble, and the remaining seven he shall keep in subjection to himself.[2]

Newton was convinced that the revived Roman Empire described in prophecy had its fulfillment in the Catholic Church, and he based his chronology of end time events on key dates of its formation. This reasoning seems to have led Newton to a dead end in his research towards a discovery of prophetic timing. Although the methods Newton used to calibrate history with the future were insufficient, the principles behind them were valid.

In the context of Rome's significance in both the spiritual force of the end times as well its ruling dominance over Jerusalem during the first advent of Christ, it is worth looking at the distance between these two cities. One would anticipate that the time/distance phenomenon would manifest.

There are exactly 1,431.81 statute miles between Rome's historic center and the temple mount foundation stone, which also equals 7,560,000 feet. This distance seems prophetically and geometrically insignificant. With respect to Rome in the end times and especially Jerusalem, the measure of distance between these two locations would seem to demand a correlation with the unifying number 2,520. This number is recorded three times in both Revelation and Daniel. Newton's works on these books inextricably linked Rome as the spiritual center of apostasy in the end times. Many other reputable eschatologists throughout history have drawn this conclusion as well. However, the distance is quintessentially 2,520.

$$7,560,000 / 3 = 2,520,000 \text{ yards.}$$
$$2,520,000 \text{ yards to Rome has } 90,720,002.21 \text{ inches.}$$
$$2,520,000 / 360 = 7,000.$$

As Newton had anticipated, the prophecy of Daniel connects through linear geometry associated with the temple.

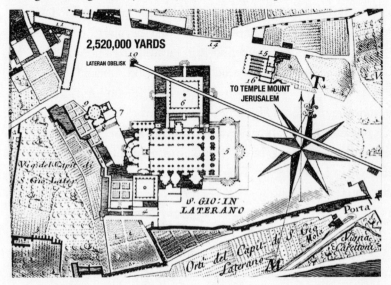

Fig. 57. Reprinted from William R. Shepherd, *The Historical Atlas* (New York: Henry Holt & Company, 1923), 24.

This measurement is taken from the temple mount in Jerusalem and the Lateran Obelisk at the site of the oldest Basilica in Rome. This is the seat of the Pope's authority in the Church, the Lateran Basilica, which is dedicated to the author of Revelation, St. John. The Catholic Encyclopedia actually states:

> The "Lateran Basilica of St. John"…ranks first among the great patriarchal basilicas of Rome. Many are unaware that it, not St. Peter's Basilica, is the cathedral of Rome and the seat of the Pope as bishop of Rome.

Among Catholics, this basilica holds the title of *ecumenical mother church* (mother church of the whole inhabited world). Because it contains the papal throne (*Cathedra Romana*), it ranks above all other churches in the Catholic Church, even above St. Peter's Basilica in the Vatican. A great many donations from the popes and other benefactors to the basilica are recorded in the "Liber Pontificalis," and its splendour at an early period was such that it became known as the "Basilica Aurea," or Golden Church. This was the period of its greatest magnificence, when Dante speaks of it as beyond all human achievements.[3]

Before the Roman Empire was converted to Catholicism, this was the site of the Lateran palace. The Lateran Obelisk, the largest standing authentic obelisk in the world, was originally from the Karnak Temple in Luxor, Egypt. This obelisk was erected over the remains of the Lateran palace.

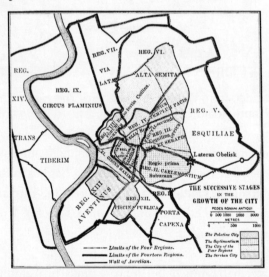

Fig. 58. The Lateran Obelisk's position at "Regio Prima" (mother church of the whole inhabited world). Reprinted from William R. Shepherd, *The Historical Atlas* (New York: Henry Holt & Company, 1923), 30.

In AD 311, Constantine gave the palace to Pope Melchiade and for about a thousand years, it continued as the principal residence of the popes. After the departure of the popes from Rome to Avignon, France and two fires, in 1307 and 1361, the palace fell from its original glory. When the popes did return to Rome in 1377, they resided first at Santa Maria in Trastevere, then at Santa Maria Maggiore, and then finally at the Vatican.

The Lateran Basilica is built over the site of the palace and has several chapels. The oldest is called the Sancta Sanctorum or Holy of Holies and dates from the 8ᵗʰ century. It serves as a private chapel for the Pope. Above its entrance is the inscription:

> *NON EST IN TOTO SANCTIOR ORBE LOCUS;*
> "There is no holier place in all the world."

On the façade of the Lateran Basilica itself is an inscription that proclaims:

SACROSANCTA LATERANENSIS ECCLESIA OMNIUM
URBIS ET ORBIS ECCLESIARUM MATER ET CAPUT

Which translates to "The Most Holy Lateran Church, Mother and Head of all churches of the city and the World."[4]

The significance of being both a "mother" and head of all Catholic Churches in the world immediately brings to mind this description from St. John's Revelation:

And upon her forehead [was] a name written, MYSTERY, BABYLON THE GREAT, THE MOTHER OF HARLOTS AND ABOMINATIONS OF THE EARTH. And I saw the woman drunken with the blood of the saints, and with the blood of the martyrs of Jesus: and when I saw her, I wondered with great admiration. And the angel said unto me, Wherefore

didst thou marvel? I will tell thee the mystery of the woman,
and of the beast that carrieth her, which hath the seven heads
and ten horn....And here [is] the mind which hath wisdom.
The seven heads are seven mountains, on which the woman
sitteth.[5]

The Jamieson-Fausset-Brown Bible Commentary from 1871, explains the content of this passage:

> Seven heads and seven mountains—The connection between
> *mountains* and *kings* must be deeper than the mere outward
> fact to which incidental allusion is made, that Rome (the then
> world city) is on seven hills (whence heathen Rome had a
> national festival called *Septimontium,* the feast of the seven-
> hilled city [PLUTARCH]; and on the imperial coins, just
> as here, she is represented as a *woman seated on seven hills.*
> Coin of Vespasian, described by CAPTAIN SMYTH [*Roman
> Coins,* p. 310; ACKERMAN, 1, p. 87])…. *The woman sitting
> on the seven hills* implies the Old and New Testament Church
> conforming to, and resting on, the world power, that is, on all
> the seven world kingdoms.[6]

The Basilica is called *Lateran* which means, "hidden frog" from
the two Latin words, *latente* (to hide), and *rana* (a frog).[7] The reason
for this strangely named place can be found in the book of *The Lives
of the Saints* by Jacobus de Voragine, Archbishop of Genoa, 1275. The
name stems from the event in which the Emperor Nero had slain his
own mother:

> The physicians and masters blamed him, and said the son
> should not slay his mother that had borne him with sorrow
> and pain. Then said he: Make me with child, and after to be
> delivered, that I may know what pain my mother suffered.

Which by craft they gave to him a young frog to drink, and grew in his belly, and then he said: But if ye make me to be delivered I shall slay you all; and so they gave him such a drink that he had a vomit and cast out the frog, and bare him on hand that because that he abode not his time it was mis-shapen, which yet he made to be kept.[8]

Nero ordered that the frog be kept as his heir at his palace in the area now occupied by the "hidden frog" Basilica. Jacobus goes on to say that after Nero committed suicide, "the Romans returned and found the frog, and threw it out of the city and there burnt it."[9]

This distasteful story has a parallel in the visions of St. John in Revelation 16:13:

And I saw three unclean spirits like frogs come out of the mouth of the dragon, and out of the mouth of the beast, and out of the mouth of the false prophet.[10]

In the Egyptian pantheon, the goddess Heqet had a frog head and was associated with childbirth and resurrection. She was believed to preside over the fetus, having a resemblance to the frog, and its development in the womb. Later in Egyptian history, she was associated with the resurrection of Osiris as the goddess who brought him back from the dead. Depictions of Heqet as a frog in the early Christian era have been found bearing the inscription "I am the resurrection."[11]

The function of Heqet as a goddess in Egypt was renounced through the plague of frogs that inundated the land and then died in heaps in Exodus 8:5. Hecate, the Greek version of the Egyptian Heqet, was portrayed as both a virgin and a whore. She was also considered a goddess of *three forms* and was portrayed as a maiden, a mother, and a crone. The frogs that issue from the mouths of the dragon, beast, and false prophet, in addition to being intimately connected to the seat of authority in Rome, seem to represent world religious forces that corrupt and oppress the Gospel.

The late Bible commentator, Albert Barnes, expanded this view nearly 150 years ago. In his book *Notes on Revelation*, Barnes connected the frogs of Revelation 16:13 with three religious world powers that, with respect to the present world scene, seem uncannily accurate.

One (frog) seemed to issue out of the mouth of the *dragon* Satan, the great enemy of the church; perhaps here Satan represents a form of Heathenism or Paganism. The idea then, is that at the time referred to, there would be some manifestation of the power of Satan in the heathen nations, which would be bold, arrogant, proud, loquacious, hostile to truth, and which would be well represented by the hoarse murmur of the frog.

> And out of the mouth of the *beast*, [is] the Papacy, as being as hostile as ever to the truth, and able to enter into a combination, secret or avowed, with the "dragon" and the "false prophet," to oppose the reign of truth upon the earth…And out of the mouth of the *false prophet* would seem then to refer to same power that was similar to that of the beast, and that was to share the same fate in the overthrow of the enemies of the gospel. As to the application of this, there is no opinion so probable as that it alludes to the Mohammedan power. The name "false prophet" would better than any other describe that power, and would naturally suggest it in future times—for to no one that has ever appeared in our world, could the name be so properly applied as to Mohammed; and what is said will be found to agree with the facts in regard to that power, as, in connection with the Papacy and with Paganism, constituting the sum of the obstruction to the spread of the gospel around the world.…The heathen, the Mohammedan, and the Papal portions of the earth still embrace so large a portion of the globe, that it might be said

that what would affect those powers now would influence the whole world.[12]

In connection with the contemporary trend of Catholic ecumenicalism, embracing all religions as valid and Barnes' identification of the frog-like spirits agrees with the context of Revelation.

As Rome appears to be the focus of the end time force of world spirituality, its distance from the temple also corresponds with the week of seven years (2,520 days) mentioned in the prophecies of Daniel and John. At the midpoint of the seven-year covenant set up by the Antichrist (at day 1,260) at which he defiles the holy place of the rebuilt temple of Jerusalem causing the sacrifices and offering to cease, the Antichrist consummates his global religious rebellion. Pertaining to this event and the duration in which it continues, Daniel 12:6 poses the question: "How long shall it be to the end of these wonders?"

[It shall be] for a time, times, and an half [1,260 days]; and when he shall have accomplished to scatter the power of the holy people, all these [things] shall be finished.[13]

The prophecy addressing the midpoint of the seven-year covenant of the Antichrist is examined in St. John's Revelation. One thousand two hundred sixty is also found in 12:6:

And the woman fled into the wilderness, where she hath a place prepared of God, that they should feed her there a thousand two hundred [and] threescore days [1,260 days].[14]

Isaac Newton wrote concerning the identity of the woman from Revelation 12:6, "Because the Church of God is frequently compared to a women therefore is this figure used chiefly to express the affliction of the Church under her enemies."[15] However, Newton also compared a woman to the nation of Israel:

[The] dispersed Jews were with child of a new polity & laboured long as a woman in travail, by the fall of their enemies to work themselves deliverance & bring it forth, but brought forth nothing: but at length when the indignation was over God should overthrow their enemies & restore Israel.[16]

Newton's summary of the woman in Revelation 12:6 indicates that Israel would become a nation again in the end times, in which the number 1,260 is prominent in the timing of Israel's persecution, but is also the beginning of its final salvation. It is an interesting feature of the city of Rome that the Tiber (dividing) River actually does divide the city. In Daniel 12:6, 1,260 is discussed by two angels on either side of *a river*, although the Elahi River (from the Hebrew root *evel*) was the scene of the prophecy, as examined in previous chapters. That there are 666 statute miles from the temple in Jerusalem to the location where Daniel received the prophecy of the Antichrist remains consistent in the *priscia theologia* suggested by Newton, since the Antichrist is also the Beast whose number is 666.

The number 2,520 is a signature of completion of plans of the Almighty and is found in both prophecy and geometry connected to the temple, the Ark, as well as the completion of creation. Its *division* represents Satan's enmity towards the completion of those plans. Revelation and Daniel both reveal the fullest expression of rebellion against God as taking place on the 1,260[th] day of the 2,520-day covenant. This is the point in which a war commences in heaven itself, the temple of God is defiled and the two witnesses of the Messiah are killed and left in the streets of Jerusalem.

The spiritual alignment of Rome against the Kingdom of God is emphasized both in the prophecies of Daniel and John. Newton and other eschatologists have written that Rome existed as an empire during Christ's first advent and will exist again at Christ's second advent. Rome was the spiritual and political authority of the world when Jesus Christ was crucified and rose from the dead. A revived Roman

Empire will oppose Christ and the resurrection of the saints at His second coming. Accordingly, the center of Rome's authority measured in distance between Jerusalem's temple (2,520,000 yards) numerically demonstrates the completion of God's plans through the spiritual opposition of Rome in the end of days.

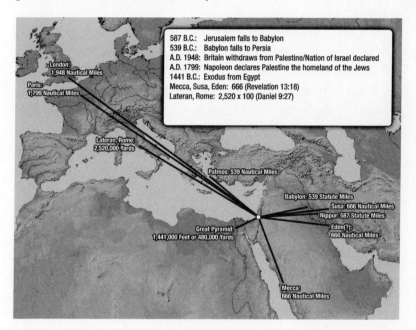

NOTES

1. Isaac Newton, *Treatise on Christ and Antichrist.* The Newton Project—University of Sussex, East Sussex London: 2007 www. newtonproject.sussex.ac.uk.
2. Ernest Leigh Bennet, *St. Cyril of Jerusalem Doctor of the Church.* Catechetical Lectures LECTURE XV. ON THE CLAUSE, AND SHALL COME IN GLORY TO JUDGE THE QUICK AND THE DEAD; OF WHOSE KINGDOM THERE SHALL BE NO END, Daniel vii. 9–14. London. Williams and Norgate 1920
3. *The Catholic Encyclopedia*, Robert C. Broderick (Editor), Virginia Broderick (Illustrator) Thomas Nelson publishers Nashville, Tennessee 1990
4. Ibid.
5. Revelation 17:5,6,7 & 9 KJV
6. Jamieson-Fausset-Brown Bible Commentary.1871. Hendrickson Publishers. Peabody, MA USA 1974.
7. E. Cobham Brewer 1810–1897. *Dictionary of Phrase and Fable.* 1898. New York: Bartleby, 2000
8. Jacobus de Voragine, *The Golden Legend or Lives of the Saints,* 1st ed., trans. William Caxton, (Princeton University Press, Princeton, New Jersey, USA 1995).
9. Ibid.
10. Revelation 16:13 KJV
11. E.A. Wallis Budge. *Egyptian Magic* (New York: Dover Publications, 1971).
12. Albert Barnes, *Notes, Explainitory and Practical, Book of Revelation.* (New York: Harper & Brothers, Publishers, 1859).
13. Daniel, 12:7 KJV
14. Revelation 12:6 KJV
15. Isaac Newton, Part of an untitled treatise on interpreting the symbolism of Biblical prophecy. Yahuda Ms. 2.1, Jewish

National and University Library, Jerusalem. The Newton
Project—University of Sussex, East Sussex London: 2007 www.
newtonproject.sussex.ac.uk
16. Ibid.

17

NEWTON'S PREDICTION

In 2003, the *Daily Telegraph* in London, England published a front-page story declaring that, according to Isaac Newton, the world would end in 2060. This was the first time that this calculation of Newton became widely known. However, various biographers and researcher of Newton's theology had encountered it since 1991 when most of his manuscripts were released on microfilm at Jewish National and University Library in Jerusalem. Newton's consideration of the year 2060 as the "time of the end" had also been published in 1980 in the book *Never at Rest* by Richard Westfall, within the context of Newton's theological views.[1]

In the 1660s when Newton believed that the end of days was imminent, there seemed no reason to work out the approximate year in which it would occur. With the Great Plague, the fire of London, and the apocalyptic fervor of the times, it seemed obvious to Newton that they had manifested. However, over the ensuing decades of his life, Newton became increasingly aware that his convictions had been premature. Near the year 1705, when Newton was in his sixties, his

concern for preventing the repetition of the same error compelled him
to invest his considerable knowledge to setting the matter of the time
of the end to rest. The paper in which Newton recorded this calculation was the subject of the article in the *London Daily Telegraph* in
2003. Very few readers understood Newton's reasoning for the date,
not being scholars of end time prophecy themselves. Newton wrote
concerning it:

> This I mention not to assert when the time of the end shall
> be, but to put a stop to the rash conjectures of fanciful men
> who are frequently predicting the time of the end, & by doing
> so bring the sacred prophesies into discredit as often as their
> predictions fail. Christ comes as a thief in the night, & it is
> not for us to know the times & seasons which God hath put
> into his own breast.[2]

Newton arrived at the year 2060 in a straightforward manner. He
believed that the last world empire at the coming of the Antichrist
would be a revived Roman Empire, a concept wholly embraced by
eschatologists in modern times. He also believed that this had actually
occurred in AD 800 through the coronation of Charlemagne by Pope
Leo III as ruler of the revived Roman Empire in the West.[3]

As described by the prophet Daniel, and John in Revelation, the
revived Roman Empire would rule for one "week," a period of 7 times
360 days, or 2,520 days total (also, remember, the value of the writing on the wall). In the midst of this week, at 1,260 days, the Antichrist will desecrate the future temple in Jerusalem. However, instead
of assigning 1,260 days of the Antichrist's reign before his desecration
of the temple, Newton assigned years. This he did realizing that the
rebuilding of the temple and the judgments of Revelation did not follow the rebirth of the Roman Empire in AD 800. None of the prophecies of the End of Days followed the coronation of Charlemagne as
Emperor of the revived Roman Empire after 1,260, nor for that mat-

ter, any of the years up until Newton's day. Therefore, he established each day with a year from AD 800, arriving at the year AD 2,060. The paper with this calculation reads as follows:

> Prop. 1. The 2300 prophetic days did not commence before the rise of the little horn of the He Goat.
>
> 2   Those day [sic] did not commence a[f]ter the destruction of Jerusalem & ye Temple by the Romans A[D] 70.
>
> 3   The time times & half a time did not commence before the year 800 in which the Popes supremacy commenced.
>
> 4   They did not commence after the reign of Gregory the 7th. 1084.
>
> 5   The 1290 days did not commence b[e]fore the year 842.
>
> 6   They did not commence after the reign of Pope Greg. 7th. 1084.
>
> 7   The difference between the 1290 & 1335 days are a part of the seven weeks.
>
> Therefore the 2300 years do not end before ye year 2132 nor after 2370. The time times & half time do n[o]t end before 2060 nor after [2344] The 1290 days do not begin [this should read: end] before 2090 nor after 1374 [sic; Newton probably means 2374].[4]

Newton's mention of the 2060 calculation exists in other manuscripts besides the one published in the *Daily Telegraph*. In a manuscript number 7.3g, f. 13v. of the Yahuda collection, Newton was even more specific about the 2060 date.

> So then the time times & half a time are 42 months or 1260 days or three years & an half, reckoning twelve months to a year & 30 days to a month as was done in the Calendar of the primitive year. And the days of short lived Beasts being put for the years of lived [sic for "long lived"] kingdoms, the

period of 1260 days, if dated from the complete conquest of the three kings A.C. 800, will end A.C. 2060. It may end later, but I see no reason for its ending sooner.[5]

Newton also recorded a clear explanation of the prophecy of Daniel that he believed established the Roman Catholic church as the last ruling Empire before the return of Christ:

Now the Senate & people of Rome I take to be the third king which was overcome by the little horn. For the old Roman Empire was a king in the sense of Daniel's prophesies....the Empire \of the Romans/ is in whose name the fourth Beast of Daniel still continued & of which Charles (Charlemagne) was made Emperor. This Rome was to be the metropolis of the little horn. And the victory of the little horn over this king was attended with greater consequences then those over the other two kings & finished the work which those victories began.[6]

Of the Pope's new power through this event and his identity as the Antichrist, Newton wrote:

For it set up the western empire which continues to this day It completed & secured Peter's patrimony to the Pope: which patrimony was the kingdom of the little horn: & it set up the Pope above all humane judicature & gave him the supremacy & a look more stout then his fellows....And being exalted above kings & declared by a Council above all humane judicature & the supreme judge of all men, he has reigned ever since with a peculiar soul & a look more stout then the rest of his fellows, & by setting up the worship of images, the abomination of desolation, he has changed times, & laws, which (1,260 years) after his rising up & becoming potent by

rooting up three of the first horns were to be given into his
hands for a time & times & half a time.[7]

Newton wrote a great deal concerning the number 1,260 and the
second advent of Christ and how they were connected in the prophecies of both the Old and New Testaments:

> When Daniel's times are done, the son of man comes in the
> clouds of heaven to receive the Empire of all the Kingdoms of
> the world, found in Dan 7:14. When Saint Luke's times of the
> Gentiles are finished, then shall be signs in the Sun & Moon;
> the Son of Man comes also in the clouds of heaven. When
> Saint John's Apocalyptical Beasts reign for 42 months with
> the witnesses 1260 days determine the Ark of the Covenant is
> seen in heaven & all the Kingdoms of the world become the
> Kingdoms of the Lord & his Christ Rev: 11.15.[8]

Newton's prediction of Charlemagne's revived Roman Empire
existing until the return of Christ was contradicted in 1806 when
Napoleon forced the Empire's dissolution.[9]

Whether or not Newton's date for the return of Christ as 1,260
years after AD 800 was correct or not, there remains a valid aspect of
his calculation. It may be that he was correct in his assumption that
there would be 1,260 years until the return of Christ at the rebirth of
the Roman Empire, but that the year he chose was incorrect. There is
an alternative year based on the allegorical meaning of prophecy.

> The Romans had fixed the birth of the city of Rome and the
> Empire in 753 BC. It was believed that the Patriarch of the
> city, Romulus had marked out the boundaries for the wall
> of Rome in this year. Known as, Ab Urbe Condita (literally,
> from the found of the city) the Roman calendar began with
> 753 BC according to the dating of Marcus Terentius Varro

(116–27 BC) whom lived at the time of the Empire itself. The traditional date of the fall of the Western Roman Empire is AD 476.[10]

Rome lay on the Tiber River, which bisected the city. Its original founding date also can be regarded in a similar bisected manner. The prophetic implication of a revived Roman Empire at the coming of the Antichrist is not outside the possibility of a supernatural time signature, a year mirroring the original on the other side of the dividing point of the era founded at the birth of Christ.[11] As has been demonstrated in previous chapters, the application of the number 2,520, and its half, 1,260, suits a variety of prophetic and geometric realities.

Using this principle, the year 753 BC designates the founding of the physical Rome and AD 753 establishes the rebirth of the spiritual Rome. Newton's count of 1,260 years from AD 753 then brings us to the future year AD 2013.

Founding of Rome	Birth of Christ	Prophetic reflection of Rome's Founding
753 B.C.	A.D. 1	A.D. 753

A.D. 753 + 1,260 = 2,013

Fig. 59. Image by author

As far as numeric symbols in the Bible that signify actual objects, 2,520 is the most temple-oriented. This is because, according to Daniel 9:27, the covenant of 2,520 days is based on the reinstitution of ritual sacrifice in a future temple in Jerusalem and 1,260 days marks its interruption. The full 2,520 days will end with the establishment of the rule of God on earth with the return of the Messiah. Jesus Christ is the subject that both the temple and the Ark of the Covenant symbolize. These topics were of great importance to Newton in his works of prophetic interpretation. The number 2,520 also predicted (in the writing on the wall) one of the most pivotal events of prophecy in the Bible and one that Newton himself anticipated: the rebirth of Israel. This gives weight to Newton's use of this number as days equaling years in his 2060 date and fits the over all scheme of *prisca theologia* in which he analyzed prophecy.

NOTES

1. Richard S. Westfall, *Never at Rest: A Biography of Isaac Newton* (Cambridge: Cambridge University, New Ed edition 1983.)
2. Isaac Newton. Yahuda MS 7.3g, f. 13v. The Newton Project—University of Sussex, East Sussex London: 2007 www.newtonproject.sussex.ac.uk
3. Einhard, *The Life of Charlemagne*, trans Samuel Epes Turner (New York: Harper & Brothers, 1880).
4. Isaac Newton, Yahuda MS 7.3o, f. 8r. Jewish National and University Library, Jerusalem. The Newton Project—University of Sussex, East Sussex London: 2007 www.newtonproject.sussex.ac.uk
5. Ibid. Newton, Yahuda MS 7.3g, f. 13v. Jewish National and University Library, Jerusalem. The Newton Project—University of Sussex, East Sussex London: 2007 www.newtonproject.sussex.ac.uk
6. Isaac Newton, *Notes on prophecies*. Yahuda Ms. 8.1, Jewish National and University Library, Jerusalem.
7. Ibid.
8. Ibid. Newton, Yahuda Ms. 23, Jewish National and University Library, Jerusalem.
9. *The American Heritage® Dictionary of the English Language*, Fourth Edition. Published by Houghton Mifflin Company. Boston, MA USA 2006
10. Some historians list AD 480 as the true date for Rome's fall. J. B. Bury, *History of the Later Roman Empire* published by Macmillan & Co., London UK 1923.
11. Author's note: The reflection of the past is the metaphor suggested here.

18

THE THRESHING FLOOR OF HEAVEN

The countryside of Wiltshire and Hampshire, England is host to one of the most enigmatic annual events of modern times. Beginning around the late spring and lasting until fall, the fields of grain in this area are pressed into complex geometric patterns. These designs were dubbed early in their appearance as "crop circles." Oftentimes, they occur around pre-existing megalithic sites, the most prominent of which is the Avebury Circle.

This phenomenon has been relegated to the "lunatic fringe" by the mainstream media of the West. However, due to the immense significance these crop manifestations possess with respect to Jerusalem, it is necessary to address. In fact, the meaning of the crop circle may reside in its connection with the temple of Jerusalem and its location on Earth.

The season of crop circles begins at the same time as Lag b' Omer and lasts until the Jewish New Year Rosh Hashanah. The number 33 is central to the Jewish festival Lag b'Omer, which is the celebration of the thirty-third day counted from the harvest of *sheaves* (omer) from Passover until the *Shavuot* (giving of the Law to Israel) on Mount Sinai. Lag B' Omer is the anniversary of the death of the author of the Zohar, Rabbi Shimon bar Yochai ca. AD 150. The Zohar, which means "the Shining Light," deals with the mystical teachings of the Torah and is the basis for Kabbalah, whose secrets are believed to bring about the coming of the Messiah.

Apparently, the feast of Lag b' Omer originated from the bar Kochba rebellion that began 33 days after Passover. Bar Kochba (whose name means "son of a star") was considered to be the messiah "at the time" and actually led a successful retaking of Jerusalem in AD 133. Bar Kochba started to rebuild the temple and began sacrifices on the temple mount that had been plowed under by the Romans. The Romans crushed the rebellion in AD 135, a feat commemorated by the shout "Hierosolyma est perdita, H.E.P., H.E.P., hurrah!" In the Zohar, Lag b' Omer is considered by mystic Jews to be a festival of the revealing (*gal*) of the future messiah; the number 33 is connected to this person as it was to Jesus.

The word *lag* is not a word, but the two letters in Hebrew that equal 33, *lamed* and *gimel*. During the week of Lag B' Omer, observant Jews read Psalms 119, the thirty-third portion of the Torah. The first verse of Psalm 119 has 33 letters. The word *lag* spelled backwards (gimel, lamed) is *gal*, which means "to reveal," as found the verse in Psalms 119:18.

Gal *einai v'abitah nifla'ot mitoratecha.*
Open (reveal to) my eyes that I may see the wonders of Your Torah.[1]

Although Lag b' Omer means the thirty-third day after harvest, it is an anagram for *gal b' omer*, "circles of pressed and twisted sheaves." One of the earliest names for Jerusalem was the city of the Jebusites, also known as Jebusi; *jebus* means "threshing place."[2]

And the border went up by the valley of the son of Hinnom unto the south side of the Jebusite; *the same [is] Jerusalem.*[3]

In threshing places of antiquity, sheaves of grain were laid out on the circular floor and trodden by oxen hitched to a pivot in the center, creating circles of flattened sheaves. The Bible is specific in designating this threshing floor as the site of the temple of Jerusalem.

Fig. 60. Image reprinted from *Illustrated Bible Dictionary*, Third Edition. M.G. Easton M.A., D.D.,Thomas Nelson New York 1897, 77.

Then Solomon began to build the house of the LORD at Jerusalem in mount Moriah, where [the LORD] appeared unto David his father, in the place that David had prepared in the threshingfloor of Ornan the Jebusite.[4]

Jesus often compared the process of farming grain to the creation of the Kingdom of Heaven on earth, the judgment at his second coming and the gathering of converts over the earth.[5] Bethlehem, the city of Jesus birth means, "city of bread"[6] and Jesus is called the "bread of Life."[7] The designation of the threshing floor as the site of the future temple aligned with the condition of humanity, destined for judgment, but prevented by God. This was set from the vantage point of David from the threshing floor. Similarly, Jesus Christ, called "the son of David,"[8] prevents judgment and death through his intercession as the bread of life.

> God sent an angel to Jerusalem to destroy it: and as he was about to destroy, Yahweh saw, and he relented of the disaster, and said to the destroying angel, It is enough; now stay your hand. The angel of Yahweh was standing by the threshing floor of Ornan the Jebusite. David lifted up his eyes, and saw the angel of Yahweh standing between earth and the sky, having a drawn sword in his hand stretched out over Jerusalem. Then David and the elders, clothed in sackcloth, fell on their faces.[9] (1 Chronicles 21:15–18)

From the temple mount in Jerusalem, to the location of the world's greatest concentration of authentic crop circles in Wiltshire, England, there are exactly 33 to 33.33 degrees of the circle of the Earth. This is in a wide swath 1,980 to 2,013 nautical miles from the temple in Jerusalem. The crop circle phenomenon began in 1980, some of which are equivalent in distance from the temple in nautical miles to their date/year of appearance.

Fig. 61. Adapted by author of map from William R. Shepherd, *The Historical Atlas* (New York: Henry Holt & Company, 1923), 51.

Fig. 62. Image by author. The number of the four cardinal directions of the earth, times 1,980, equals the mean diameter of the earth in statute miles.

NOTES

1. Psalms 119:18 KJV
2. Strong's Hebrew Dictionary # 2982 *James Strong Exhaustive Concordance of the Bible*. AMG Publishers edition, World Bible Publishers, Inc. 1986 Iowa Falls, Ia.
3. Joshua 15:8 KJV
4. 2 Chronicles 3:1 KJV
5. Matthew 13: 25 KJV
6. Ibid. Strong's Hebrew Dictionary. # 1035
7. John 6: 35 KJV
8. Mark 12: 35 KJV
9. 1 Chronicles 21:15–18

19

AMERICA

The United States is the greatest economic and military power in modern times. Though many theologians and eschatologists have dismissed America's significance in end-time prophecy, the illuminated elite has not. The ancient order of Free Masonry had a spiritual design for America at its inception. The location of Washington DC was selected according to the tenets of mystical toponomy, "occult significance in earth location."[1] As the ruling center of America, the longitude of the Federal Capitol building sits exactly on the 77th meridian, 00 minutes, 33 seconds. The latitude is 38 degrees, 53 minutes, 25 seconds.[1] In fact, the whole of the Washington DC complex was arranged in latitude and longitude that relates to the number 77. The latitude at 38.5 degrees is half of 77 degrees.

Seventy-seven is a number from biblical narrative associated with the ancient patriarch Lamech. According to the extra-biblical texts the Book of Jasher, the Talmud, and Midrash, Lamech accidentally killed Cain.[2] Because Lamech understood God's sevenfold curse on anyone harming Cain, Lamech cursed anyone harming him 70 plus 7 times. Axiomatically, since God himself swore to revenge Cain, Lamech's curse was directed against God.

The date of America's founding, 1776, is twice 888—the number in Greek letters for Jesus. The secret meaning of this date is discovered in the understanding of the two advents of Jesus Christ.

According to the occult elite, America's supernatural reason for being is to initiate the second coming of Christ. To signify the second advent, the number of his name is doubled, and yields 1776. However, the occult version of Jesus Christ is based on a Gnostic interpretation of his divinity. According to this theology, Jesus was the incarnation of Lucifer. His death on the cross is represented in this framework as the symbol of Mercury, or caduceus of a snake on a pole. This is a corruption of the Gospel originating from before the founding of Christianity. This is oftentimes cited as an argument against the veracity of Christianity. However, there can be no doubt that the spiritual forces that are in rebellion against God were present throughout history. The forces of evil have followed a set agenda to prevent the establishment of God's kingdom on earth.

In Gnostic legend, Cain, the first son of Eve, was produced through her union with Lucifer. As explained earlier, the pagan god Thoth was the prototype of the Greek Hermes and Roman Mercury. Thoth (*tau-oath,* "marked with an oath") was considered the person of Cain.[3] The knowledge that Cain spread across the antediluvian world originated from both his divine origin and the intercession of angelic beings aligned with Lucifer. The symbolic events of the Exodus are interpreted as Moses' interaction with Lucifer and not Elohim, the father of Adam. Parallel to this, all the symbols presented in the Old Testament are distorted to fit the Gnostic paradigm. Especially emphasized is the serpent on the pole that Moses erected in the desert. Jesus took upon himself the sin of the entire world. As the serpent on the pole saved the Israelites from death, so in like manner did Jesus with his death on the cross. The subtle difference between the Gnostic switch of Jesus with Lucifer in the Gospel is hallmark of the serpent as named in the Bible, *nachash.* The first mention of Satan in the Bible describes him in the guise of a serpent: "Now the serpent, [nachash] was more subtle than any beast of the field that the Lord God had made…"[4]

The number of Mercury is 88, which equals the time in Earth days it takes for the planet Mercury to make one revolution around the sun. Its closeness to the sun in the astronomical sense, and his capacity of messenger between gods and men establishes him as a corrupted version of Christ. As Mercury is closest to the sun, the Greek Helios (god of the sun) is his superior. The Gnostics consider this arrangement to be parallel with Christ's relationship to God the father, or, according to their occult identities, father Lucifer, the god of light, and the son Mercury, bringer of the light. Additionally, light or illumination stands for knowledge itself. In connection with this, the word "church," universally referred to in the feminine, originated from Circe, the Greek name of the daughter of Helios.

> They called her [Circe] and she came down, unfastened the door, and bade them enter. They, thinking no evil, followed her, all except Eurylochus, who suspected mischief and stayed outside. When she had got them into her house, she set them upon benches and seats and mixed them a mess with cheese, honey, meal, and Pramnian wine but she drugged it with wicked poisons to make them forget their homes, and when they had drunk she turned them into pigs by a stroke of her wand, and shut them up in her pigsties. They were like pigs—head, hair, and all, and they grunted just as pigs do; but their senses were the same as before, and they remembered everything.[5]

This myth gives insight to the Gospel account of the Gerasene demoniac. When Jesus exorcised the man of the legion of demons, they fled into a herd of pigs and drowned themselves in the Sea of Galilee, or literally, the "sea of the circle." It serves as a statement against the pagan origin of the Church of Rome that has corrupted the tenets of

Christianity. It is known that William Tyndale translated the Greek word *ekklesia* as "congregation" in his English Bible of 1526, and only used the word "church" for heathen temples in Acts 19:37.[6]

When King James authorized the English version of the Bible in 1611, he established fifteen rules that bound the translators. Article 3 stated, "The old Ecclesiastical Words [are] to be kept, viz. the Word Church not to be translated Congregation, etc."[7]

The Bible scholar Andrew Edgar in his work *The Bibles of England* explained the King's reason for superimposing the word "church" over *ekklesia*:

> James believed in the divine right of kings, and held that this right was hereditary, and that the king was responsible to God alone, and not to his subjects. As "Defender of the Faith" and head of the State church, he came into opposition with the Puritans on the one hand and the Catholics and their papal claims on the other. In his struggles with both he was motivated by a combination of religious and political considerations.[8]

This corruption of the Bible by King James (with the sun goddess, "Circe") pales in comparison to the distortions of Christianity made by the first King of Catholic Rome. When Constantine converted pagan Rome to Catholicism, he superimposed Christian motifs over pre-existing sun worship cults. He himself worshipped the god *Sol Invictus* (the invincible sun) until his death. Constantine declared *dies Solis*, "Sun-day," as the official day of rest for the empire on March 7, AD 321, minted coins bearing Helios crowned with the spiked rays, and established Christ's nativity on the pagan date of the birth of the sun, December 25.[9]

The imagery of Revelation involves the same circumstance. This is especially manifest in the feminine version of the "church" as a "solar" counterfeit of the ecclesia.

The waters which thou sawest, where the whore sitteth, are
peoples, and multitudes, and nations, and tongues. And the
woman which thou sawest is that great city, which reigneth
over the kings of the earth.[10]

And upon her forehead [was] a name written, MYSTERY,
BABYLON THE GREAT, THE MOTHER OF HARLOTS
AND ABOMINATIONS OF THE EARTH.[11]

New York City shares the title "The Capital of the World," and
has the Statue of Liberty in its harbor.[12] The Statue of Liberty was
designed by Frédéric-Auguste Bartholdi in 1875. Before beginning
the project, Bartholdi sought a commission for the construction
of a giant statue of Isis, the Egyptian Queen of Heaven, to over-
look the Suez Canal. The design of the statue of Isis was of "a robed
woman holding aloft a torch."[13] Modeled closely on the Colossus of
Rhodes, an image of Helios, the Statue of Liberty wears the same
spiked crown and holds a torch. The torch was originally intended
to be a cup, but later the flame was added to its center, which, according to Revelation 14:4 means, "having a golden cup in her hand
full of abominations and filthiness of her fornication."[14] Twenty-five
windows in the crown are intended to symbolize gemstones found
on the earth and the heaven's rays shining over the world. The seven
rays of the statue's crown represent the seven seas and continents of
the world.[15] The most intriguing connection to Revelation that the
Statue exhibits is not in its appearance, but in its distance from the
temple in Jerusalem.

America has long been considered a utopian land, designated by
the founding fathers as a country of freedom and liberty. Its laws are
clearly based on Plato's philosophy, and is largely extracted from his
work *Laws*. The Platonic relationship is defined by the mutual benefit
shared between citizen and state. This value was emphasized by Plato
as embodied in the number 5,040. As the perfect city of Magnesia was

designed around this number, a city that is dedicated to the commerce of the entire modern world, such as New York, should relate to it in some way. The Statue of Liberty is 5,706 statute miles from Jerusalem. This is 5,040 plus 666.

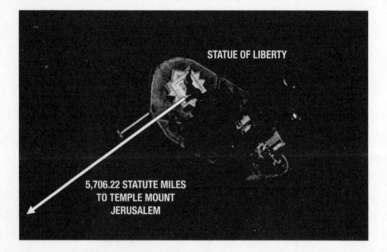

STATUE OF LIBERTY

5,706.22 STATUTE MILES
TO TEMPLE MOUNT
JERUSALEM

Fig. 63. Courtesy of NASA World Wind

The phrase "Babylon has fallen, has fallen" is found once in the Old Testament in Isaiah 21:9, and twice in the New Testament in Revelation, 14:8 and 18: 2. This is due to the fact that Babylon fell in 539 BC, and that Babylon the Great, the future city and world religious system, will fall at the end of days. From the perspective of the prophets, the same spiritual force designated both cities. This idea was reflected in the number that appeared on the wall of Belshazzar's palace on the eve of Babylon's fall. Not only does it define the perfect proportion of God's creation and design of prophecy, it also had the metaphorical meaning that Daniel interpreted in that the kingdom was weighed, balanced, and divided. Similarly, the number of Plato's Magnesia, 5,040, pertains to the second fall of Babylon. Jerusalem temple center expresses the judgment of God against the center of the world. The number incorporates both the number of its demise as well as the number of the beast found in Revelation.

"America" can be found in the Bible spaced 17 letters apart in Daniel 3:3. This is the shortest equal distance letter skip that appears throughout the entire text from Genesis to Revelation.

Fig. 64. Image by author

From the beginning of Daniel 3:3 until the last letter of America in the text, there are 33 Hebrew words. America is spaced 17 letters apart in 33 words:

$$33 / 17 = 1.941176479$$
$$\text{and } 1.941176479 \times 2 = 3.88235.$$

By moving the decimal place to the right one number, the exact latitude of the Washington DC is found. After all, 38.8235 decimal degrees is 38.50 degrees in minutes and seconds. Daniel 3.3–5 reads:

Then the princes, the governors, and captains, the judges, the treasurers, the counselors, the sheriffs, and all the rulers of the provinces, were gathered together unto the dedication of the image that Nebuchadnezzar the king had set up; an obelisk and they stood before the image that Nebuchadnezzar had set up. Then an herald cried aloud, To you it is commanded, O people, nations, and languages, That at what time ye hear the sound of the cornet, flute, harp, sackbut, psaltery, dulcimer, and all kinds of music, ye fall down and worship the golden image that Nebuchadnezzar the king hath set up.[17]

In modern times, the largest obelisk in the world is the Washington monument in Washington DC. At 555 feet tall, it is also 6,660 inches tall.[18]

The history of Daniel 3:3 is also important. Between 587 BC and 586 BC, Nebuchadnezzar destroyed the temple in Jerusalem and brought the Jews into exile in Babylon. Shadrach, Meshach, and Abednego were among the select Jews who served in the court of Nebuchadnezzar as his counselors. However, these men refused to worship the obelisk and were thrown into the fiery furnace. Daniel witnessed the fall of Babylon by the hand of King Cyrus between 538 BC and 539 BC. It was Cyrus who released the Jews from captivity to build the temple in Jerusalem. It is an often unrecognized fact that the name Cyrus, the liberator of the Jews, means "he who possesses the furnace."[19]

Because the Bible code of America, a country born in 1776, is found in Daniel 3:3, a relationship seems to exist between America's founding date and the chapter and verse of this referenced passage in Daniel:

$$1776 / 3.3 = 538.$$

As is mentioned above, 538 BC fell to King Cyrus, who ultimately freed the Jews from their exile. Furthermore,

$$17.76 \times 33 = 586,$$

which is the year that Babylon destroyed the temple of Jerusalem.

These years can also be calculated using 77 degrees west longitude of Washington DC. This number is a hidden symbol of the Babylon captivity of Judah:

$$77.07 \times 7.7 - 7 = 586 \text{ BC (the beginning of Judah's exile),}$$
$$\text{and } 77 \times 7 = 539 \text{ BC (the end of Judah's exile).}$$

There were 49 years from the early calculation of the exile 587 BC to the late calculation of the return 538 BC. This means that between the first temple's destruction in 587 BC by the Babylonians until the second temple's destruction in AD 70 by the Romans, there were:

$$657 \text{ years (587 BC + 70 AD)}$$

These are all 365-day solar years.

The strange thing is, in biblical 360-day years, the same duration is 666 years:

$$666 \times 360 \text{ days} = 239{,}760$$
$$239{,}760 \ / \ 365.2425 \text{ solar days} = 656.44058 \text{ solar years}$$
$$656.44058 - \text{AD } 70 = 586 \text{ BC}$$

If the numbers of the "America" code in Daniel 3:3 are multiplied,

$$17 \text{ spaces} \times 33 \text{ words} = 561$$

It is important to note that 561 BC is a year that is equally spaced between the destruction of the temple of Jerusalem and the decree by Cyrus to "rebuild" the temple. In fact, according to the "America" code, 561 BC may have actually been the year in which Nebuchadnezzar erected the obelisk.

Interestingly, America's founding date factors into the number of the beast of Revelation in an intriguing way:

$$1776 + 666 \times 6 = 5772.$$

As it just so happens, 5772 is the Jewish calendar year for 2012. The proportion between the Jewish year of 2012 and the founding date of America is "hexagonal." In other words:

$$5772 - 666 \times 6 = 1776.$$

This proportion can also be broken down in the following manner:

$$12 \times 333 + 1776 = 5772$$
$$5772 \times 77 \text{ (degrees longitude of Washington DC)} = 444,444$$
$$5772 \times 38.5 \text{ (degrees latitude of Washington DC)} = 222,222$$
$$444,444 + 222,222 = 666,666$$
$$77.7.7 \text{ west to } 33.33.33 \text{ east} = 6640.6666 \text{ nm} / 3.3 = 2012$$
$$.1212121212\ldots$$

From Jerusalem's temple mount to the world's tallest obelisk in Washington DC there are 5,133 nautical miles.

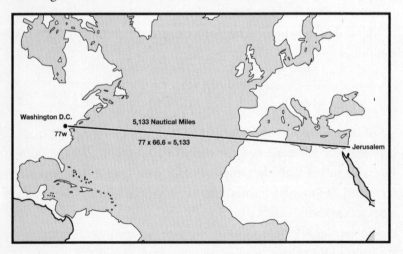

Fig. 65. Image by author

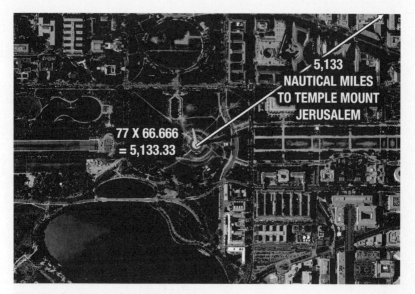

5,133
NAUTICAL MILES
TO TEMPLE MOUNT
JERUSALEM

77 X 66.666
= 5,133.33

Fig. 66. Courtesy of NASA World Wind

The aforementioned text of Daniel 3:3 containing the "America" code and the rest of the passage from Daniel 3:3–5 describes "all nations" being forced to worship the "image." America and historical Babylon were the nexus of the civilized world because both were superpowers that all nations were obliged to submit to in some respect, whether they benefited or not. In this light, Daniel 3:3–5 seems not only a record of the "image worship" event during the Babylonian exile, but also a prophecy concerning the Antichrist in the same vein as Matthew 24:15: "When ye therefore shall see the abomination of desolation, spoken of by Daniel the prophet, stand in the holy place, (whoso readeth, let him understand)."[20]

Jesus was referring to the prophecy in Daniel 11:31, in which he says, "And they shall pollute the sanctuary of strength, and shall take away the daily sacrifice, and they shall place the abomination that maketh desolate."[21] This prophecy concerning the Antichrist is mentioned again in Revelation:

And [he] deceiveth them that dwell on the earth by the means
of those miracles which he had power to do in the sight of
the beast; saying to them that dwell on the earth, that they
should make an image to the beast, which had the wound
by a sword, and did live. And he had power to give life unto
the image of the beast, that the image of the beast should
both speak, and cause that as many as would not worship the
image of the beast should be killed.[22]

Death for those who refuse to worship the image of the beast is
paralleled in Daniel: "And whoso falleth not down and worshippeth
shall the same hour be cast into the midst of a burning fiery furnace."[23]
In order for this prophecy to occur, the temple of Jerusalem must be
built. Daniel 12:11 states that Jewish temple rituals will be renewed
and then interrupted before the return of Christ. In Matthew 24:15–
16, Jesus Christ warned, "Therefore when you see the 'abomination
of desolation,' spoken of by Daniel the prophet, standing in the holy
place (whoever reads, let him understand), then let those who are in
Judea flee to the mountains."[24]

The prophet Daniel himself asked the question, "When will be
the end of these things?" (literally "the later time" of these things). His
answer: "Go thy way, Daniel: for the words [are] closed up and sealed
till the time of the end."[25]

Perhaps we have finally arrived at the end. It may be that words of
Daniel's prophecy are beginning to be unsealed.

Ezekiel 33 containing 33 verses underscores the importance of
"watching" in order to warn the faithful of coming troubles:

Son of man, speak to the children of thy people, and say unto
them, When I bring the sword upon a land, if the people
of the land take a man of their coasts, and set him for their
watchman: (Tzapha) If when he seeth the sword come upon
the land, he blow the trumpet, and warn the people; Then

whosoever heareth the sound of the trumpet, and taketh not warning; if the sword come, and take him away, his blood shall be upon his own head. He heard the sound of the trumpet, and took not warning; his blood shall be upon him. But he that taketh warning shall deliver his soul. But if the watchman see the sword come, and blow not the trumpet, and the people be not warned; if the sword come, and take [any] person from among them, he is taken away in his iniquity; but his blood will I require at the watchman's hand.[26]

A similar warning is found in reference to the return of Christ in the New Testament in Revelation 3:3:

Remember therefore how thou hast received and heard, and hold fast, and repent. If therefore *thou shalt not watch*, I will come on thee as a thief, and *thou shalt not know what hour I will come upon thee.*[27] (Emphasis added)

Jesus used the word "watch" so often in warning that followers of his return raised some interesting possibilities. In each instance, the word in Greek is *gregoreuo,* meaning

1) to watch
2) to rise from the dead (1 Thessalonians 5:10)

This word is from the root *egeir,* which means

1) to arouse, cause to rise
   a) to arouse from sleep, to awake
   b) to arouse from the sleep of death, to recall the dead to life[28]

In modern times, the unit of time is according to "the year of our Lord," and is counted by using the *Gregorian* calendar. Timothy 3:16

states that "all scripture is given by inspiration of God."[29] Under the same inspiration, the authors of the Gospel rendered the words of Jesus in the Greek language. The word "watcher" has revealed much concerning the nature and timing of the End of Days. Did Jesus choose this word intentionally as a clue for the time of his return?

Take ye heed, watch and pray: for ye know not when the time is. [For the Son of man is] as a man taking a far journey, who left his house, and gave authority to his servants, and to every man his work, and commanded the porter to watch.

Watch ye therefore: for ye know not when the master of the house cometh, at even, or at midnight, or at the cockcrowing, or in the morning: Lest coming suddenly he find you sleeping. And what I say unto you I say unto all, Watch.[30]

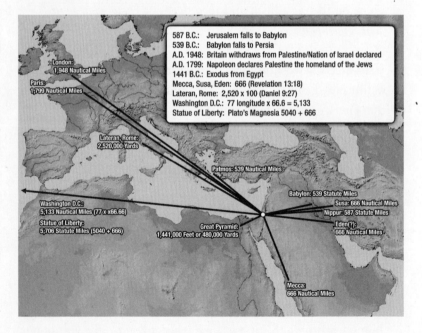

587 B.C.:   Jerusalem falls to Babylon
539 B.C.:   Babylon falls to Persia
A.D. 1948: Britain withdraws from Palestine/Nation of Israel declared
A.D. 1799: Napoleon declares Palestine the homeland of the Jews
1441 B.C.: Exodus from Egypt
Mecca, Susa, Eden: 666 (Revelation 13:18)
Lateran, Rome: 2,520 x 100 (Daniel 9:27)
Washington D.C.: 77 longitude x 66.6 = 5,133
Statue of Liberty: Plato's Magnesia 5040 + 666

London: 1,948 Nautical Miles
Paris: 1,799 Nautical Miles
Lateran, Rome: 2,520,000 Yards
Patmos: 539 Nautical Miles
Washington D.C.: 5,133 Nautical Miles (77 x x66.66)
Statue of Liberty: 5,706 Statute Miles (5040 + 666)
Great Pyramid: 1,441,000 Feet or 480,000 Yards
Babylon: 539 Statute Miles
Susa: 666 Nautical Miles
Nippur: 587 Statute Miles
Eden(?): 666 Nautical Miles
Mecca: 666 Nautical Miles

NOTES

1. Michael A. Hoffman II. *Secret Societies and Psychological Warfare.* Published by Independent History and Research Coeur d' Alene, Idaho 2001
2. Google Earth, 5 Oct. 2006.
3. J.H. Parry (Author)2. *The Book of Jasher,* (New York: Artisan Publishers 2007 J.H. Parry & Company, 1887).
4. Genesis 3:1 KJV
5. Homer, *The Odyssey,* Book 10, 210. Robert Fitzgerald (Translator) New York. Farrar, Straus and Giroux; Seventh edition 1998
6. Andrew Edgar, *The Bibles of England,* (Paisley and Paternoster, London:, UK 1884).
7. James Baikie, *The English Bible Its Story* (Lippincott: Philadelphia, USA 1928).
8. Herbert Gordon May, *Our English Bible in the Making* (Westminister Publisher Philadelphia USA, 1952).
9. Ramsay MacMullen, *Christianity and Paganism in the Fourth to Eighth Centuries,* (New Haven, Connecticut USA:Yale University Press, 1997).
10. Revelation 17:15, 16 KJV
11. Revelation 17:5 KJV
12. Author's note: The location of the Statue is closer to New Jersey but it technically belongs to New York. Tourist information from Statue of Liberty National Monument & Ellis Island New York, NY 10004
13. The National Park Service Historical Handbook Series No. 11 Washington, D.C. 1954 History.
14. Revelation 14: 4 KJV

15. Bernard Weisberger, *Statue of Liberty: 1st Hundred Years*, (Published by Horizon Book Promotions. Cape Town, South Africa.1988).

16. Ibid.

17. Daniel. 3.3–5 KJV

18. Monuments and Memorials: Washington Monument, The National Park Service, U.S. Department of the Interior, 5 Oct. 2006.

19. Strong's Hebrew Dictionary #3565, 3566 *James Strong Exhaustive Concordance of the Bible.* AMG Publishers edition, World Bible Publishers, Inc. 1986 Iowa Falls, Ia.

20. Matthew 24:15 KJV

21. Daniel 11:31 KJV

22. Revelation 13:14–15 KJV

23. Daniel 3:6 KJV

24. Matthew 24:15–16 KJV

25. Daniel 12: 8, 9. KJV

26. Ezekiel 33:6 KJV

27. Revelation 3:3 KJV

28. Ibid. BlueLetter Bible, 1996–2002, 5 Oct. 2006.

29. 2 Timothy 3:16 KJV

30. Mark 13:33–37 KJV

20

CONCLUSION

The temple's re-establishment during the last seven years is an expression of God's design for humanity. It represents the Word of God through its geometry, rituals, and location and is the ultimate statement of prophecy and law of God. As coexisting in eternity and the material world, the temple also symbolizes the possibility of transformation of men to immortality. The Ark was the focal point of God's presence in the temple, dwelling in time while remaining eternal. This is represented in the linguistic metaphor of eternity arcing the temporal. The Gospel explains that humanity can be made immortal through the encountering Christ, whom the Ark within the temple symbolizes. This is the ultimate intent of God for the sons of Adam, to be revealed as the sons of God. It is also the purpose driving the last events before the coming of the Messiah. Everything centers on the resurrection of the dead and the change of mortals to immortals. Isaac Newton understood this. He believed in a physical resurrection at the return of Christ. More over, he wrote of the transformation to incorruption of the living saints:

Wheresoever the body is thither will the Eagles be gathered together Luke 17:37. That is where the bodies of the saints are at the coming of our Lord, thither will the Angels go to carry them up into the Air to meet the Lord at his coming. Matthew 24:31 & 1 Thessalonians 4:17.[1]

The goal of revealing of the "sons of God" has been obscured by the influence of rebels from the spiritual realm. They have exercised deception over the world from the beginning.

At the midpoint of the seven-year covenant with the Antichrist, a temporal gate will open. With its opening, the framework of time will be amended. The rebel "watchers," having an immortal nature, will be thrust through into the confines of time and space on the earth. This is described in Isaiah 24:22 and 23:

And it shall come to pass in that day, [that] the LORD shall punish the host of the high ones [that are] on high, and the kings of the earth upon the earth. And they shall be gathered together, [as] prisoners are gathered in the pit, and shall be shut up in the prison, and after many days shall they be visited.[2]

Simultaneous to this event, those of the human race, having been changed to an immortal state by Christ's finished work on the cross, will pass through the temporal gate to a dimension of timelessness:

Thy dead [men] shall live, [together with] my dead body shall they arise. Awake and sing, ye that dwell in dust: for thy dew [is as] the dew of herbs, and the earth shall cast out the dead.[3]

And many of them that sleep in the dust of the earth shall awake, some to everlasting life, and some to shame [and] everlasting contempt.[4]

For I know [that] my redeemer liveth, and [that] he shall stand at the latter [day] upon the earth: And [though] after my skin [worms] destroy this [body], yet in my flesh shall I see God.[5]

Open ye the gates, that the righteous nation which keepeth the truth may enter in...[6]

Come, my people, enter thou into thy chambers, and shut thy doors about thee: hide thyself as it were for a little moment, until the indignation be overpast. For, behold, the LORD cometh out of his place to punish the inhabitants of the earth for their iniquity.[7]

For he bringeth down them that dwell on high; the lofty city, he layeth it low; he layeth it low, [even] to the ground; he bringeth it [even] to the dust.[8] Therefore rejoice, [ye] heavens, and ye that dwell in them. Woe to the inhabiters of the earth and of the sea! for the devil is come down unto you, having great wrath, because he knoweth that he hath but a short time.[9]

The legends concerning Cain and his son Enoch have, superimposed within them, the dual meaning of *ir*, which means "watcher" in Hebrew.[10] Genesis records that Cain built the first city and named it after his son Enoch, but this was not the prophet of the pseudepigraphic book of Enoch. However, the Enoch in this case described the "watchers" with same word, *ir*.[11] These were the angels that descended to Earth before the flood to teach mankind the arts of civilization. The corrupting arts included the building of cities, also called *ir* in Hebrew.[12]

The stories of Cain and Enoch have the conflict between men and the law of God at their core. They also describe mankind corrupted by spiritual beings given authority over the kingdoms of the earth in enmity with God and His kingdom of Heaven. Man by himself is powerless to resist the influence of angelic beings. His destructive path, though blazed by the first-born human, Cain, was interrupted by the saving power of God. The mark of that power, the *tau*, is linked to all the aspects of the ubiquitous rebellion of men and angels alike.

The angels "watch" mankind's progress towards immortality. The city (designated ir) of their greatest concern and diligent watch is Jerusalem. It is there that the mark of Cain manifested in its total power. It is at the "cross," where the ankh and the tau symbolically culminated in the death and resurrection of Christ. Men, guilty even of murder, find protection from the penalty of death at the cross in Jerusalem. It is through these diametrically opposed forces, death and life, murder and salvation, that the symbols representing the crucifixion of the Messiah connect. The meaning of the name Enoch (chanuch, "initiated" or "dedicated") connects to the temple in Jerusalem as we have seen. His life on Earth lasted 365 years according to the Bible. The letters of the name Jerusalem equal 365 x π.

ידושלם
600 30 300 6 200 10

=1,146 (365 x π)

JERUSALEM

Fig. 67. Image based on design courtesy of Wikipedia, "Image: Jerusalem coat of arms," http://en.wikipedia.org/wiki/Image: Jerusalem-coat-of-arms.svg.

Jerusalem is also the city by which our present era of time is anchored. The calendar of this era is fittingly, the *Gregorian* (to watch, or rise from the dead). Because of the promise of resurrection, the centrality of Jerusalem in the world and the spiritual universe was represented in stylized maps from the Crusades as a circle of the earth surrounding a "T."[13]

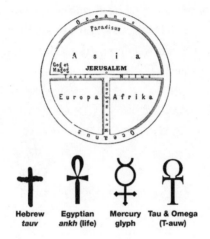

Fig. 68. Reprinted from Isidore's Etymologiarum (T-O map), 1472, with additional glyphs by author.

This map and "T" symbols have the dualistic connection to the conflict of evil with good, darkness with light, and death with life. As the cross of Christ was the instrument of his death, it is also the instrument of our salvation and eternal life. While on the cross, in Jerusalem at the center of the earth, Jesus Christ paid the full price for the sins of the whole world. The cross of Jerusalem embodies the *prisca sapientia* and the *prisca theologia* of the ancients. The powers behind Mercury, Nebo, and Thoth in the role of pagan prophets, strive to obscure the saving act of Jesus on the cross. They will continue to distort the truth until the final escape from death is realized.

We have seen that pivotal events in history are connected in time and space to Jerusalem. From the perspective of heaven, all events are linked to that one place on earth. It is the doorway through which humanity meets the God of Israel.

Newton did find the key.

And many nations shall come, and say, Come, and let us go up to the mountain of The Lord, and to the house of the God of Jacob; and he will teach us of his ways, and we will walk in his paths: for the law shall go forth of Zion, and the word of God from Jerusalem.[14]

NOTES

1. Isaac Newton, *Untitled treatise on Revelation* (Section1.1) Jewish National and University Library, Jerusalem: Yahuda Ms. 1.1a Transcribed by Rob Iliffe summer 1998. The Newton Project—University of Sussex, East Sussex London: 2007 www.newtonproject.sussex.ac.uk
2. Isaiah 24:22, 23 KJV
3. Isaiah 26:19 KJV
4. Daniel 12:2 KJV
5. Job 19:25, 26 KJV
6. Isaiah 26:2 KJV
7. Isaiah 26:20, 21 KJV
8. Isaiah 26:5 KJV
9. Revelation 12:12 KJV
10. Strong's Hebrew dictionary # 5894 *James Strong Exhaustive Concordance of the Bible*. AMG Publishers edition, World Bible Publishers, Inc. 1986 Iowa Falls, Ia
11. Ibid. Strong's Hebrew # 5892 & 5894
12. Michael A. Knibb, *The Book of Watchers (1 Enoch 1–36) The Ethiopic Book Of* (Oxford: Clarendon Press, 1978).
13. Alfred W. Crosby, *The Measure of Reality : Quantification in Western Europe, 1250–1600*. (Cambridge: Cambridge University Press, 1996).
14. Micah 4:2 KJV

√

Epilogue

THE PERSISTENCE OF "CIRCLES & THIRDS" IN THE HISTORY OF THE TEMPLE OF JERUSALEM

Jesus answered and said unto them,
Destroy this temple, and in three days I will raise it up.

—JOHN 2:19

The numbers 33, PI (3.14159265…), and 360 are prevalent in all major historical dates of the First and Second Temples in Jerusalem. These values are seen most often connected with the 360-day prophetic year used in the Old Testament. These numbers also reinforce the theme of "a circle." For example: In November of the year 333 BC, Alexander the Great conquered the Persians and ended their rule over Jerusalem.[1] Alexander brought the "3rd" world-governing power into existence according to Daniel the prophet. Flavius Josephus recorded that Alexander himself performed a sacrifice in the Temple of Jerusalem one year later.[2]

Exactly half 333 (prophetic 360-day year) years later in 168/7 BC, the Greek, Antiochus Epiphanes, desecrated the Temple of

Jerusalem. This event began the Maccabeus rebellion in 166.6 BC or half 333 in solar years. In 165/4 BC the Temple was rededicated by Judas Maccabee.[3]

In 63 BC, Pompeii ended Greek rule in Judea and captured Jerusalem, beginning the fourth world empire (Rome) predicted by Daniel the prophet.[4]

Between 166.6 BC and 63 BC, there were 103.6 years on the Gregorian calendar.

33 x PI = 103.6 (If 103.6 represents prophetic years, it is 102.1 when converted to solar years. If 103.6 represents solar years, it is 105.1 in prophetic years.)

105.1 + 63 = 168.1 BC,
the desecration of the Temple by Antiochus Epiphanes.
102.1 + 63 = 165.1 BC,
the rededication of the Temple by Judas Maccabeus.

The destruction of the First and Second Temples was separated by 657 solar years (587 BC by the Babylonians and AD 70 by the Romans). However, 657 solar years is exactly 666 prophetic years.

666 divided by 33 = 20.18181818…This number,
multiplied by PI equals the year when
Rome began ruling Israel in AD 63.

The latitude and longitude of Jerusalem is 31.46 North, 35.14 East. These coordinates added together equal 66.6

The Hebrew letters of the name "Jerusalem" equal 1,146 or the number of days in a year, 365 x PI. The same number is found in the sum of the name "Leviathan," meaning a connected serpent or circled serpent.[5]

The name "Jebusi" (a place trodden down or a threshing floor) was the original name of Jerusalem and site of the Temple.[6] The Hebrew letters in the name Jebusi equal 88.

When the year of the First Temple's dedication by Solomon in "960" BC is divided by the number of the name of the Temple site "88," the dividend is:10.9090909090909090...This number x 33 = 360, the number of degrees in a circle.

Perhaps the most significant correlation between the "circle" and the history (and future) of the Temple lies in the year of the dedication of the First Temple of Solomon in 960 BC.

PI times 960 = 3,015.928947...
Could this number also represent prophetic years?

If we assume that this number represents prophetic years with 360 days, the conversion to 365.242-day, solar years is 2,972.64394861.

If this figure stands for the number of total years from the dedication of the First Temple of Solomon in 960 BC until the dedication of the Last Temple that will be built before the Second Coming of Christ, the date indicated is AD 2012.

2,972 years
- 960 BC
= AD 2,012

The conversion to 365.242-day, solar years is:

3,015.928947 x 360 = 1085734.4210806 days...
divided by 365.242 = 2,972.64394861...solar years.

Is AD 2012 the appointed time of completion for world influence over the Temple in Jerusalem? Is this the year that the circle of our age draws to a close?

We know that Jesus died and rose again at 33-years-old and performed most of his miracles in Galilee, meaning "circuit." The root of Galilee is "Gal," formed by the two Hebrew letters Gimel (3) and Lamed (30), which equal 33.

The Sea of Galilee is also called in Latin, "Tiberius." In Rome the *Tiber* River divides the city from north to south. The divided circle is indicative of the number PI, as the diameter of any circle x PI equals its circumference.

The average water level of the Sea of Galilee, indicated by its ancient shoreline, is 640 feet below sea level. Perhaps not coincidentally, Israel was captured by Muslim Arabs in 640 AD. [7]

$$640.4 \times PI = 2012$$
$$639 \times PI = 2007$$
$$641 \times PI = 2013.7$$

As we have seen, the name "Galilee" reoccurs as one of the most prominent symbols in the Gospel narratives connected with the ministry and resurrection of Christ. It is mentioned in the Annunciation of Mary's conception by the Angel Gabriel.

And in the sixth month the angel Gabriel was sent from God unto a city of Galilee, named Nazareth. (Luke 1:26)

After this, when Joseph and Mary left to be counted in the census, they traveled to Bethlehem, which lies on North 31 degrees, 41 minutes, 59 seconds or PI x 10.

But after I am risen again, I will go before you into Galilee. (Matthew 26:32)

Ye men of Galilee, why stand ye gazing up into heaven? This same Jesus, which is taken up from you into heaven, shall so come in like manner as ye have seen him go into heaven. (Acts 1:11)

Perhaps the consistent pairing in the Gospel of the "circuit" with the resurrection of Jesus Christ is telling us about His "Second" Coming and the resurrection of His Church, which after all, also has the meaning, "a circle."

NOTES

1. Katharine Wiltshire, *The British Museum Timeline of the Ancient World* (New York: Palgrave Macmillan, 2004), 50.
2. Flavius Josephus, "Jewish Antiquities," 11.317–345, Translator William Whiston, *New Complete Works of Josephus* (Grand Rapids: Kregel,1999), 977.
3. James C. VanderKam, *An Introduction to Early Judaism* (Grand Rapids: Eerdmans Publishing, 2001), 19–20.
4. Katharine Wiltshire, *The British Museum Timeline of the Ancient World*, First Edition (New York: Palgrave Macmillan, 2004), 75.
5. James Strong, *Exhaustive Concordance of the Bible.*, (Iowa Falls: AMG Publishers, 1986), 804.
6. Ibid, James Strong, 721.
7. Katharine Wiltshire, *The British Museum Timeline of the Ancient World*, First Edition (New York: Palgrave Macmillan, 2004), 89.

APPENDIX

Temple Mount Foundation Stone, Jerusalem Israel
31°46'43.45" N 35°14'05.87" E

London Stone, London England
51°30'43.70"N 0°05'32.52 W

Mile marker Paris Island, Paris France
48°51'12"N 2°20'56.18" E

Mecca, Saudi Arabia
21°26'55" N 39°48'1" E

Babylon center, Iraq
32°32'0.0" N 44°24'56.0" E

Susa (Shush) canal between rivers, Iran
32°08'41".0 N 48°18'33".0 E

Nippur (Nuffar) center, Iraq
32°07'48.0" N 45°14' 40.0" E

Washington Monument, Washington D.C. USA
38°53'22.0" N 77°02'07.0" W

Statue of Liberty, New York Harbor, NY, NY USA
40° 41'21.0" N 74° 02' 40.0" W

Lateran Obelisk, Rome Italy
41° 53'12.60" N 12° 30'17.30" E

Great Pyramid, Giza Egypt
29° 58'48.40" N 31° 08'08.0" E

The FAI Sphere distance calculation:
Cosine a = (Cosine Latitude A x Cosine Latitude B x Cosine
(Longitude A - Longitude B)) + (Sine Latitude A x Sine Latitude B)
Earth's radius = 3958.75 Statute miles (3,440.06479 Nautical miles)